Computing Research
Survival Manual

A practical handbook for beginners

Online at: https://doi.org/10.1088/978-0-7503-5017-4

Computing Research Survival Manual

A practical handbook for beginners

Haruna Chiroma
Computer Science and Engineering Department, University of Hafr Al Batin, Hafr Albatin, Saudi Arabia

Jemal H Abawjy
School of Information Technology, Deakin University, Australia

IOP Publishing, Bristol, UK

ISBN   978-0-7503-5017-4 (ebook)
ISBN   978-0-7503-5015-0 (print)
ISBN   978-0-7503-5018-1 (myPrint)
ISBN   978-0-7503-5016-7 (mobi)

DOI   10.1088/978-0-7503-5017-4

Supplementary material is available for this book from https://doi.org/10.1088/978-0-7503-5017-4.

Version: 20230801

IOP ebooks

British Library Cataloguing-in-Publication Data: A catalogue record for this book is available from the British Library.

Published by IOP Publishing, wholly owned by The Institute of Physics, London

IOP Publishing, No.2 The Distillery, Glassfields, Avon Street, Bristol, BS2 0GR, UK

US Office: IOP Publishing, Inc., 190 North Independence Mall West, Suite 601, Philadelphia, PA 19106, USA

The book is dedicated to Zaid Jemal Abawjy

Contents

Preface   **xv**

Author biographies   **xvi**

1   Computing disciplines ecosystem and origin of research   **1-1**

1.1   Introduction   1-1

1.2   Computing disciplines   1-3
    1.2.1   Computer science   1-3
    1.2.2   Software engineering   1-4
    1.2.3   Computer engineering   1-5
    1.2.4   Information systems   1-5
    1.2.5   Information technology   1-5
    1.2.6   Cybersecurity   1-6
    1.2.7   Data science   1-6
    1.2.8   Emerging areas: artificial intelligence   1-7

1.3   Comparing the focus of the seven disciplines within the computing ecosystem   1-7

1.4   Scientific research in computing   1-8
    1.4.1   Types of research   1-8

1.5   Research philosophy and origin of research in computing   1-10
    1.5.1   Origin of research in computer science   1-11
    1.5.2   Origin of research in software engineering   1-12
    1.5.3   Origin of research in information systems   1-13
    1.5.4   Origin of research in information technology   1-13
    1.5.5   Origin of research in data science   1-14
    1.5.6   Origin of research in cybersecurity   1-14
    1.5.7   Origin of research in computer engineering   1-15

1.6   Comparing research methods in discipline within the computing ecosystems   1-15

1.7   Generic procedure for computing research   1-17

1.8   Features of quality and bad research   1-17

1.9   MSc, PhD and undergraduate project in computing   1-18

1.10 Organization of the book   1-18

1.11 Summary   1-19

    References   1-20

2	**Computing search engines and bibliographic databases**	**2-1**
2.1	Introduction	2-1
2.2	The computing academic databases	2-2
	2.2.1 Clarivate Analytics Web of Science	2-3
	2.2.2 Scopus	2-4
	2.2.3 Comparing the Scopus and Web of Science	2-5
	2.2.4 DBLP computer science bibliography	2-6
	2.2.5 ACM digital library	2-9
	2.2.6 Ei-Compendex	2-12
	2.2.7 IEEE Xplore	2-12
	2.2.8 ScienceDirect	2-15
	2.2.9 Springerlink	2-16
	2.2.10 PubMed	2-16
	2.2.11 Google Scholar	2-17
2.3	Comparing the academic search engines: similarities and differences	2-18
2.4	Summary	2-21
	References	2-22

3	**Systematic literature review from a computing perspective and research problem formulation**	**3-1**
3.1	Introduction	3-1
3.2	Why conduct literature search and systematic literature review?	3-2
3.3	Systematic literature review, narrative review and metadata analysis: differences	3-4
	3.3.1 Approach for conventional review	3-5
	3.3.2 Synthesis of existing evidence and research problem	3-5
3.4	Proposed systematic literature review methodology for computing	3-6
	3.4.1 Focus and selection of research topic	3-6
	3.4.2 Motivation	3-8
	3.4.3 Keywords	3-9
	3.4.4 Research questions	3-9
	3.4.5 Literature search and data sources	3-10
	3.4.6 Study selection procedure	3-10
	3.4.7 Exclusion and inclusion criteria	3-10
	3.4.8 Inclusion and exclusion of papers	3-11
	3.4.9 Screening based on introduction and conclusion (optional)	3-12

	3.4.10	Stopping the search and the number of articles required for the SLR	3-12
	3.4.11	Data extraction and synthesis	3-13
	3.4.12	Answers to research questions	3-13
	3.4.13	Systematic literature review quality assessment	3-13
	3.4.14	Discussion	3-15
	3.4.15	Limitations	3-15
	3.4.16	Challenges and future research opportunities	3-16
3.5	The brief structure of systematic literature review		3-16
3.6	Common mistakes in conducting systematic literature review		3-16
3.7	Research problem formulation		3-18
	3.7.1	Developing problem statement	3-18
	3.7.2	The problem statement–computer science perspective	3-19
	3.7.3	Research questions	3-19
	3.7.4	Aim and objectives of the research	3-20
	3.7.5	Significance of the research	3-22
	3.7.6	Research scope	3-22
3.8	Summary		3-22
	References		3-23

4	**Computing research tools and resources**		**4-1**
4.1	Introduction		4-1
4.2	Research productivity tools		4-2
	4.2.1	Reference management software	4-2
	4.2.2	EndNote	4-3
	4.2.3	Plagiarism detection tool	4-5
	4.2.4	Spelling and grammar checkers: Ginger Software spelling and grammar checker	4-8
	4.2.5	Google documents	4-9
	4.2.6	ShareLaTeX	4-9
	4.2.7	Backup tools	4-10
	4.2.8	Finding a suitable journal for submitting a paper	4-10
4.3	Computing research tools		4-11
	4.3.1	Software engineering	4-12
	4.3.2	Information systems and information technology	4-12
	4.3.3	Data science	4-16
	4.3.4	Libraries and frameworks	4-17

4.4	Computer engineering	4-20
	4.4.1 Gem5 simulator	4-20
	4.4.2 Webots	4-20
4.5	Hardware and software platforms	4-21
4.6	Summary	4-22
	References	4-24

5 Computing datasets and data engineering   **5-1**

5.1	Introduction	5-1
5.2	Large-scale datasets as today's reality compared to small-size datasets	5-2
	5.2.1 Definition of big data	5-3
	5.2.2 Characteristics of big data	5-3
	5.2.3 Case studies	5-5
	5.2.4 Content large-scale data format	5-5
	5.2.5 Challenges regarding big data	5-6
5.3	Benchmark, real-world and synthesis datasets	5-7
5.4	Characteristic of real-world datasets	5-8
	5.4.1 Missing values	5-8
	5.4.2 Inaccurate values	5-9
	5.4.3 Imbalanced data	5-9
	5.4.4 Outliers and noise	5-10
	5.4.5 Redundant and irrelevant features	5-11
5.5	Case study: collecting data from a real physical environment—smart city	5-11
5.6	Knowing your dataset	5-12
5.7	Cross-datasets	5-13
5.8	Dark datasets	5-13
5.9	Research data management	5-13
	5.9.1 Storing, preservation and discarding	5-14
	5.9.2 Safety, security and confidentiality	5-15
	5.9.3 Third party access	5-15
	5.9.4 Data storage facilities	5-15
	5.9.5 Data retention and publication	5-16
	5.9.6 Confidentiality management	5-16
	5.9.7 Responsibilities of researchers on data and developing a data management plan	5-16

5.10   Research data repositories and sources   5-17
     5.10.1   IEEE DataPort   5-17
     5.10.2   University of California Irvine machine learning repository   5-21
     5.10.3   Kaggle and Code Ocean   5-21
     5.10.4   GitHub platform   5-22
     5.10.5   Google Dataset Search   5-22
     5.10.6   Quantitative and qualitative means of data collection   5-23
     5.10.7   Knowledge discovery in database 99—DARPA,   5-24
             ADFA Linux and NSL-KDD
5.11   Features engineering   5-24
5.12   Summary   5-26
     References   5-27

6   Methodology from a computing perspective   6-1

6.1   Introduction   6-1
6.2   Research methodology in computing   6-2
     6.2.1   Process   6-3
     6.2.2   Modeling   6-3
6.3   Relating the methodology to the computing disciplines   6-4
6.4   Algorithms   6-4
     6.4.1   Algorithm performance analysis   6-5
6.5   Solving real-world problems using algorithms   6-6
     6.5.1   Existing algorithm   6-6
     6.5.2   Modified algorithm   6-6
     6.5.3   New algorithm   6-7
6.6   Conceptual framework   6-7
6.7   Comparative study: hardware and software   6-8
6.8   Case studies   6-9
     6.8.1   Case study 1: software engineering   6-9
     6.8.2   Case study 2: cybersecurity   6-13
     6.8.3   Case study 3: cybersecurity   6-14
     6.8.4   Case study 4: data science   6-16
     6.8.5   Case study 5: computer science   6-18
     6.8.6   Case study 6: information systems   6-18
     6.8.7   Case study 7: computer engineering   6-21
     6.8.8   Case study 8: information technology   6-22
6.9   Summary   6-23
     References   6-23

7   Scientific publishing in computing: beginners guide   7-1

7.1   Introduction   7-1

7.2   PhD/MSc thesis, journal and conference proceedings publications   7-3

7.3   Tips for developing an excellent journal paper   7-4

    7.3.1   Title of the paper   7-4

    7.3.2   Abstract   7-4

    7.3.3   Keywords   7-5

    7.3.4   Introduction   7-5

    7.3.5   Theoretical background   7-5

    7.3.6   Methodology   7-5

    7.3.7   Results and discussion   7-6

    7.3.8   Conclusions   7-6

    7.3.9   References   7-7

7.4   Common reasons for desk rejection and tips to avoiding it during initial screening   7-7

    7.4.1   Disregard for journal aims and scope   7-8

    7.4.2   Poor grammar, writing and formatting   7-8

    7.4.3   Ethical issue: plagiarism/self-plagiarism   7-8

    7.4.4   Insufficient contribution or lack of novelty   7-9

    7.4.5   Resubmitting a rejected paper to a new journal without modification   7-9

    7.4.6   Duplicate submission   7-9

    7.4.7   Poorly developed paper   7-10

    7.4.8   Poor literature reviews   7-10

    7.4.9   Failure to respond to feedback   7-10

    7.4.10   Lack of relevance to an international audience   7-10

7.5   Cover letter   7-11

7.6   Research highlights   7-12

    7.6.1   Highlights   7-12

7.7   Supplementary materials   7-13

7.8   Suggesting reviewers for a researcher's own paper   7-13

7.9   Quality measurement in computing publications   7-13

    7.9.1   Peer review in the research community   7-14

    7.9.2   Peer review cycle   7-14

    7.9.3   Types of peer review in the research community   7-15

7.10   Responding to reviewer comments   7-17

7.11   Handling of rejections   7-19

7.12 Understand different publishing models—open access,   7-20
     subscription, and hybrid
     7.12.1 Open access journals   7-21
     7.12.2 Subscription journals   7-21
     7.12.3 Hybrid journals   7-21
7.13 Summary   7-21
     References   7-22

8   Research ethics in computing   8-1

8.1 Introduction   8-1
8.2 Research ethics from the perspective of computing   8-2
     8.2.1 Trust   8-4
     8.2.2 Privacy   8-4
     8.2.3 Consent   8-4
     8.2.4 Inclusion and digital divides   8-5
     8.2.5 Visual ethics   8-6
     8.2.6 Research ethics using wearable cameras   8-6
8.3 The six domains of research ethics   8-6
8.4 Research misconduct   8-8
     8.4.1 Plagiarism   8-8
     8.4.2 Disciplinary action against plagiarism   8-9
     8.4.3 Plagiarism types   8-9
     8.4.4 Authorship   8-10
     8.4.5 Conflict of interest   8-11
8.5 Tips to avoid conflict of interest   8-12
     8.5.1 Participation in editorial board   8-12
8.6 Avoiding research misconduct   8-12
8.7 Ethics committees and institutional research boards   8-13
8.8 Research ethics in the context of disciplines in computing 8-14
     8.8.1 Ethics in software engineering   8-15
     8.8.2 Ethics in computer science   8-16
     8.8.3 Ethics in information system   8-18
     8.8.4 Ethics in cyber security   8-19
     8.8.5 Ethics in data science   8-20
     8.8.6 Ethics in information technology   8-21
     8.8.7 Ethics in computer engineering   8-22

8.9   Negative research results and tips to get published   8-22

    8.9.1 Publishing negative results   8-23

8.10 Summary   8-24

    References   8-24

9   Emerging research trends in computing   9-1

9.1   Introduction   9-1

9.2   Emerging research topics in computing   9-2

    9.2.1 Computer science   9-3

    9.2.2 Computer engineering   9-5

    9.2.3 Cyber security   9-9

    9.2.4 Software engineering   9-11

    9.2.5 Information systems, information technology and data science   9-12

9.3   Selected research problems   9-13

    9.3.1 New generation artificial neural networks   9-14

    9.3.2 Emerging Internet of Things research areas   9-15

    9.3.3 The role of emerging 6G in unmanned aerial vehicle cellular   9-16
             communications

    9.3.4 Nature inspired algorithms for global optimization problem   9-17

    9.3.5 Software requirement engineering for blockchain applications   9-17

    9.3.6 Network security   9-18

9.4   Artificial intelligence future prediction   9-19

9.5   Summary   9-20

    References   9-20

Preface

Research methodology is the core component of any valid research. There is no consensus on methodology for computing but this book attempts to provide a guide on conducting research from the perspective of computing instead of the commonly written books on general research methodology or niche areas within the computing discipline itself.

Ph.D., M.Sc., undergraduate and early-stage researchers in industry and academia are often challenged with identifying research problems, choosing research areas, convincing supervisor's/advisors and deciding on which methodology to apply in the research within a specific computing discipline. After determining the methodology, then comes the issue of how to apply it. In all, having a dense snatch of these remains essential for beginners. This book contains a detailed research procedure from the perspective of computing – Computer Science, Software Engineering, Information System, Information Technology, Data Science, Cybersecurity and Computer Engineering. The book can equip the readers with an understanding of the differences among the computing disciplines ecosystem; understanding of the sources of credible, complete, accurate and updated computing literature; procedure for conducting systematic literature review from the perspective of computing; developing research problems; research tools needed to implement research ideas; sources of datasets repositories and feature engineering; identification of trending research topics; a guide on how to draft an excellent manuscript or extract from a thesis/dissertation for submission to journals and ethics in conducting research in different computing research areas. Lastly, the book points out how to overcome potential challenges in a journey to research and high impact journal publications.

The book is of great importance to postgraduate students, undergraduate and early-stage researchers as it comprises the step-by-step procedure of how to conduct research from the beginning of writing a thesis/project up to publishing in top journals and conferences.

For expert researchers such as professors, the book can be an excellent teaching/ instructional material for delivering research course content to learners. For teaching and presentation purposes, the book contains slides conveying the key points in the book, which are available at https://doi.org/10.1088/978-0-7503-5017-4.

Author biographies

Haruna Chiroma

Haruna Chiroma is an Assistant Professor at the University of Hafr Al Batin, College of Computer Science and Engineering, Saudi Arabia. He received his B.Tech., M.Sc., and Ph.D. in Computer Science and Artificial Intelligence from Abubakar Tafawa Balewa University, Bayero University Kano, and University of Malaya, respectively. He is ranked in the top 2% most influential scientists by Stanford University. He is an academic editor of Computational and Mathematical Methods in Medicine (ISI WoS/Scopus Indexed), Associate Editor of IEEE Access (ISI WoS/Scopus Indexed) 2018 – 2021, Editorial board member for IAES International Journal of Artificial Intelligence, (Scopus Indexed), Associate Editor for TELKOMNIKA, Indonesia (Scopus Indexed), and Editorial board member for Recent Advances in Computer Science and Communications (Scopus Indexed). He is also currently guest editing special issues. His research interests include artificial neural networks, machine learning and artificial intelligence. He has published over 155 academic articles relevant to his research interest in different venues. He is an invited reviewer for over 60 ISI WoS/ Scopus indexed journals. He has been a technical programme committee member for more than 50 international conferences, workshops and symposia. Presently, Chiroma is supervising M.Sc. and Ph.Ds. students and graduated many M.Sc. and 2 Ph.D candidates.

Jemal H Abawjy

Jemal H Abawjy is a Full Professor with the School of Information Technology, Faculty of Science, Engineering, and Built Environment at Deakin University, Australia. He is currently the Director of the Parallel and Distributing Computing Laboratory. He is a Senior Member of the IEEE Technical Committee on Scalable Computing, the IEEE Technical Committee on Dependable Computing and Fault Tolerance, and the IEEE Communication Society. His leadership is extensive, spanning industrial, academic, and professional areas. He has served on the Academic Board, Faculty Board, the IEEE Technical Committee on Scalable Computing Performance Track Coordinator, Research Integrity Advisory Group, Research Committee, Teaching and Learning Committee, and Expert of International Standing Grant and External Ph.D. Thesis Assessor. He has delivered over 70 key-note addresses, invited seminars, and media briefings and has been actively involved in the organization of over 250 national and international conferences in various capacity, including Chair, General Co-Chair, Vice-Chair, Best Paper Award Chair,

Publication Chair, Session Chair, and Program Committee. He has also served on the editorial board of numerous international journals and currently serving as an Associate Editor of the IEEE Transactions on Cloud Computing, International Journal of Big Data Intelligence, and International Journal of Parallel, Emergent and Distributed Systems. Prof. Abawjy has also guest edited over 20 special issues. He is actively involved in funded research supervising large number of Ph.D. students, postdoctoral, research assistants, and visiting scholars in the area of cloud computing, big data, network and system security.

Chapter 1

Computing disciplines ecosystem and origin of research

In this chapter, we provide an overview of computing and the seven disciplines that make up the computing ecosystem: computer science, computer engineering, software engineering, information systems and information technology. We further discuss the two newly emerged disciplines, cybersecurity and data science. Emerging areas (e.g. artificial intelligence) are defined. To correct misconception about the computing disciplines, the origin and differences among the computing disciplines are outlined and discussed. For easy understanding by readers, taxonomies, figures and tables were created to give readers visual representation of the differences and origins of the disciplines. Scientific research in computing, procedure for scientific research, types of research in computing, and features of good and bad research are discussed. We go further to discuss the origin of research in each of the disciplines. We believe the misconception about the computing disciplines among computing students and graduates will vanish after reading this chapter. In addition, readers will be properly guided on research areas for a specific discipline in the computing ecosystem.

1.1 Introduction

Computing is not a single discipline but a combination or family of different disciplines with different focus. Computing is defined as any goal oriented activity that requires computers, benefits from computers or creates computers. Therefore, computing involves the design and building of computer components including hardware and software for different purposes such as processing, structuring, and management of different types of information, scientific studies that require the use of computers; making computer systems act intelligently; the creation and application of communications and entertainment media; the findings and assembling of information that is relevant to a particular purpose, etc. The list of the computing

doi:10.1088/978-0-7503-5017-4ch1

purposes is endless and vast. There are many areas of specialization in computing, which makes it virtually impossible for a single individual to specialize in all the components of computing. Thus, students are required to earn a degree in different disciplines of computing to prepare them for entering society as computing professionals. Each discipline in computing has its own focus based on the problems and issues addressed by the discipline. However, in the 1960s the computing disciplines were just three: computer science, electrical engineering and information systems (Shackelford *et al* 2006). Figure 1.1 shows a visual representation of the different purposes of using computers.

There is a misconception among the students and graduates of computing on the differences among the different disciplines in computing. As a University professor, I often ask graduates and students to distinguish computer science (CS) from information technology (IT) or information systems (IS). In some cases, asked to differentiate the disciplines in computing, there is hardly a graduate or student of any of the disciplines that can clearly explain the differences correctly because of a misconception about the disciplines.

Therefore, in this chapter we have decided to explain clearly the definitions of the disciplines according to the Association for Computing Machinery (ACM), the world-leading organization of computing that dictates the pace of computing in the world. This can help to correct the misconception about the various disciplines that make up the family of computing. If a graduate or student has a clear distinction of the different disciplines, the applicant can conduct research in the appropriate research area without mixing the research areas or trying to propose a research proposal in a different discipline from the discipline in which the applicant is intending to earn a degree. For example, a student that intends to get an MSc or PhD in CS, the research contribution should be in CS, similarly, for an MSc or PhD degree in IS, the research contribution should be in IS. Therefore, it is mandatory for the student to understand the differences to be able to conduct research in the appropriate discipline. An overview of the computing disciplines is discussed to clearly explain the distinction among the family of the computing disciplines to correct any misconception.

Figure 1.1. Computing—goal oriented activities requiring computers.

1.2 Computing disciplines

Currently, the seven disciplines in the computing ecosystem are as follows: CS, computer engineering (CE), software engineering (SE), data science (DS), Cybersecurity (CyS), IS and IT as presented in figure 1.2. The differences of the seven computing disciplines based on different focus are explained in the subsequent sections.

1.2.1 Computer science

The CS discipline witnessed rapid progress and it was accepted as an academic discipline. CS initially appeared as a discipline in the 1970s, especially in American colleges and universities. At the beginning, there was controversy about the legitimacy of CS as an academic discipline. Critics argued that CS is a vocational specialization for technicians that has its research platform from mathematicians or programmers, while proponents argued that CS has its own identity. In the 1990s, CS advancement led to the development of research, knowledge, and innovation which extended from theory to practice. Therefore, the controversy about the legitimacy of CS as an academic discipline varnished. CS extends from its theoretical and algorithm foundation to progress in robotics, computer vision, intelligent systems, bioinformatics, etc. The responsibilities of computer scientists are categorized into three: (1) design and implementation of software, supervising programmers and informing programmers on new approaches; (2) creating new approaches to using computers—networking, database, human–computer

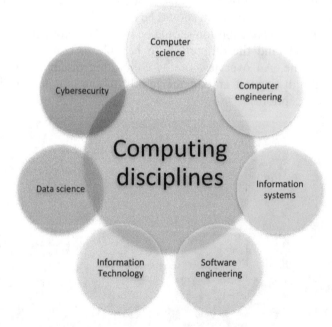

Figure 1.2. The taxonomy of the computing disciplines.

interaction, robotics, etc; (3) development of an effective method of solving computing problems, e.g. the best method of storing information in databases, exchange of data over the internet and display of complex images as well as the determination of the best performance algorithm (Shackelford *et al* 2006).

1.2.2 Software engineering

SE emerges as an academic discipline area from computer science, as shown in figure 1.3. The emergence of SE became necessary because of increasing complexity, cost and difficulties in producing reliable software. In addition, one individual would not be able to understand the whole program, and the various components of the program that interact in an unpredictable manner. The term SE emerged from a conference sponsored by NATO in Garmisch, Germany in 1968. SE is mainly concerned with the development and maintaining of software systems, including complex software and safety critical applications that are reliable, efficient, cost effective and capture all the user requirements. The software engineering discipline differs from other engineering disciplines because of the intangible and discontinuous nature of the software operation. SE combines the principles of mathematics, CS and engineering practices. SE mainly focuses on rigorous methods of designing and building software that reliably works as it is supposed to work (Shackelford *et al* 2006).

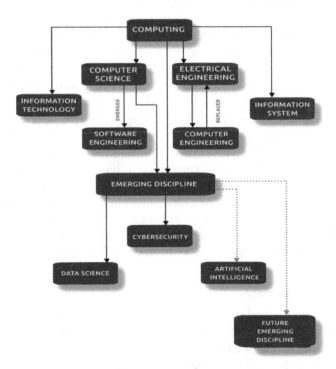

Figure 1.3. Emergence of the computing disciplines.

1.2.3 Computer engineering

Before the breakthrough of the invention of chip-based microprocessors, electrical engineering was among the computing family because computers used vacuum tubes and subsequently transistors. The advent of the microprocessor in the mi-1970s prompted the emergence of the CE discipline. CE was within electrical engineering before it split into CE and electrical engineering, as shown in figure 1.3.

CE is mainly focused on design and construction of computers, including computer-based systems. CE involves the learning of hardware, software, communications, and their interaction. The theories, principles, and practices of CE are from electrical engineering and mathematics. Subsequently, these were applied for solving problems of designing and developing computers and computer-based systems. CE students study software development but mainly focus on digital devices software and their interfaces. The emphasis in CE is more on hardware than software, or there could be some balanced emphasis. Examples of devices that require embedded software are as follows: cell phones, digital audio players, digital video recorders, alarm systems, x-ray machines and laser surgical equipment (Shackelford *et al* 2006).

1.2.4 Information systems

Before the 1990s, IS specialists mainly focused on the computing requirement of the business world. The expansion of the role of computers and organizations triggered more information available than had ever been seen before. The organizational processes were increasingly being enabled by computing technology. As such, the problems of managing the information became complex and challenging. Thus, IS grew into a complex field of study. IS mainly focuses on the combination of IT solutions and business processes so as to meet the required information of businesses and enterprises. This can enable businesses and enterprises to achieve their objectives in an effective and efficient manner. IS is more to do with information and it is considered the technology as a means to generate, process and distribute information. IS professionals are more concerned with information that is generated from the computer to help business and enterprises achieved their target. The professionals are responsible for determining how information and technology based business can be used to improve competitive advantage. The IS professionals have a key role to play in the determination of organization information systems and provide specification, design and implementation. Therefore, organizational practice and principles must be understood by IS professionals (Shackelford *et al* 2006).

1.2.5 Information technology

IT began to emerge in the late 1990s when computers sprung up as an essential working tool in many organizations and networked computers became the backbone of the information in the organization. Applications of the computers enhance productivity, but also reduce productivity if problems exist in the computing infrastructure. Thus, IT departments were created in corporations and organizations saddled with the responsibility of ensuring smooth working of the computing infrastructure. At the end of the 1990s, universities and colleges started developing programs in IT for graduates with the mix of the right knowledge and skills to meet these basic requirements. IT has two meanings: firstly, IT is frequently referred to as computing and secondly, in academia, it is a discipline that prepares students to meet the needs of business, government, healthcare, schools etc in terms of computer technology. IT emphasis is more on the computer technology than the information it conveys. Today's organization needs to have systems working properly, secured, and upgraded, maintained, and replaced when the need arises. Employees in organizations need the support of the IT staff that understand both the computer systems and software and are committed to solving related problems in the computer systems (Shackelford *et al* 2006).

1.2.6 Cybersecurity

The development of CyS can be traced back to when the first mainframe computers were created. Security systems on multiple levels were created for the protection of the device and its goals. As time passes, the need for national security continues growing to the extent of complex and sophisticated technology based security guards. In the early development of CyS, it was a simple process mostly involving physical classification of documents in view of the fact that the main threat to security was largely physical involving equipment theft. However, as cyberspace expanded, the reliance of society on the cyber infrastructure has increased exponentially, and the threat to the environment is rapidly increasing. CyS starts with computer security building on the foundation of information security and information assurance (ACM 2017).

The shortage of human resources in CyS prompted the emergence of CyS to develop the required talent. As a result, programmes on CyS started springing up across the computing ecosystem for establishing cybersecurity programs. By August 2015, ACM recognized the need for the establishment of the cybersecurity curriculum to create a task force in conjunction with other scientific computing societies on CyS education for the development of a comprehensive cybersecurity curriculum to serve as a guide for cybersecurity education. The new CyS program is developed based on the foundation of the five computing disciplines: CS, IS, IT, CE and SE. The ACM joint task force defined CyS as the discipline in computing that involved technology, people, information and processes to guarantee operation within the context of adversaries. It ensured the security of a computer systems by creating, operating, analysing and testing of the computer systems. The CyS discipline is interdisciplinary in nature because it cut across law, policy, ethics and management of risk (ACM 2017). The emerging field of CyS is now a discipline within the computing ecosystem, as shown in figure 1.3.

1.2.7 Data science

Viewing the conversation on DS, the ACM in August 2017 created a task force to explore the possibility of adding it to the computing ecosystem with an articulation for its role in the computing ecosystem specific discipline contributions to the emerging discipline area. The joint task force was charged with the responsibility to define the computing contributions to the emerging discipline and discuss a guide on the competencies specific to computing in DS to serve as a benchmark to the departments offering DS as a program. The emergence of DS as a discipline is related to the generation of large-scale data across multiple domains. The rapid expansion of large-scale raw or structured data are seen in science, engineering, social sciences, business, humanities and engineering as opportunities for discovery and making informed decisions. The large-scale nature of the data is beyond human analysis with the intervention of automated processes. DS merges domain data, CS, and statistics for analyzing the data to extract new or useful information. Each component of DS has its own role. For instance, the domain generates the data; analysis, modeling and inference are performed by statistical tools and mathematics and lastly, CS provides data access, management, security and using modern computer architecture for processing (ACM 2021). The emerging field of DS is now a discipline within the computing ecosystem, as shown in figure 1.3.

1.2.8 Emerging areas: artificial intelligence

The computing curriculum is expanding rapidly with new emerging disciplines trying to form part of the computing ecosystem. Subsequently, a variety of educational disciplines that focus on the cross-domain is expanding. Among them, recently, artificial intelligence (AI) (see figure 1.3) is attracting very high interest and it is believed to be complex in nature. AI is not a completely new concept as it has its roots back in the 1950s. However, AI witnessed a tremendous boost in the last decade. Robotics in AI has become a popular field in computing. However, at the time of writing this chapter there is no formal ACM curricula to serve as a guiding principle for departments running an AI programme, though it is expected to emerge in the near future (ACM 2021). As computing is becoming complex with the need for additional disciplines, we expect the emerging of additional disciplines in the computing ecosystem.

1.3 Comparing the focus of the seven disciplines within the computing ecosystem

The computing disciplines have progressed to seven, as shown in figure 1.4 from three in 2004, as described in the previous sections that clearly distinguish between the disciplines. We believe the misconception about the computing disciplines among computing students and graduates will disappear after reading this chapter. To provide a summary of the differences that exist among the seven computing disciplines, we created this section to give the reader the main focus for each of the disciplines. The summary of the main focus for each of the computing disciplines is provided in table 1.1 for easy reference to the main focus of each discipline.

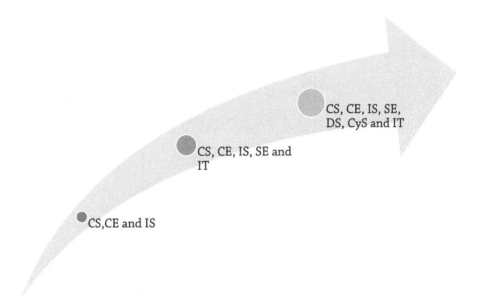

Figure 1.4. Progression of computing disciplines.

1.4 Scientific research in computing

The major mechanism for the advancement of development in computing is typically initiated by research (Glass *et al* 2004). Since there is no universally accepted definition of research, it varies across different research communities. Therefore, in this chapter we try to give the general definition of research before narrowing it to computing.

Research is a process of conducting certain activities systematically such as administering and analyzing a survey questionnaire, performing experiments, ethnography/observing participants, development of root definition and proposing conceptual models. These techniques are generally well defined sequence operations that form research activities to produce a predictable outcome (Mingers 2001). Another definition of research is that it is a process of achieving goals to find new outcomes and development of human knowledge. Before delving into scientific research, science is the experience gained by humans based on experiment or experience. The process to achieve these goals is referred to as scientific research (CIKD 2020). Research in computing deals with artificial phenomena unlike natural science which deals with natural phenomena. Scientific research in computing is the investigation of the world related to computing to discover new knowledge, performance improvements, models, applications, interpret existing knowledge or knowledge that is incomplete related to any aspect of the computing ecosystem (Salim 2015).

1.4.1 Types of research

There are two main categories of research, which will be discussed before relating them to computing. The reader needs an understanding of the different types of

Table 1.1. Comparing the main focus for each of the disciplines in computing.

Discipline	Algorithms foundation	Creation of new computing method	Computer design and construction	Embedded software	Complex software development	More information solution than the computer	More computer solution than the information	Extensive data analytics	Computer systems security
CS	✓	✓	✗	✗	✗	✗	✗	✗	✗
SE	✗	✗	✗	✗	✓	✗	✗	✗	✗
CE	✗	✗	✓	✓	✗	✗	✗	✗	✗
IS	✗	✗	✗	✗	✗	✓	✗	✗	✗
IT	✗	✗	✗	✗	✗	✗	✓	✗	✗
CyS	✓	✗	✗	✗	✗	✗	✗	✗	✓
DS	✗	✗	✗	✗	✗	✗	✗	✓	✗

research in general terms before narrowing them to computing. Researches are in different forms but in a broad category, research is categorized into two different classes. The two main classes of the research are as follows.

1.4.1.1 Fundamental or basic research

Fundamental or basic research is conducted to gain new scientific theories as well as expand the horizon of science in different areas. In this category of research, the main focus is on scientific theories through the discovery of principles or rules. Typically, in fundamental research, the application of the outcome in the real world is given less attention and it is mostly performed in the laboratory, on animals, etc. It is found that psychologists are highly interested in this type of research (CIKD 2020). However, the basic research cuts across different research domains including computing. We have basic research in computing, which refers to research that expands the understanding of theories through discovery processes in relation to computing. For example, Chiroma *et al* (2016) proposed the training of an artificial neural network using a flower pollination algorithm instead of the commonly used backpropagation algorithm. Rehman *et al* (2021) proposed a new team formation algorithm for the formation of an expert team called search space reduction team formation, based on communication cost and graph reduction. It is proposed for the extraction of experts for collaboration. The researches are considered as basic research because the results gave less attention to real-world applications, they only expanded the understanding of the algorithms.

1.4.1.2 Applied research

Applied research is the second category of research. It is conducted very fast to swiftly solve problems and take the required action. In applied research, the outcome/finding/discovery of fundamental research is used to solve problems or more simply putting fundamental research into action. Applied research is mainly focused on real-world applications and scientific matters unlike the fundamental research that is highly theoretical. Typically, applied research is not conducted in a laboratory in view of its nature, it is conducted to tackle social, political, etc realities in society (CIKD 2020). We have applied research in computing, which refers to research that puts fundamental research into action through application processes in direct relation to computing. For example, during the COVID-19 pandemic, robots were applied for the collection of patient samples for diagnosis to minimize the chances of spreading the virus (Sarker *et al* 2021). This research can be considered as applied because it puts fundamental research into action.

1.5 Research philosophy and origin of research in computing

The system of beliefs and assumptions about research on developing knowledge is called philosophy of research. In simple terms, it is the activities carryied out when conducting research in a particular research field. When conducting research, knowingly or unknowingly, researchers make certain assumptions at different stages of the research process (Burrell and Morgan 1979). These assumptions can be epistemology—assumption about knowledge development, ontology—realities encountered in the process of the research, and axiology—the extent to which your values influence the research. A well-grounded assumption determines the credibility of the research philosophy that underpins the choice of the methodology, strategies of the research, data collection techniques and analysis (Saunders *et al* 2009). In computing, the research philosophy differs depending on the research field in which the research is conducted as there is no universally accepted research methodology for computing ecosystems. The methodology deployed in human–computer interaction research differs from the methodology for conducting research in machine learning (ML) or IS. Chapter 6 discusses research methodology in the context of each discipline in computing.

1.5.1 Origin of research in computer science

Research in CS has struggled with identity. The CS discipline has a strong background from mathematics theories, for example, the Turing machine and the halting problem—computational complexity theory; the relational model, expressive power of query languages—databases, etc. CS also has an engineering background that led to machines that have changed society. The research in computers is derived from the same discipline. The mathematical approach has axioms, postulates, proofs and the engineering approach has quantity, measurement and comparing. CS has traditional emphasis on publishing research papers in conferences instead of journals as practiced by other disciplines, though it has been a subject of debate in the research community. Currently, publication is the common practice for quantifying scientific output. For that reason, pressure is mounting on PhD students to publish in peer reviewed journals for organizing their PhD around the collection of the published papers. The common practice is for the PhD student to have workshop papers outlining the idea of the research, especially in the beginning of the process; halfway into the PhD one is expected to published two conference papers with some preliminary findings; journal publications summarizing major findings of the research. Based on these activities, a computer scientist is expected to publish a significant number of papers in peer reviewed venues and should have a good understanding of the peer review cycle to increase their success rate. In CS research, the methodology differs depending on the nature of the research to be conducted, as explained below (Demeyer 2012).

1.5.1.1 Formal
The methodologies applied in formal methodology are used for proving effectiveness of algorithms and systems about their facts. An example is the formal specification of a software component for allowing automated verification of the components implemented. For algorithms, time or space complexity of the algorithm can be measured or a measure can be made of the performance of the algorithm in terms of correctness or solution quality (Amaral *et al* 2011).

1.5.1.2 Experiment

Experimental method in computing science is used for the evaluation of a newly generated solution for a certain problem. The phases of the experimental evaluation are two-fold, namely, exploration and evaluation. In exploration, the system under evaluation is observed to help identify questions about the system that are seeking an answer. The question identified in the exploration phases seeks for answers in the evaluation phase (Amaral *et al* 2011). For example, to improve the solution quality of an artificial neural network algorithm, the algorithm is trained using the cuckoo search algorithm. It is then applied to predict the crude oil price. To measure the performance of evolutionary algorithms, baseline algorithms were applied for the prediction of the crude oil price. The performance of the evolutionary neural network in crude oil price prediction is compared with the baseline algorithms, and it was found that the evolutionary neural network performs better than the baseline algorithms (Chiroma *et al* 2015).

1.5.1.3 Build

This methodology involves building of artefacts. The artefact build should be new or add new features to an already existing artefact to make it a research. The artefact constructed can be a physical or software based system (Amaral *et al* 2011). This methodology can be deployed in human–computer interaction as it involves the design, development and evaluation of the artefact.

1.5.2 Origin of research in software engineering

The emergence of research in SE has been shrouded in controversy by suffering from identity crises that prompted advocacy for well-grounded research methodology for SE research. Research in SE gives strong emphasis on teamwork and processes. The emphasis on team has led to the issue of team dynamics as well as cognitive factors, therefore, psychology and sociology research methods were borrowed in SE research. Other research methodology in SE involved case studies for investigating real-life contemporary phenomena in their real context (Demeyer 2012). SE research hinges on processes but there is a growing interest in empirical methods. The empirical methods comprise experiment, surveys, metrics, case studies and field study used for the investigation of SE processes (Singer and Vinson 2002).

One of the goals of SE research is to come up with effective processes of constructing and evolving large-scale software because of the following challenges: large teams, complexity, dynamic requirement, quality and disruptive technology. An effective process can instil discipline in the development of the system and improves its quality. Many of the scientific research techniques if used in SE research can give effective processes or tools that can be used in reality. For instance, models development for software structure and behaviour, proof of concept development, experimentation with developers and users. Having an intense experience of the techniques can lead to the processes of model-driven development, improved collaborative strategies, and assistive tools for both of them (Elio *et al* 2011).

1.5.3 Origin of research in information systems

IS has a long history in conducting research within the computing ecosystem and data derived from society and businesses. IS has long been recognized since the emergence of computers that automate business processes and transactions. IS emerged to unravel the design and implementation of systems for providing information at the right time to the right people. This concept defined early research in IS. As such, it entailed the comprehension of individual and executive data requirement, therefore, it captures and manages data by designing the required structure and interface for accessing and using the data. It is not out of place to claim that IS scholars set the stage for big data in the early days of computing in view of the fact that they were equipped with the technique of storing, managing, processing and understanding the complexity of data (Agarwal and Lucas 2005). IS researchers have a broad perspective in enterprises compared to other functional business areas, thus creating a strong synergy between business models and data. The emphasis in IS research is on business transformation and creation of value from the data but putting less emphasis on the algorithms. IS researchers were criticized for heavy cross-domain research but they perceive it as a strength not a weakness considering the data rich environment in today's world (Agarwal and Dhar 2014). The research method suitable for application in IS research has been a subject of debate with the three research methods in consideration for IS researchers being positive, interpretivist and critical. But the positivist framework has taken the centre stage since 1988 and it keeps growing (Mingers 2001). Research in IS has been predominantly conducted on the impact of information technology artefact on users, teams and the organization (Hevner and Chatterjee 2010). IS researchers are expected to conduct research that has productive application of IT to organizations as a whole, including management (Zmud 1997).

1.5.4 Origin of research in information technology

The potential of IT to impact positively and negatively in organizations has attracted scientific attention. Another factor that attracted scientists is the pervasiveness of IT phenomena in the present information society. Scientists believe that these phenomena can be explained with scientific theories in the hope that scientific research will improve IT practice. The scientific interest in IT is classified into two: descriptive and prescriptive. The goal of descriptive research in IT is to understand the nature of IT, whereas prescriptive aims to improve performance of IT. The classification trigger debate in the IT research community is about scientific research in IT. This debate is not surprising because it is common in the field that it is activity involving the production and use of knowledge. Arguably, the research in IT aims at developing the IT system, improve IT practice is successful compared to the attempt to understand IT. Research in IT deals with artificial phenomena, unlike natural science that deals with natural phenomena that can be created and studied (Simon 1981). The research methods in IT are dominated by the collection of data and assessing the data (March and Smith 1995).

IT research studies the changes about an artefact in an environment and changes in the components. The framework for research in IT involves research activities and research output. Research in IT develops and evaluates constructs, model, method and instantiation. These artefacts are theorized and the theories are justified. Subsequently, they build and evaluate IT artefacts. The research activities involve build, evaluate, theories and justify. IT research is expected to address a design problem facing the practitioners. The problem has to be conceptualized and a suitable solution constructed. The solution is implemented and evaluated using the appropriate criteria. The justification for the working or otherwise of IT systems is to be established for IT to make progress considering both the IT systems and the operating environment (March and Smith 1995).

1.5.5 Origin of research in data science

John Tukey in 1962 predicted the merging of statistics and computers to speed up data analysis that would take a long time to complete when processed manually, shorten it to hours rather than the days it typically takes. In preparing for future challenges, Cleveland (2001) plans to train data scientists to cope with the future challenges in data analytics. An action plan was prepared, in which Cleveland described the procedure to increase the technical expertise and the range of the data analysts including the specification of six areas to departments in Universities. Cleveland promoted the development of resources for research in the six areas: multidisciplinary investigations, models and methods, computing with data, pedagogy, tool evaluation and theory that give the foundation of DS. Subsequently, the plan was applied to government and corporate research. In business and academic research DS has become important. Research in DS has expanded to include informatics, biological science, healthcare, humanities, social science, and medical sciences (Foote 2016). The technique of DS must be learned by the specialist to broaden the understanding of the world while the non-specialist needs literacy skills to be productive members of society in the 21st century world's workforce as data continues accumulating unprecedentedly and the world is dominated by data (Press 2013).

1.5.6 Origin of research in cybersecurity

Research in CyS began from the efforts made by the 'phreaker' or by phone freaking. It was the movement for studying and understanding telephone communication systems manipulation. It was reverse engineering where phreakers learned the working of the telephone system and its operation. The goal was to manipulate the communication system to gain free services especially long-distance calls. Phreaking was the first CyS research dilemma showcasing duality and ethics for CyS. As others gained knowledge for gaining free phone calls the line of legality was crossed (Edgar and Manz 2017). The first worm was created by a graduate student to investigate how large was the internet. The worm spread on the internet using multiple exploits of vulnerable services. The student made a mistake in the worm propagation strategy whereby machines were infected multiple times including denial of service operations. The approach to inserting code in a computer forcefully was tagged as illegal and unethical. The graduate student was the pioneer convicted for cybercrime under the computer fraud and abuse act (Edgar and Manz 2017).

Research methods in CyS are categorized into two, namely, formal theoretical and simulation. The theoretical method of CyS research mostly crosses over to other research fields. For example, cryptography and cryptanalysis are research areas in CyS that cross the boundary into mathematics, linguistics and theory of computations. In some cases, theoretical research in CyS can make it divergent to other categories of research because of its multidisciplinary nature. The key idea in CyS theoretical research is the definition of the abstract ideas based on mathematics or computational models to represent cyberspace. The choice of CyS research methods, theoretical or simulation, depends on the availability of resources at the researcher's disposal and the research interest. The choice of simulation method can be considered if the research is working with an already established theory or is close to getting a theory that is defined and one wants to evaluate it under different conditions. Also, the simulation can be adopted if there is no theory and the concept couldn't be defined with mathematical notations. On the other hand, a formal theoretical method can be adopted for the research if there is no define theory but it can be constrained and the situation modeled using mathematics like the formal method (Edgar and Manz 2017).

1.5.7 Origin of research in computer engineering

The research in CE originated as a result of the advent of the processor in place of the vacuum tube for executing instructions in the computer. Research in CE deals mainly with the design and implementation of computer-based systems, more from the hardware aspect of the computer system than the software. Thus, CE research comprised both the hardware and software as well as experiment and theories. Research in CE is extended to embedded systems, device design automation, communication protocols, high performance systems, cyber physical systems, computer architecture, distributed systems, computer networks, VLSI architectures, design of energy efficient device, reliable real-time computer systems, etc as outlined by the University of California Irvine and University of California Davis department of electrical engineering and CS and department of electrical and CE, respectively.

1.6 Comparing research methods in discipline within the computing ecosystems

The previous section discusses the origin of research in each computing discipline. The research methods in the seven different disciplines in the computing ecosystem differ depending on the discipline as well as research philosophy. Each of the disciplines has its own research focus and emphasis, therefore, the research methodology will definitely be different. A summary of the differences that exist in the different disciplines is presented in table 1.2 to give readers the opportunity to compare and contrast. This will give the reader a clear perspective of the differences.

Table 1.2. Comparing research methodologies in different computing disciplines.

Computer science	Software engineering	Information systems	Information technology	Computer engineering	Data science	Cybersecurity
• Formal • Experiment • Build • Process • Model	• Processes • Survey • Case study • Empirical • Metrics • Field study	• Positive • Interpretivist • Critical	• Design • Build • Implementation • Evaluation • Grounded theory	• System design, implementation	• Data analytics	• Theoretical • Simulation • Implement

1.7 Generic procedure for computing research

This section presents the summary of the research process in computing but the details can be found across the chapters in the book. The process of conducting research in computing differs from discipline to discipline within the computing ecosystem depending on the objective and nature of the research. However, a general procedure exists, the discipline to conduct the research is chosen depending on the research area the student is pursuing to obtain a degree such as a PhD, MSc or BSc in CS, DS or IS. Rigorous literature review should be conducted by the researcher based on a topic from the discipline the student intended to earn the degree in to establish the research problem before proposing the methodology to solve the problem established from the literature (see chapter 3 for literature review and problem formulation). Then, the nature of the research methodology depends on the discipline to conduct the research. For example, in SE, case study or experiment can be chosen depending on the nature of the research to be conducted in the SE discipline.

The method of the data collection depends on the type of research methodology adopted, for example, if a survey is selected, a questionnaire or interview can be adopted for the collection of the data. If experiment is chosen in CS, the data collection can be done through observations. After the data collection, data engineering is applied to improve the quality of the data before feeding the data to an algorithm for analytics.

Different techniques for data analysis are available in different disciplines within the computing ecosystem, it also depends on the nature of the data, objective of the research, etc, for example, an interview conducted to gather qualitative data can be analysed using NVivo, and data collected based on observations from experiment in CS can be analysed using algorithms.

1.8 Features of quality and bad research

The research conducted should be of high quality. As such, all the features of quality research should be upheld for the research to be regarded as a quality research. Trust is the backbone of all research, a researcher is expected to be trustworthy and always conduct research by upholding all the research ethics. The features of good research should be as follows: the research conducted should be based on the works of other researchers (establishingd the problem from literature review); the methodology used in the research should be in detail in such a way that it can be replicated by another researcher to get the same result; the research can be applicable to another domain; the research should be on the foundation of theory and logical rationale; it is possible to conduct the research clearly; there is the ability to generate new questions; the research should have the potential for impact in society; data is from a credible source and sufficient for the research; there should be no hidden assumption in the research; analysis of the data should be properly performed; the conclusion of the research has to be from the data used to conduct the research (Salim 2015).

On the other hand, the features of bad research are outlined as follows: plagiarism —stealing of other researchers' work and claiming it as one's own; falsification of data to support an argument; misrepresentation of information in the research; poor data from questionable sources; use of incomplete data to conduct the research; misleading of participants and readers. The features of bad research are the complete opposite of the features of good research (Salim 2015). See chapter 8 for research ethics in computing.

1.9 MSc, PhD and undergraduate project in computing

In computing, a PhD, MSc and first degree can be earned having satisfied all the institutional criteria for graduation. The PhD degree is the highest qualification that can be earned.

Extensive study and intellectual efforts by a candidate are required. The two major things that a PhD candidate has to accomplish includes mastering of the particular subject matter comprehensively and substantial extension of the body of knowledge about a subject (Salim 2015). Earning a PhD degree means that the candidate is a full-blown professional researcher with the capacity to conduct research that is of interest to the research community, and has a command of the subject and capacity to perform peer review (Phillips and Pugh 1994). Good PhD research is expected to have publication potential or have part of the work in press or published as evidence of the publication status of the research. There are universities that require part of the PhD research to be published before the PhD candidate graduates. An MSc is earned when the student shows evidence of critical reasoning and reasonable gain of knowledge and literature awareness. Subsequently, they should adopt the methodology to solve a problem. An undergraduate project is for earning a first degree, the candidate is expected to show a well-structured account of convincing study, solution of a problem or experimental results (Salim 2015). PhD/MSc can be completed by publications instead of the traditional thesis/ dissertation approach. For PhD/MSc the candidate is required to publish a number of related papers and compile the published papers sequentially with logical flow as the thesis/dissertation. The number of papers to publish varies across institutions. For example, in University of Malaya, graduation by publication requires the PhD candidate in any of the computing disciplines to publish at least three papers in ISI WoS—SCIE indexed journals, while for an MSc at least two published papers in ISI WoS—SCIE indexed journals (University of Malaya PG Handbook 2020).

1.10 Organization of the book

The book is logically organized into different chapters as follows:

Chapter 2: *Computing search engines and bibliographic databases*—In this chapter, different academic databases related to computing such as the Web of science, Scopus, ACM digital library, DBLP computer science bibliometric, Sciencedirect, Springerlink, IEEExplore, and Ei compendia are discussed.

Chapter 3: *Systematic literature review from computing perspective and research problem formulation*—The chapter discusses the procedure for conducting extensive systematic literature review from the perspective of computing before presenting the stages involve in developing problem formulation.

Chapter 4: *Computing research tools and resources*—The chapter discusses the tools required by researchers to implement a conceptual idea to ease the work of the researcher and improve the researcher's productivity.

Chapter 5: *Computing datasets and data engineering*—Considering the critical nature of data in research, we have dedicated this chapter to discuss different types of datasets and sources of the datasets for easy access to researchers. Data engineering and technique for managing research datasets are discussed.

Chapter 6: *Methodology from computing perspective*—This is the heart of the book that discusses methodology from the perspective of computing. Case studies were used to demonstrate the methodology from the different perspectives of the computing disciplines—CS, SE, IS, DS, CyS, CE and IT. The steps in developing a conceptual framework based on the problem established from the literature is discussed.

Chapter 7: *Scientific publishing in computing: beginners guide*—In this chapter, common mistakes that always lead to desk rejection of papers and what editors and reviewers are always looking for in a research paper are highlighted and discussed. The peer review process, responding to reviewer's comments, dealing with rejections, research highlights, cover letter, supplementary materials, and recommending reviewers for the researcher's own paper are all contained in the chapter. The chapter spells out the differences between thesis, journal paper and conference paper. We spell out the stages involved in developing journal paper—abstract, keywords, introduction, theoretical background, methodology, results and discussion, conclusions and references.

Chapter 8: *Research ethics in computing*—This chapter discusses ethics in computing research to provide readers, especially new researchers, with the ethics involving research misconduct, its implications and ways to avoid misconduct.

Chapter 9: *Emerging research trends in computing*—This chapter provides brief discussion on the emerging research directions in different aspects of computing for researchers to easily identify the trending topics in computing.

1.11 Summary

In this chapter, we provide an overview of computing and the five disciplines that make up the computing ecosystem: CS, CE, SE, IS and IT. We further discuss the two newly emerged disciplines, CyS and DS. Emerging areas (e.g. AI) are defined. To correct misconception about the computing disciplines, the origin and differences among the computing disciplines are outlined and discussed. For easy understanding by readers, taxonomies, figures and tables are created to give readers visual representation of the differences and origins of the disciplines. Scientific research in computing, procedure for scientific research, types of research in computing, features of good and bad research are discussed. We go further to discuss the origin of research in each of the disciplines. We believe the misconception about the computing disciplines among computing students and graduates may disappear after reading this chapter.

References

ACM 2017 *Cybersecurity Curricula 2017 Curriculum: Guidelines for Post-Secondary Degree Programs in Cybersecurity* (New York: ACM)

ACM 2021 *Computing Competencies for Undergraduate Data Science Curricula: ACM Data Science Task Force* (New York: ACM)

Agarwal R and Dhar V 2014 Big data, data science, and analytics: the opportunity and challenge for IS research *Inform. Syst. Res.* **25** 443–8

Agarwal R, & Lucas Jr. H C 2005 The Information Systems Identity Crisis: Focusing on High-Visibility and High-Impact Research MIS Quarterly **29** 381–98

Amaral J N, Buro M, Elio R, Hoover J, Nikolaidis I, Salavatipour M, Stewart L, & Wong K 2011 About Computing Science Research Methodology. http://webdocs.cs.ualberta.ca/~amaral/courses/603/readings/research-methods.pdf (Accessed: 14 October 2021)

Burrell W G & Morgan G 1979 Sociological Paradigms and Organizations Analysis (London: Heinemann)

Canadian Institute for Knowledge Development—CIKD 2020 Types of scientific research https://cscitconf.cikd.ca/ (accessed 19 November 2021)

Chiroma H, Khan A, Abubakar A I, Saadi Y, Hamza M F, Shuib L, Gital A Y and Herawan T 2016 A new approach for forecasting OPEC petroleum consumption based on neural network train by using flower pollination algorithm *Appl. Soft Comput.* **48** 50–8

Chiroma H, Abdulkareem S and Herawan T 2015 Evolutionary Neural Network model for West Texas Intermediate crude oil price prediction *Appl. Energy* **142** 266–73

Cleveland W S 2001 Data science: an action plan for expanding the technical areas of the field of statistics *Int. Stat. Rev.* **69** 21–6

Demeyer S 2012 Research methods in computer science *IEEE 27th International Conference on Software Maintenance, ICSM 2011 (Williamsburg, VA, September 25–30)*

Edgar T and Manz D 2017 *Research Methods for Cyber Security* (Oxford: Syngress)

Elio R, Hoover J, Nikolaidis I, Salavatipour M, Stewart L and Wong K 2011 About computing science research methodology https://webdocs.cs.ualberta.ca/~amaral/courses/MetodosDePesquisa/papers/Amaral-research-methods.pdf (Accessed: 11 December 2021)

Glass R L, Ramesh V and Vessey I 2004 An analysis of research in computing disciplines *Commun. ACM* **47** 89–94

Foote K D 2016 *A brief history of data science* https://dataversity.net/brief-history-data-science/ (accessed 19 November 2021)

Hevner A and Chatterjee S 2010 Design science research in information systems *Design Research in Information Systems* (Boston, MA: Springer), pp 9–22

March S T and Smith G F 1995 Design and natural science research on information technology *Decis. Support Syst.* **15** 251–66

Mingers J 2001 Combining IS research methods: towards a pluralist methodology *Inf. Syst. Res.* **12** 240–59

Phillips E M and Pugh D S 1994 *How to Get a PhD* 2nd edn (Buckinghamshire: Open University Press)

Press G 2013 A very short history of data science *Forbes Magazine* https://forbes.com/sites/gilpress/2013/05/28/a-very-short-history-of-data-science/ (Accessed 19 November 2021)

Rehman M Z, Zamli K Z, Almutairi M, Chiroma H, Aamir M, Kader M A and Nawi N M 2021 A novel state space reduction algorithm for team formation in social networks *PLoS One* **16** e0259786

Salim N 2015 *UCP 0010 – research methodology (slides)* (Department of Information Systems, Faculty of Computing, Universiti Teknologi Malaysia)

Sarker S, Jamal L, Ahmed S F and Irtisam N 2021 Robotics and artificial intelligence in healthcare during COVID-19 pandemic: a systematic review *Rob. Autom. Syst.* **146** 103902

Saunders M, Lewis P and Thornhill A 2009 Understanding research philosophies and approaches *Res. Methods Bus. Stud.* **4** 106–35

Shackelford R, McGettrick A, Sloan R, Topi H, Davies G, Kamali R, Cross J, Impagliazzo J, LeBlanc R & Lunt, B. 2006 Computing Curricula 2005: The Overview Report ACM SIGCSE Bulletin, **38** 456–7

Simon H A 1981 *The Sciences of the Artificial* 2nd edn (Cambridge, MA: MIT Press)

Singer J and Vinson N G 2002 Ethical issues in empirical studies of software engineering *IEEE Trans. Software Eng.* **28** 1171–80

University of Malaya PG Handbook 2020 Institute of Graduate Studies, University of Malaya, Guidelines for the degree of doctor of philosophy program by publication mode (prior publications)

Weber R 1987 Toward a theory of artifacts: a paradigmatic base for information systems research *J. Inf. Syst.* **1** 3–19

Zmud R 1997 Editor's comments *MIS Q.* 21 xxi–ii

Chapter 2

Computing search engines and bibliographic databases

The pattern of information retrieval changes as a result of internet development, especially Web 2.0. Academic search engines and bibliometric databases are used by researchers to retrieve credible publications. Different academic databases exist for different disciplines and area of specialization. However, the focus of this chapter is academic search engines indexing computing scientific publications. The reputable search engines for retrieving scientific computing publications are outlined and discussed. We believe that after reading this chapter, the reader will be conversant with the world largest and comprehensive academic search engines and bibliometric databases indexing computing scientific literature that researchers rely on for discovery and retrieval of computing specific content that is accurate, reliable, complete and updated. It can make it easy for new and novice researchers to access reputable scientific publications in computing—computer science (CS), computer engineering (CE), software engineering (SE), cybersecurity (CyS), information systems (IS), data science (DS) and information technology (IT).

2.1 Introduction

A lot of information exists on the internet having its own share of the good, the bad and the ugly side like the physical world. The internet is experiencing a surge of information on a daily basis without control. Disinformation, poor literature without credible source and fake news keep proliferating on the internet, uncontrollable to the extent that the internet community see it as a source of serious concern. The academic community is not immune to the distortion of literature on the internet. Many questionable sources of academic literature are flooding the internet such as predatory journals, conferences, seminars, workshops and symposia. In such predatory venues, any work submitted can be published as long as the author is willing to pay the publication fees. These type of venue for publication don't subject the submitted manuscript to any form of rigorous peer review process as demanded by the typical practice in the academic community. On the other hand, the identity of some credible journals are being hijacked by fraudulent individuals to deceive reputable researchers into submitting research work thinking it is the authentic website of the original journal. Many researchers and students fall into this trap unintentionally. Predatory publication venues dilute science with questionable and fake results, and scam scholars.

Developing a research manuscript for submission to a credible journal/conference requires the researchers to build the manuscript with literature from credible sources. No matter how excellent the research results, if the literature is built around predatory/fake journals and conference papers, the manuscript cannot be accepted in a credible/reputable journal for publication. Submitting a manuscript for publication to a credible journal requires the literature to be built with literature from top reputable publication venues.

To respond to the issues raised in the previous paragraph, the academic search engines and bibliographic databases (ASEBDs) were developed to index only reputable academic literature. Researchers and students can only focus on ASEBDs as the source of literature for conducting research to avoid falling into the trap of predatory literature.

Internet technology has revolutionized the pattern of information retrieval from the traditional offline system. Notably, in the late 1990s, the ASEBDs began to receive more attention from scholars and students as tools they used to access up-to-date and relevant information for scientific investigations (Haines *et al* 2010). Gradually, the ASEBDs become the widely acceptable services to retrieve up-to-date scientific publications, therefore, increasingly replacing the traditional offline system of information retrieval (Haines *et al* 2010, Gusenbauer 2019). It makes the ASEBDs the standard databases for accessing scientific publications.

The ASEBDs are of different categories depending on the literature indexed in the database. For example, Web of Science (WoS) and Scopus ASEBDs index literature across multi-disciplines such as science and technology, social science and humanities. ASEBDs disciplines can be specific, like the Ei-Compendix that indexes only literature from engineering disciplines, or DBLP computer science bibliography that only indexes literature from computing disciplines. However, this chapter mainly focuses on the computing ASEBDs because the focus of the book is purely for readers interested in computing research.

The purpose of writing this chapter is to outline and discuss computing ASEBDs to properly guide students and new career researchers pursuing scientific discovery in computing on the ASEBDs for use in retrieving reputable computing literature. This can shield the students and new career researchers from falling into the trap of predatory literature.

2.2 The computing academic databases

There are 10 computing ASEBDs, as shown in figure 2.1, indexing literature on computing. Among the 10 ASEBDs, DBLP computer science bibliography (DBLP)

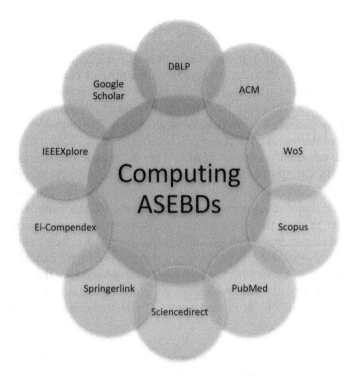

Figure 2.1. Computing academic search engines and bibliographic databases.

and ACM digital library index only literature emanating from computing disciplines. The other eight ASEBDs index computing literature and publications from other disciplines. The ASEBDs discussed are not the exhaustive list of ASEBDs indexing computing literature but certainly these are the top ASEBDs for computing literature. The subsequent sections outline and dicuss the ASEBDs.

2.2.1 Clarivate Analytics Web of Science

From the perspective of computing, WoS covers scientific publications from CS, CE, SE, CyS, IS, DS and IT classified under Science Citation Index Expanded (SCIE).

The Clarivate Analytics WoS is multidisciplinary and the most powerful academic search database in the world, covering over 34 000 journals, well-organized with ideas from almost one billion, seven hundred million references from at least one hundred and fifty five million or more different areas of specializations at different period of time. And following the inventor of the citation index for research literature, the legacy of Dr Eugene Garfield, WoS has been the highest academic research database in terms of efficiency that delivers sufficient discovery, access, and assessment from the top-notch published papers as well as information with regards to citation. This platform cuts across provincial, professional, data as well as patent indexes to the WoS Core Collection, the actual global citation index. This platform is encyclopedic in searching standard and world class literature that connects with well-organized peer-reviewed journals and is able to uncover unique information through the help of well-assembled metadata and citation connections (Clarivate 2022).

Research data is rapidly growing. Data provides the opportunity to confidently understand and make a decision by revealing meaningful insights between current and past findings, associates, sponsorship and effects of research. The WoS Core Collection which involves more than twenty one thousand peer-reviewed journals, excellent globally published journals (as well as open access journals); more than two hundred and five thousand conference proceedings; and more than one hundred and four thousand editorially chosen books. The databases pay more attention to Medline, BIOSIS Citation Index, and Zoological data; a focus specified chronicle involves Derwent Innovation Index (patent) as well as data citation index which includes datasets and data studies. It includes other databases that shed additional ideas from other parts of the globe such as the Russian Science Citation Index, KCI Korean Journal database, as well as SciELO Citation Index. Traversing through all relevant databases available on the platform, it extracts content capturing numerous study areas, nature of chronicles, and formats and determines the citation linkage between various contents. The WoS core collection only indexes journals' extraordinary thorough editorial work and abiding by best publishing practice (Web of Science Group 2022).

2.2.1.1 Criteria for title selection for inclusion in Web of Science

The WoS Editors are free to determine the extraction of recently added titles as well as re-assessment of already available titles found in the WoS. The Editors have the right to decline any journal from any Clarivate product or service if the publisher's editorial policy or business norms retrogressively affect the journal quality, or its impact with regards to surrounding literature of the subject. WoS Editors may also reject titles from being active any time in case there is failure of meeting up to expected standardized quality, failure of adhering to ethical standard, or if any case fails to meet up with the laid down rules or norms by the Editors. In case a journal is rejected from coverage, the journal indexing will no longer be associated with the WoS commencing immediately on a date decided by the WoS Editors, additionally, articles published at the end of the set date will not be indexed. The WoS Editors' resolution on every issue with regards to journal coverage is final (Web of Science Group 2022).

2.2.2 Scopus

The Scopus search engine is an academic database organized by independent experts in the subject matter. The Scopus database was launched in November 2004 and now covers more than twenty five thousand one hundred titles from more than five thousand international publishers. It is known to unveil an up-to-date review of the overall contribution resulting from studies in the areas of science, technology, medicine, social science together with arts and humanities (Research Intelligence 2020). Scopus combines comprehensive, well drafted abstracts by experts and a citation database with data that is enriched as well as linked publications across multiple disciplines. Scopus enables librarians, researchers and principal R&D experts to get ideas for making informed and reliable decisions in taking an action. Scopus has been the choice of leading educational institutions, businesses as well as organizations owned by government authorities from as far back as 2004. Superior quality, data coverage and advance analytic tools are provided by Scopus in a single platform. Typically, Scopus provides assistance in the following aspects:

- Checking copyright or ownership of publication including promoting the privacy of the scholars' data;
- Giving power for efficient and effective monitoring of research trends;
- Empowering the performance, reputation and ranking of institutions;
- Promoting the zeal of funding authorities to enhance the rate of the funding.

The Scopus database has remained the best choice when it comes to researchers pushing for groundbreaking scientific discovery, agencies of government whose responsibility is to assess research and ranking institutions carrying out evaluation. In all, there are more than five thousand academic, corporate and government organizations that make use of Scopus, it is considered as the original point through which the worldwide research intelligence portfolio emanates (Scopus 2022).

2.2.3 Comparing the Scopus and Web of Science

The world of scientific research today keeps publishing a large number of papers from different fields and disciplines. It is pertinent, therefore, to assess the most efficient databases that are objectives for literature searches. To this end, WoS and Scopus seem to be the giants that provide the most comprehensive and efficient databases for literature searches. Besides the services of rendering literature searches, these two platforms rank journals' impact, prestige and influence based on their productivity and the total citations received (Aghaei Chadegani *et al* 2013).

The most widely used databases in the field of science for literature search are the WoS and Scopus. According to Thomson Reuters (ISI), WoS has been the major source of academic databases as well as a publications bank where all science related disciplines have been stored over numerous years. Nevertheless, in 2004, Elsevier Science established the Scopus database, which is fast becoming another means apart from WoS. The most up-to-date and robust database for literature (searchable citation as well as abstract) sources has been known to be Scopus. The introduction of Scopus challenged the existence of WoS because of their similarity in structure and content. The struggle for superiority between WoS and Scopus has been known to be enormous because they are both expensive to subscribe to at the same time. Hence, by unveiling the new citation database, Scopus, there is need for scientific libraries to determine the best citation database that preserves the necessary requirements. This contest has propelled improvements in the services provided by the databases. There are studies conducted to compare and uncover the spread, characteristics as well as bibliographic capacities of both Scopus and WoS. The critical comparison being carried out between WoS and Scopus has been established that both of them are constantly being enhanced. The comparative studies carried out revealed that best choice between the two databases relies on which particular specialization aspect is being considered. Moreover, other scholars show interest in comparing certain evaluations to figure out the most reliable repository in terms of area of specialization and time under consideration. So far, no study has successfully exposed a clear winner between the two databases. At the moment, between the two databases, which one supersedes the other? Which one should be adopted? Answers to these questions are yet to be concluded (Aghaei Chadegani *et al* 2013).

2.2.4 DBLP computer science bibliography

The University of Trier was first to unveil the DBLP which was then monitored by Schloss Dagstuhl—Leibniz Center for Informatics, this is the freely available bibliographic center dealing mainly with computer science journals as well as proceedings; figure 2.2 shows the search engine interface.

The DBLP project1 contains more than 1.3 million items of metadata information mostly used for publications in computer science as well as other related disciplines. It indexes a large portion of the digital libraries center for the ACM, IEEE Computer Society as well as Springer, including many other smaller ones. DBLP can be accessed freely and has a large amount of data (Reitz and Hoffmann 2010). DBLP was first an acronym from the *database systems and logic programming* (DBLP) for research scholars team from the University of Trier, Germany. The DBLP was originally intended for publications from this field of research; however, it was later broadened to include various areas of computer science while maintaining the abbreviation. However, DBLP was sometimes labeled as '*Digital Bibliography & Library Project*' but that is not actively in use. The DBLP group is based in Schloss Dagstuhl branch offices on Campus II of the University in Trier, Germany (DBLP 2021).

DBLP was established towards the end of 1993. It was initially meant to be an experimental web server, later achieving increased fame with Xmosaic browsers and the NCSA HTTP server as of then, but it gradually grew to become a famous free data source accessed by the entire computer science group. The DBLP team has a defined mission, supporting computer science scholars for their day-to-day activities by ensuring availability of bibliography metadata as well as sites for the electronic edition of publications for free. It is on record that more than four million four hundred thousand published papers have been recorded by more than two million two hundred thousand authors on the DBLP platform as of January 2019. Hence,

Figure 2.2. DBLP bibliography home page. Image credit: Schloss Dagstuhl, DBLP.

there are almost forty thousand indexed journals, over thirty nine thousand conferences as well as workshop proceedings, with over eighty thousand monographs (DBLP 2021).

The concept of the DBLP bibliography was inspired by a PhD thesis, where the author's proof-of-concept turned out to be an interesting concept that attracts online users. The thesis outlined a view of a reproduced set of tabular representations of what is contained in the table of contents (TOCs) for essential proceedings and journals with regards to area of database system and logic programming. The TOCs were entered and restructured using only HTML, that were declared to be present in the database world mail list, by creating hypertext originally from the name of every author to a particular page illustrating the individual's publications and a statistically independent network for the formed TOC ranking. The author's profile further links to their co-authors including respective TOC pages, hence forming a kind of research social network and 'person–publication network' for the author (DBLP 2021).

However, the resulting effects available on the author's page have demanded that there must be one-on-one direct connection linking an individual as well as the individual's page. This led to the need for tedious name normalization and therefore increased maintenance of the DBLP. Another issue, probably an abnormal resolution available in academic territory is found to be that the DBLP has been established to be known as a service provider but not a research project. The development of new features has always been traded off against taking care of what is available to a certain acceptable or reasonable standard. In many instances, decisions are based in accordance with what the container holds. The view being held is that what has been witnessed earlier for updating a complicated software collection is how costly it is in terms of time rather than the result obtained on a majority of a single user modus operandi. To date, a database management system has not been applied on the authoritative version of the DBLP (DBLP 2021).

Two students, in the year 1996, from the University of Wisconsin developed versions of the program that handles DBLP using DBMS SHORE that is object-oriented based, and another student re-conducted the experimental analysis using DB2 generated from IBM. The two versions of the software were operational, but require a lot of time in order to be continuously and successfully run with the dynamic nature of machines as well as variety of operating systems involving the Linux and Unix families. In 1997, the DBLP team won ACM SIGMOD Service prize including the VLDB Endowment Special Recognition Award (DBLP 2021).

An anthology project assisted in making the DBLP the most up-to-date bibliography of the database field with the aim to expand the DBLP scope for inclusion of virtually every computer science field. The study area forms the basic aspect of computer science with powerful connections linking other study areas such as systems, information retrieval, programming languages, algorithms, complexity theory, etc. Students were hired towards this direction with help from Microsoft Bay Area Research Center and Jim Gray. Other areas of DBLP that are not connected to the database are still in progress, and responses are being received of the usefulness for researchers (Ley 2002).

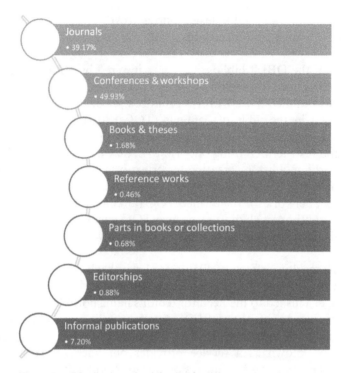

Figure 2.3. Distribution of publication in different types of document.

There are two search algorithms embedded in the DBLP: there are a series of textual comparison algorithms for the author search algorithmic application running in the entire document within all available authors' names. There is a direct title searching from the TOC_OUT document. The two search engines are C programs enabled by the HTTP demon through a CGI interface. Orderly searching has not affected the rate of execution, but substring matching author or title words without (Boolean) operators, stemming, ranking and so on. The rate of service delivery is not sufficient (Ley 2002). Figure 2.3 presents the percentage of the type of documents in DBLP as at 15 May 2021 with journals and workshops having the highest percentage of publications.

2.2.4.1 DBLP scope
The publications in DBLP are only based on computer science. The DBLP only prioritizes international publications, mainly in English language with some deviations in respect to this ruling. Due to insufficient space to handle the entire available publications, DBLP gives priority to the literature with very high credibility that is of value to the computer science community. It is impossible to indicate the start and end of a particular scientific research because of the interweaving between disciplines, thus, DBLP includes hybrid publications cutting across disciplines as long as the publication is of interest to the computer science research community. The scope of the DBLP unexhausted topics is spelled and they try to categories the topics in

different computing discipline as follows: the scope of DBLP topics shows that the DBLP covers scientific publications across the computing disciplines. For example, CS publications in DBLP cover AI, database, soft computing, distributed systems, etc; CE covers computer architecture, robotics and control, embedded systems, integrated circuits, automation, etc; CyS covers IT security, cryptography, formal methods, legal aspects, etc; DS covers decision support systems, visualization, machine learning, data mining, legal aspects, etc; IS covers business information systems, information theory, legal aspects, decision support systems, etc; SE covers systems software, software requirements, legal aspects, etc; IT covers legal aspects of computing, IT security, networks, etc (DBLP 2021).

2.2.5 ACM digital library

The ACM digital library (figure 2.4) indexes its publications such as journals, conference proceedings, technical magazines, newsletters and books. A large portion of ACM literature has been published online, which makes it possible to link online scholarly literature. In an effort for a bigger project that will ensure automatic connection between the literature published by the scholars and the address, efforts for the analysis of the PDF document were carried out. The ACM digital library had been considered to be the experimental corpus (Bergmark *et al* 2001). The ACM digital library combines different systematically organized online complete textual publications published by scholars. The ACM digital library is a guide to computing literature, a comprehensive bibliographic database that focuses exclusively on the field of computing. It provides a well-meaning avenue through which various authors, works, organizations and specific circle are linked together (ACM 2021a). ACM digital library is the world largest digital library dedicated to computing, covering the entire spectrum of literature in computing disciplines. ACM digital library constitutes different categories of publications such as journals, magazine, proceedings, books and conferences. The subsequent sub-sections outline the features of each.

Figure 2.4. ACM digital library interface.

2.2.5.1 Journal

There are over fifty peer-reviewed journals by ACM in different fields involving computing disciplines and IT areas. The ACM's high-impact, peer-reviewed journals can be accessed both in print and online, and constitute an exclusive repository of computing transformations, covering evolving development and established computing research emanating from both practice and theory. The editors of ACM journal are top researchers in their respective research areas working to ensure rapid publication of emerging concepts and discoveries (ACM 2021b).

2.2.5.2 Magazine

A set of seven ACM magazines deliver contents such as articles, news and ideas conceived by rational leaders from the computing and IT community. Some of the ACM magazines are as follows: *Flagship Magazine*, *Communications of the ACM*, ACM's magazine written, edited by and for students, *XRDS: Crossroads*, captivating pieces are issued to the readers which compel them to return monthly (ACM 2021c).

2.2.5.3 Proceedings

Each year, ACM organizes a conference to discuss state-of-the-art research from different researchers across the world. The conference proceedings cover the changes that cover the various areas of computing by ensuring the publication of peer-reviewed research discoveries, papers invited from ACM conferences, workshops and symposia. ACM and its Special Interest Groups (SIGs) hold over one hundred and seventy conferences, symposia and workshops yearly (ACM 2021d).

2.2.5.4 Books

ACM Books comprises research monographs and graduate papers, developed by computer scientists and practitioners leading in different aspects of computing. These books focus on practitioner-level professional books, graduate-level textbooks, research monographs, and books encapsulating the history and social effect of computing that transcend established and emerging computing fields. The ACM books cover all the different areas of computer science, matched to researchers, educators, practitioners and students. The ACM Books editorial board is made up global famous experts who serve as a symbol to the field's major study areas (ACM 2021e).

2.2.5.5 Conferences

The ACM conference, workshops, and symposia attract thousands of experts from different fields of computing who converge to discuss cutting edge and leading researches in their respective fields annually. The papers presented at the events are considered for inclusion in the published proceedings. ACM and ACM SIGs take the responsibility of the sponsorship of over one hundred and seventy computing conferences, workshops, and symposia around the globe. Many of these conferences achieve an outstanding level in their respective fields, attracting attendees from across the world (ACM 2021f).

2.2.5.6 ACM computing classification system

The ACM computing classification systems (CCS) of 2012 ACM replaced the 1998 version of the CCS. The CCS version of 1998 had been known to be the default computing CCS. The 2012 ACM version was upgraded by including web semantic application for poly-hierarchical ontology. The 2012 ACM version allows for easy searching and presentation of topics visually in respect to the Digital Library. It depends on a semantic vocabulary as the only origin of classifications as well as conceptualizations that demonstrates the computing state-of-the-art profession which is open to structural changes as it develops in the future. ACM makes provision for an instrument within the visual display format in order to accelerate the use of CCS categories to forthcoming papers and processes to ensure that the CCS remains updated. The CCS visual display has both interactive and flat views of the classification tree. The latest classification system is said to play a key role in developing individuals searching the ACM Digital Library interface to supplement the traditional bibliographic search. Authors should note that giving the required indexing and retrieval information under ACM CSS is an essential way for research works to be prepared for publication by ACM Press. The author benefits due to the fact that accurate categorization gives the reader fast content reference, accelerating the search for related literature, and also enable searches for work in ACM's Digital Library and online resources (ACM 2021g).

2.2.5.7 Securing the ACM digital library

Although ACM put in place measures for the promotion of security as well as the appropriate utilization of the Digital Library, nevertheless, ACM depends on the professional integrity of the community it renders service to ensure a secured facility. Different initiatives have been established by the ACM Headquarters staff to support the dynamic nature of the digital library. The manuscript submitted by ACM authors now are accepted in different formats. These manuscripts are automatically transformed to SGML for onward submission to the in-house publication system of the ACM. The manuscripts undergo a series of editing before being compiled into issues and published online. The metadata for each article is handled and taken care of in the ACM's primary database before automatically producing the bibliographic reference pages. There are processes available that enable journal information directors to include additional details to the pages (Denning 1997).

2.2.5.8 The library content

The online library is in line with the notion of the bibliographic reference page. All information linked with an article can be accessed through the page. Bibliographic reference pages generally involve information about the authors, journal, the published paper, index terms from the ACM CSS, brief comment from the ACM Computing reviews, and a link to the published paper full content. The bibliographic reference pages give the starting foundation for search in the library. The complete contents of published papers are basically produced in PDF due to the desirable features such as smaller file size and free PDF reader (Acrobat Reader) for viewing documents online. Before 1996, PDF scanned images were used to produce articles on ACM's digital library. The articles produced from 1996 to date enjoy the professional touch of the ACM's publishing system, and, consequently, are smaller in size making it easy for simple analysis (Denning 1997).

2.2.6 Ei-Compendex

The Ei-Compendex is the world's largest and comprehensive academic database available for engineering literature. It has more than twenty million peer-reviewed engineering publications cutting across one hundred and ninety engineering disciplines indexed in the database. The engineering index Thesaurus is used for the selection of publications to be indexed in the database to ensure the discovery of engineering literature as well as retrieval. Ei-Compendex is the engineering academic database that engineering students and professionals depends on to get reliable literature. Retrieving information from Ei-Compendex gives engineers confidence that the literature is of high quality, complete, relevant and accurate. Ei-Backfile was founded in 1884, and gives an all-inclusive view of engineering historical revolutions between 1884 and 1969, with more than one million seven hundred thousand million digitized records. Ei-Backfile and Ei-Compendex give 130 years of comprehensive overview of literature originating from engineering disciplines, which can only be found in the engineering community. The Ei-Compendex is a valuable resource to students preparing for research in engineering disciplines. On other hand, expert researchers can use it to update knowledge on the new areas of engineering research, developing manuscripts for publication, writing proposals for research grants and discovering the trending topics in engineering. It is really a leading engineering information platform for discovery (Elsevier 2021a).

2.2.7 IEEE Xplore

The Institute of Electrical and Electronics Engineers (IEEE) Xplore digital library (see figure 2.5 for the interface) is a tremendous resource for discovery of scientific knowledge and technical content, comprising more than two hundred journals, three million conference papers, ten thousand technical standards, five thousand books

Figure 2.5. IEEE Xplore home page.

and hundreds of courses published by the IEEE and its publishing partners. About twenty thousand documents are uploaded to IEEE Xplore monthly. The platform gives accessibility to over five million documents, most highly-cited publications of the world in engineering, computer science and electronics. There are different categories of access to full text documents in IEEE Xplore which include:

- Institutional subscription;
- Exclusive subscription for IEEE members and IEEE society members;
- Individual online purchase of document with discount given for IEEE members.

IEEE Xplore provides categories of documents shown in figure 2.6 and is explained below (IEEE 2021).

2.2.7.1 Books
Books are published jointly by the IEEE Press, the IEEE Computer Society Press and with John Wiley & Sons in the areas of computer, electrical, and software engineering under the Wiley-IEEE Press and Wiley-IEEE Computer Society. Services are provided such as recent bibliographic details on every functioning title in all programs, PDF chapters, the preface as well as complete TOC for every book title. Institutions can purchase a subscription to all books, individuals can also purchase any book (with discounted price for IEEE members). furthermore, IEEE members have the benefit to access any book free with a copyright date more than

Figure 2.6. The content of IEEE Xplore collections.

three years ago. When available, book pages give a link to the Wiley website with available hardcover and book editions to be purchased.

2.2.7.2 Conference publications
Over 1700 leading-edge conference proceedings annually are published by IEEE. These proceedings are recognized in academia worldwide which ranges from electrical engineering, computer science, and other related fields. Different fields of interest publication found in the database include the following: bioengineering, communication, networking and broadband technology, computing and processing, robots and control systems among others.

2.2.7.3 Courses
Furthermore, with the IEEE-USA professional development courses, IEEE Xplore conducts courses online in the IEEE learning network. Courses are provided in different fields such as aerospace, bioengineering, communication, computing and processing, networking and broadcasting, signal processing and analysis, transportation, robotics and control systems among others.

2.2.7.4 Journal and magazines
IEEE publishes top ranking journals, letters, transactions and magazines in different disciplines related to science, technology and education such as the electrical engineering, biotechnology, computing, power and energy, telecommunications and many other extra technologies.

2.2.7.5 Standards
IEEE is among the key players in developing global standards for industries like power and energy, biomedical and healthcare, telecommunications, information assurance, information technology, nanotechnology, and transportation. All the IEEE approved standards and unapproved/approved draft standards can be accessed via IEEE *Xplore* to IEEE Standards Online and IEL subscribers. Standards can be purchased individually through IEEE Xplore.

2.2.7.6 Information about drafts
The unapproved and approved draft standards can be accessed online with no additional cost. Unapproved drafts are proposed IEEE standards. More so, IEL subscribers can buy an add-on package that contains draft standards. It is important to note that uncompleted drafts which are under development may not be made available as such, only drafts that are up-to-date are included and can be accessed. Anyone using unapproved standards does that at their own risk.

2.2.7.7 Information about archived standards
The relegated (archived) standards may only have value as historical documents but are not up-to-date IEEE standards as such, and may either be removed, replaced, or overshadowed by other standards. The IEEE is not responsible for anyone using these archived documents.

2.2.7.8 Summary of the IEEE Xplore content collection

The content of journals, magazine, letters and transaction publications dates back to 1884 with some selected content. The IEEE Xplore indexed publications from journals published by IBM, Beijing Institute of Aerospace Information, Tsinghua University Press and American Geophysical Union date back to 1930. From 1988, conference proceedings published by IEEE, IET and VDE VERLAG have been published in The IEEE Xplore. Standards and specification based on IEEE are published since 1948. IEEE are in partnership with Wiley Press, Wiley Telecom, MIT Press and Morgan & Claypool for published books. The best conferences, seminars and workshops courses in interactive format form part of the IEEE Xplore content (IEEE 2021).

2.2.8 ScienceDirect

ScienceDirect research database provides a broad span of reliable, excellent, inter-professional research and erudite literature, for teachers, students, librarians and researchers around the world. Intuition from published research is important to come up with the new ideas that facilitate research and development. In order to promote scientific innovation, researchers globally depend on the peer-reviewed research available in ScienceDirect. There are over eighteen million scientific, technical and medical publications from 1823 up to today. ScienceDirect provides comprehensive and up-to-date and trending in-depth insights into the world's most pressing questions. Different services are provided on the scienceDirect platform such as providing personal recommendation based on reading history, what peers are reading as well as the newest Scopus citation data. It provides custom alerts, quickly comprehending basic terms as well as perfectly translating concepts within the scholarly literature by using ScienceDirect topics. ScienceDirect constitutes different fields as follows (Elsevier 2021b):

- Physical sciences and engineering: these constitute disciplines from the theoretical to the applied.
- Life sciences: literature covering journal articles and book chapters presenting original research, comprehensive analysis, up-to-date theory and more on foundational science to the latest novel research.
- Health sciences: provides updates in the area of medical growth for research stimulation as well as enhanced patient care, covering education, reference information and decision support.
- Social sciences and humanities: journals and books shed more light on historical context, latest developments, theories, applications, trending topics, etc.

ScienceDirect provides excellent content as well as intelligent search options, corporate researchers, scientists, chemists and engineers can (Elsevier 2021b):

- Come up with latest product concept or improve products that are already existing.

- Use the already existing research to learn to prevent deadlock and rapidly authenticate claims.
- Provide decisions for projects around methods, materials and safety.

2.2.9 Springerlink

Springerlink is an academic search engine own by Springer-Verlag a pre-eminent scientific publishing house, building a reputation for excellence over a period spanning more than 150 years. It is an online collection of comprehensive publications. It is a reliable source of information for leading researchers to keep up-to-date with recent developments and trending topics. All the publications across different disciplines such as scientific, engineering, computing, humanities, medical, education etc published by Springer are indexed in Springerlink for easy access. The publications are from journals, reference work entries, video, protocols and book series publishing conference proceedings, authored books, edited books and others. The content that is accessible through the website such as the image, text, photograph, logos, visual interface, user interface, computer code, trademark, programs, graphics, etc are owned by Springer.

2.2.10 PubMed

The PubMed academic database with interface, as shown in figure 2.7, enables free search and retrieval of biomedical including life sciences literature. Also, the PubMed indexed literature from related disciplines like behavioral sciences, bioengineering and chemical sciences to enhance global and personal health. PubMed has more than thirty three million citations and abstracts. PubMed became available online from 1996 with the National Center for Biotechnology Information maintaining it at the U.S. National Library of Medicine (NLM). However, PubMed does not include articles' full text but provides links to the publishers of the articles from online sources when available or from PubMed Central. There are components that make the PubMed database effective and efficient such as the MEDLINE that has been found to be the biggest element that makes up the essential articles indexed

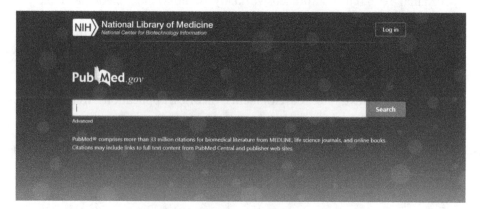

Figure 2.7. PubMed interface for literature search.

with medical subject headings. The second biggest component is the citations for the PubMed Central articles that archive articles' full text (PubMed 2021).

2.2.11 Google Scholar

This is a literature search engine that indexes article metadata or the article in full text cutting across different disciplines and different format of publishing articles. Google Scholar indexes literature from the sources as depicted in figure 2.8. Google Scholar utilizes the operation of crawlers or robots for the searching of literature files based on some specified criteria to be included in the findings of the search (Google Scholar). It has been estimated since 2014 that between 80% and 90% of the articles indexed in Google Scholar were written in English with approximately hundred million articles. The study adopted mark and recapture method for conduct the research (Khabsa and Giles 2014). In 2019, it is estimated that the records in Google Scholar were three hundred and eighty nine million, and it is believed to be the academic search engine with the most comprehensive content (Gusenbauer 2019).

Google Scholar offers the following benefits to users (Google Scholar n.d.):
- Explore all scholarly literature from any suitable location.
- Find out more about related works, citations, authors and publications.
- Find the whole document via the library or website owned by the user.
- Maintain latest updates in respect of every research area.

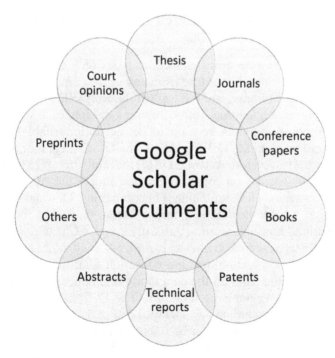

Figure 2.8. Literature indexed in Google Scholar search engine.

- Find out those citing your publications and users can create a public author profile.

  Google Scholar metrics gives simple means through which authors can rapidly measure visibility and impact of recent articles emanating from scholarly publications. The Google Scholar metrics provide an overview of the current citations accumulated by different publications to help researchers identify the venue to publish new research findings.

- To begin, the user can browse the uppermost hundred publications available in different languages, ordering by recent 5 years H-index and the H-median. To view the most cited published articles as well as the individuals that cite the publications, click on the Google Scholar accumulated H-Index. It also displays the articles and the citations that the H-index is derived from.

- Google Scholar can find more about published articles in respect of area of research interest. To have a condensed overview of publications in broad research areas, the user can choose interested research areas from the left column, for example, engineering and computer science.

- In exploring certain area of research, the broad research area is selected by clicking on the link of the 'Subcategories' and selecting among the options available, for instance, database and information systems.

- It can be browsed by research field with publications available in English language. The search for a particular publication can be performed in other languages by words in the titles.

2.3 Comparing the academic search engines: similarities and differences

The ASEBDs discussed in the previous sections index only computing literature or its content indexed substantial literature from any of the computing disciplines. The DBLP and ACM digital library are the top two largest ASEBDs in the world that only focus on literature emanating from computing disciplines in which researchers from the computing community rely on to get accurate, reliable, complete and updated information. Unlike DBLP, ACM digital library indexes only peer-reviewed literature. However, despite the DBLP indexing literature from computing disciplines, it mainly focuses on computer science, unlike the ACM digital library whose scope spans across all the disciplines in computing. This makes ACM digital library the largest academic database in the world that only focuses on peer-reviewed computing literature. Contrary to DBLP and ACM digital library, IEEE Xplore mainly focuses on electrical and electronics engineering literature but diverges to index science, technology and education literature. As a result, IEEE Xplore contains literature from all the computing disciplines. IEEE Xplore and Ei-Compendex both index engineering literature. The Ei-Compendex focuses mainly on engineering literature including CE. Detailed comparison of IEEE Xplore, ACM digital library and Ei-Compendix can be found in Tomaszewski (2021). However, other computing discipline literature can partially be found in the Ei-Compendex because some computing series like the famous Lecture Notes in Computer Science is indexed in Ei-Compendex where literature across the computing disciplines is published in the series because of interweaving between disciplines despite that it mainly focuses on computer science. Sciencedirect and Springerlink index literature from different disciplines including all the computing disciplines published by Elsevier and Springer-Verlag, respectively.

PubMed is mainly for indexing medical literature but computer science literature is part of the content because of bioinformatics. Different computing disciplines create synergy between medical and computing, for example internet of medical things, thus, literature from computing disciplines is partly contained in PubMed. Lastly, Google Scholar differs from the nine other ASEBDs in view of the fact that it indexes genuine reputable literature from top ranking WoS/Scopus journals, conferences, magazines, books, etc but unfortunately it also contains publications from predatory venues. Manuscripts/literature that never go through a peer review cycle are contained in Google Scholar. It is the researcher that filters the publication credibility, rejecting predatory and questionable sources based on experience. However, Google Scholar gives a broad view of the literature published in the other ASEBDs at a central point for the purpose of comparison or analysis. The WoS and Scopus comparison is already discussed in section 2.3. All the ASEBDs discussed in this chapter index journals, conference proceedings, magazine, books, edited books, symposia and workshops. A summary of the differences and similarities of the ASEBDs is presented in table 2.1 and attributes of the ASEBDs in table 2.2. Despite the fact that the ASEBDs were created a few decades ago, the documents coverage period spans to over a century because of the digitization of the traditional publications that predated digitization.

The volume of records in the ASEBDs is dynamic as the databases are updated constantly by indexing more literature. So, the volumes of records keep on changing. Before now, a few ASEBDs like the DBLP and Google Scholar indexed preprints, but recent development indicates that preprints have been launched by some of the top ASEBDs to incorporate preprint versions of manuscripts. For example, Scopus

Table 2.1. Comparing the academic search engines and bibliometric databases based on computing content.

	CS	IT	CE	IS	CyS	DS	SE
Web of science	Yes	Yes	Yes	Yes	Yes	Yes	Yes
Scopus	Yes	Yes	Yes	Yes	Yes	Yes	Yes
ACM digital library	Yes	Yes	Yes	Yes	Yes	Yes	Yes
DBLP	Yes	Yes	Partial	Partial	Yes	Yes	Yes
IEEE Xplore	Yes	Yes	Yes	Yes	Yes	Yes	Yes
PubMed	Yes	Partial	Partial	Partial	Partial	Partial	Partial
ScienceDirect	Yes	Yes	Yes	Yes	Yes	Yes	Yes
Springerlink	Yes	Yes	Yes	Yes	Yes	Yes	Yes
Google Scholar	Yes	Yes	Yes	Yes	Yes	Yes	Yes
Ei-Compendex	Yes	Yes	Yes	Partial	Yes	Yes	Partial

Table 2.2. The attributes of the academic search engines and bibliometric databases.

Search engine	Owner	Established online	Volume of records	Main focus	Documents coverage period	Accessibility
Web of science	Clarivate analytic	1997	>171 million	Multi-discipline	1900 to date	Subscription
Scopus	Elsevier	2004	>87 million	Multi-discipline	1788 to date	Subscription
ACM digital library	ACM	X	>3.4 million	Computing	1908 to date	Subscription
DBLP computer science	University of Trier	1993	>6.4 million	Computer science	1936 to date	Freely available
IEEE Xplore	IEEE	2000	>5.4 million	Electrical and electronic engineering	1884 to date	Subscription
ScienceDirect	Elsevier	1997	>18 million	Multi-discipline	1823 to date	Subscription
Springerlink	Springer	1996	>10 million	Multi-discipline	X	Subscription
PubMed	National library of medicine	1996	>22 million	Medical	1809 to date	Freely accessible
Ei-Compendix	Elsevier	1967	>20 million	Engineering	1970 to date	Subscription
Google Scholar	Google	2004	>389 million	Multi-discipline	1700 to date	Freely available

launched preprints as one of its document types via arXiv, MedRxiv, etc, IEEE Xplore via TechRxiv and recently Ei-Compendex via arXiv. A preprint is a manuscript that has not passed through the peer review cycle. Details on the ASEBDs can be found in (Hull *et al* 2008), especially information on ASEBDs' early stages of development.

2.4 Summary

In today's world, the pattern of retrieving information because of the internet revolution and the quest for green computing has drastically changed with the internet at the forefront of leading the changes. Just like the physical world, the internet has its own share of challenges regarding disinformation and questionable academic literature. The academic community is not immune to the distortion of literature on the internet. Many sources of academic literature are flooding the internet such as predatory journals, conferences, seminars, workshops, books, and symposia. In predatory venues, any manuscript submitted can be published as long as the author can pay for the article processing charge. Predatory publication venues dilute science with questionable and fake results, and scam reputable scholars.

The ASEBDs are used by researchers to retrieve credible and authentic academic publications. Different academic databases exist for different disciplines and areas of specialization. However, this chapter focuses on ASEBDs containing substantial computing scientific publications or that focus only on computing. The reputable ASEBDs for retrieving computing publications such as the Web of science, Scopus, ACM digital library, DBLP computer science bibliography, ScienceDirect, Springerlink, IEEE Xplore, and Ei-Compendex were discussed, the full list is presented in table 2.3. We believe after reading this chapter, the reader will be conversant with the best ASEBDs indexing only computing literature or where

Table 2.3. The academic search engines and bibliometric databases focusing on computing or that contain substantial computing literature.

Academic database	URL
ISI Web of Science	https://apps.webofknowledge.com/
Scopus	https://www.scopus.com/
IEEE Explore	http://ieeexplore.ieee.org/
Google Scholar	https://scholar.google.com/
ScienceDirect	http://www.sciencedirect.com/
Ei-Compendix	https://www.elsevier.com/solutions/engineering-village/content/compendex
ACM Digital Library	http://dl.acm.org/
PubMed	https://pubmed.ncbi.nlm.nih.gov/
Springerlink	http://www.springer.com/
DBLP computer science bibliography	http://dblp.uni-trier.de/

their content has substantial computing literature. It can make it easy for new and novice researchers to know how to access reputable scientific publications in computing disciplines.

References

ACM 2021a *ACM Digital Library* https://dl.acm.org/about (accessed 6 December 2021)

ACM. 2021b *ACM Journals* https://dl.acm.org/journals (accessed 6 December 2021)

ACM 2021c *ACM Magazines* https://dl.acm.org/magazine (accessed 6 December 2021)

ACM 2021d *ACM Proceedings* https://dl.acm.org/proceedings (accessed 6 December 2021)

ACM 2021e *ACM Books* https://dl.acm.org/books (accessed 6 December 2021)

ACM 2021f *ACM Conference* https://dl.acm.org/conference (accessed 6 December 2021)

ACM 2021g *ACM Computing Classification Systems* https://dl.acm.org/about (accessed 6 December 2021)

Aghaei Chadegani A, Salehi H, Yunus M, Farhadi H, Fooladi M, Farhadi M and Ale Ebrahim N 2013 A comparison between two main academic literature collections: Web of Science and Scopus databases *Asian Soc. Sci.* **9** 18–26

Bar-Ilan J, Peritz B C and Wolman Y 2003 A survey on the use of electronic databases and electronic journals accessed through the web by the academic staff of Israeli universities *J. Acad. Librariansh.* **29** 346–61

Bergmark D, Phempoonpanich P and Zhao S 2001 Scraping the ACM digital library *ACM SIGIR Forum* 35*(September 2001)* (New York: ACM), 1–7

Clarivate 2022 *Web of Science Platform* https://clarivate.com/webofsciencegroup/solutions/webofscience-platform/?msclkid=ad6783e2ba4511ecb29c506020e52809 (accessed 12 April 2022)

DBLP 2021 *Frequently Ask Questions* https://DBLP.org/faq/index.html (accessed 12 May 2021).

Denning P J 1997 The ACM digital library goes live *Commun. ACM* **40** 28–9

Elsevier 2021a *Ei-Compendex* http://stpaulschester.org/compendex.html (accessed 12 May 2021)

Elsevier 2021b *ScienceDirect* https://elsevier.com/solutions/sciencedirect (accessed 12 July 2021)

Google Scholar n.d. About. https://scholar.google.com/intl/en/scholar/about.html (accessed 12 July 2021)

Gusenbauer M 2019 Google Scholar to overshadow them all? Comparing the sizes of 12 academic search engines and bibliographic databases *Scientometrics* **118** 177–214

Haines L L, Light J, O'Malley D and Delwiche F A 2010 Information-seeking behavior of basic science researchers: Implications for library services *J. Med. Libr. Assoc.* **98** 73–81

Hull D, Pettifer S R and Kell D B 2008 Defrosting the digital library: bibliographic tools for the next generation web *PLoS Comput. Biol.* **4** e1000204

IEEE 2021 *IEEE Xplore Resources and Help* https://ieeexplore.ieee.org/Xplorehelp/overview-of-ieee-xplore/about-ieee-xplore (accessed 12 July 2021)

Khabsa M and Giles C L 2014 The number of scholarly documents on the public web *PLoS One* **9** e93949

Ley M 2002 The DBLP computer science bibliography: evolution, research issues, perspectives *Int. Symp. on String Processing and Information Retrieval (September 2002)* (Berlin: Springer), 1–10

PubMed 2021 *National Library of Medicine* https://pubmed.ncbi.nlm.nih.gov/about/ (accessed 6 December 2021)

Research Intelligence 2020 *Scopus Content Coverage Guide* https://elsevier.com/__data/assets/pdf_file/0007/69451/Scopus_ContentCoverage_Guide_WEB.pdf?dgcid=RN_AGCM_Sourced_300002811&sf233436297=1 (accessed 12 April 2022)

Reitz F and Hoffmann O 2010 An analysis of the evolving coverage of computer science sub-fields in the DBLP digital library *Int. Conf. on Theory and Practice of Digital Libraries (September 2010)* (Berlin: Springer), 216–27

Scopus 2022 *Scopus Preview—Scopus—Welcome to Scopus* https://scopus.com/home.uri (accessed 12 April 2022)

Tomaszewski R 2021 A study of citations to STEM databases: ACM Digital Library, Engineering Village, IEEE *Xplore*, and MathSciNet *Scientometrics* **126** 1797–811

Web of Science Group 2022 *Brows, search, and explore journals indexed in the Web of science* https://mjl.clarivate.com/home?msclkid=ad656632ba4511ec9dbb55ab50c3b4ac (accessed 12 April 2022)

Chapter 3

Systematic literature review from a computing perspective and research problem formulation

Systematic literature review and problem formulation are fundamentals to the creation of new knowledge. The purpose of this chapter is to equip the reader with the procedure to conduct a systematic literature review from the perspective of computing and formulate a research problem from the literature for the reader to understand how to situate the research problem within the context of the existing body of knowledge. In this chapter, the differences that exist among metadata analysis, systematic literature review and narrative reviews are discussed for the readers to have a clear understanding of the differences. The chapter proposes a methodology for conducting an extensive systematic literature review from the perspective of computing and describes in detail the process of research problem formulation. The step-by-step guides in formulating the research problem are outlined and discussed. We believed that this chapter will be of great significance to both novice and expert researchers as it can provide a guide to novice researchers in systematic literature review from the perspective of computing and research problem formulation. On the other hand, it can add value to expert researchers.

3.1 Introduction

Already published works are critical in the development of new knowledge. Researchers conduct literature review by the analysis, interpretation, and critical evaluation of the existing literature. Conducting a critical literature review provides opportunities for the researcher to detect the pattern of already published results, understand the depth and details of the knowledge in the exiting literature before identifying and formulating the research problem for further exploration. One of the best ways to situate a study within the existing literature is through the traditional literature review that has been in practice for a long time. However, an alternative to the traditional literature review has been proposed called systematic literature review (SLR) (Mohamed Shaffril *et al* 2021).

SLR was first conceived by James Lind in 1753, who published an SLR paper that aimed to provide a brief and impartial summary of the evidences published in the literature. The attention of the research community to SLR was little until the 1970s and 1980s when the attention of the research community began to grow exponentially because of the need for improving the state-of-the-art synthesis of evidences (Clarke and Chalmers 2018).

The large body of literature is associated with different problems. One of the problems is the assessment of the state-of-the-art body of knowledge that can be comprehensively recorded. The best way to conduct a review of the existing evidences is through SLR. The formal development of the SLR in the 20th century was motivated by the expanding body of research together with the demand for systematic summarization of available evidences for informing decisions from both stakeholders and consumers (Meerpohl *et al* 2012)

It is worth properly documenting the process of SLR more especially for new career researchers/authors. SLT help authors refine their knowledge about a particular subject area they are interested in, to gain tremendous novel ideas and be equipped with the critical skills for analysis and synthesis of existing studies. The SLR has been prominent in the healthcare community. However, subjects outside of healthcare have started gradually adopting the SLR as an approach for conducting a systematic comprehensive review of published literature (Peričić and Tanveer 2019). The SLR has now penetrated almost every aspect of the subject areas classification such as science, engineering, social sciences, art and humanities, etc. There is no SRL method from the perspective of computing that is universally accepted by the computing research community to the best of the authors' knowledge. However, there is an attempt to propose a guide for SLR in computer science (Weidt and Silva 2016) and software engineering (Kitchenham *et al* 2009).

The SLR methodology from the perspective of computing including all the subject areas: computer sicence (CS), computer engineering (CE), software engineering (SE), information systems (IS), information technology (IT), data science (DS) and cyber security (CyS) is scarce in the literature. This chapter is intended to propose an initial guide for SLR from the perspective of computing.

3.2 Why conduct literature search and systematic literature review?

Postgraduate students, new career researchers, undergraduates and expert researchers need SLR to have a comprehensive understanding of a certain research topic. For novice researchers, the SLR can be used as initial reading material, while expert researchers can use it to easily identify the areas that need novel approaches from a new perspective. Figure 3.1 depicts a visual representation of the benefits of SLR.

Conducting SLR provides the means of indicating the knowledge of the author in understanding a particular research area including the vocabularies, variables, theories, methodology, phenomena, and history of the research area. Conducting SLR gives authors an opportunity to know the influential voices and research groups

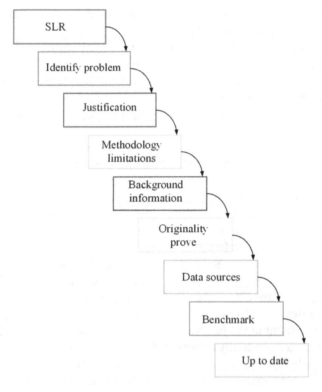

Figure 3.1. Visualization of the SLR benefits.

in the research area (LeCompte *et al* 2003). SLR involves the searching of literature, evaluation and collation of all relevant published evidences to give a comprehensive interpretation of the results (Gilbody *et al* 2005).

SLR offers a number of benefits to researchers, especially new career researchers, expert researchers and postgraduates students. The benefits of SLR outlined in the literature are as follows: SLR gives a comprehensive picture of the already published results regarding a particular research topic; SLR simplifies the identification of a research problem with justification; it highlights the limitations of already published methodology that can be improved upon by prospective researchers (Eagly and Wood 1994). SLR can be utilized to pinpoint research questions that have clear answers based on the available evidence in the literature without the need to conduct any further study (Chalmers and Glasziou 2009). SLR provides comprehensive background information/theories required to understand a propose study. It shows proof of the research originality. The importance and significant of the research topic is established by SLR. SLR helps in providing the motivation for choosing a particular research methodology or developing a theoretical/conceptual framework. It indicates that the researcher demonstrates mastery of the research topic and is conversant with recent happening in the research area. It helps researchers to identify sources of data and benchmarks (Salim 2015). Therefore, SLR is highly recommended to postgraduate students starting research who wish to effectively evaluate the chosen research area and understand it before developing a proposal that can be situated in the current body of knowledge (Weidt and Silva 2016).

3.3 Systematic literature review, narrative review and metadata analysis: differences

Apart from SLR, there are other types of review, namely, narrative and metadata analysis. This section provides the differences that exist among the different types of reviews. The differences, pointed out in Hodgkinson and Ford (2014), are as follows:

SLR involves the method of assembling evidences published in the literature based on a formulated research question. It is subsequently evaluated systematically according to scientific excellence before integrating it for more consideration or more formal review process exclusion. It mostly requires the involvement of a multiple number of evaluators before final judgement (Hodgkinson and Ford 2014). More formally, SLR is the systematic approach to the collection, critical evaluation, integration and presentation of results from different published research on a particular research question or interesting research topic. SLR has the benchmark for evaluating the quality and magnitude of the results published about a research question or interesting research topic. SLR simplifies the accurate understanding of the topic compared to the traditional literature review. SLR uses standard method-ology for the review for systematic searching of the literature, filtering, reviewing, interpretation, critiquing, synthesis and reporting of the results obtain from different publications about the chosen topic/domain of interest (Pati and Lorusso 2018).

Unlike SLR, the **narrative review** is believed to be the most popular approach to literature review. In this type of narrative review approach authors move straight to critiquing the collected literature in the form of written narrative review for assessing the documents. The main problem of the narrative review is that it is subjectivity that is inherent. However, narrative reviews have the advantage of quickly generating new research questions to find direction for future research and summarize the limitations of the previous approaches published in different studies. The narrative review is sensitive to the potential of bias regarding the coverage and evaluation of the available literature about the review topic. On the other hand, when the narrative review is crafted carefully by placing the content of the SLR in the context before inserting the concluding remarks section that make conclusions about it is implication for the building of new theory in the future, empirical research, development of alternative methods and implications for theory and practice, then it can be concluded that including the SLR techniques only improves the quality of the manuscript and proposal (Hodgkinson and Ford 2014).

Metadata analysis is adopted to be included as part of the SLR methodology in the case where the evidences considered for the problem are limited to only quantitative. Quantitative studies can be embedded in the SLR provided they satisfy the criteria for inclusion set by the authors. In this case, the outcome of the studies in each individual study is arranged in a tabular form based on the systematic main features of each study that can contribute to the conclusions deduced from the SLR.

The criteria for exclusion and inclusion in this approach are explicit much more like in the conventional metadata analysis (Hodgkinson and Ford 2014).

3.3.1 Approach for conventional review

The four main stages involved in the conventional review are outlined as follows (Salim 2015):
    i. Problem formulation: refer to the topic or the research area under consideration and the main components issue.
    ii. Literature search: searching for materials from the academic databases relevant to the research area under consideration for exploration.
    iii. Data evaluation: selecting the relevant literature that report significant contributions about the research area under consideration.
    iv. Analysis and interpretation: this section provides discussion and the conclusion about the relevant literature under consideration.

3.3.2 Synthesis of existing evidence and research problem

In this section, we explain the establishment of a research problem based on the synthesis of existing evidences in the context of healthcare before presenting it in the context of computing.

The best way to inform a decision about healthcare is through SLR, as it is widely recognized by the research community. The full potential of SLR has not been fully utilized. The evidence that exists in the literature typically limits the knowledge of the researcher in taking informed decisions because it frequently highlights the limitations in important areas. The research problem, sometimes called the research gap, refers to the situation where the researcher's ability to draw conclusions is limited. Stakeholders involved in prioritization can further developed research problems as the research needs. The research needs can be categorized as the areas in which the problem in the existing evidences limit the ability of the patient, clinicians and policy makers to take informed decisions. Developing research agenda, decision about research funding and study designs necessarily requires the identification of the research problem. Researchers looking for research direction from SLR often get frustrated due to insufficient information about the details of the future research direction (Robinson *et al* 2011). SLR can provide one of the best approaches to take decisions about computing depending on the computing disciplines. Available evidences mostly limit taking decisions about computing because of the limitations highlighted in certain critical areas. Research problems in computing can be identified when stakeholders such as computing researchers, practitioners, users and policy makers fail to take decisions because of limitation in available evidences. For example, Musa *et al* (2022) presented SLR on the applications of deep learning algorithms in ECG. The paper provided research problems existing in the available evidences and suggestions for future research direction.

3.4 Proposed systematic literature review methodology for computing

In our attempt to propose uniform SLR methodology for computing, we propose SLR methodology for computing as discussed in this section. The stages involved in the proposed methodology were adopted from different studies to conduct SLR in the context of computing. The proposed phases are as follows: focus and selection of research area, motivation, keywords, research questions, literature search and data sources, study selection procedure, data extraction and synthesis, extraction of answers related to research questions and SLR quality assessment. Details of each phase are discussed in the following sections.

3.4.1 Focus and selection of research topic

Focus of the SLR

In the focus, the review constructs are defined to decide what to be included or excluded in the review process (Randolph 2009). As defined in Randolph (2009), the major components of the study to focus on during the review process are basically four: result of the study, methodology, theories, practices/applications. Mainly, literature review focuses on outcomes of the researches conducted. Literature review is the synthesis and analysis of research outcome not the listing of bibliography, summary of the literature and making conclusions as defined by the educational resource information center. They went further to suggest that research outcome helps to identify research rationale and lack of information in a certain research outcome is identified with the help of outcome-oriented review, thereby assisting in the establishment of justification for the outcome of the research. Secondly, the review can focus on the research methodology, the review that focuses on the research methodology for investigation mainly focuses on investigating the key variables, measures and data analysis techniques as well as the informed outcome-oriented research. Such type of review helps in identifying the weaknesses and strengths of the methodology, analyzing the differences that exist in research practice across different groups, time or settings. A combination of outcome and methodology review may identify the approach that informs the research outcome. Methodological review can form the basis for the rationale in justifying the proposed dissertation research in case the already published methodologies have been found to be flawed from the perspective of the methodology. Next, a review can focus on the perspective of theories. In this case the review can establish already published theories, the relationship that exists between the theories and the extent to which the theories have been investigated by the research community. When a dissertation aims to improve a new theory, theoretical review is appropriate for such a research focus. A rationale can be established from the theoretical review by identifying where theory is lacking or there is an insufficiency of existing theory to justify the proposal of new theory. The review can also come from the perspective of practice or application. This type of review mainly focuses on how a particular intervention has been applied or studies how a group of people intend to perform a certain practice. This type of review can help to identify the practical requirement that has not being met (Randolph 2009). Figure 3.2 depicts review focus for the SLR.

Figure 3.2. Focus of the review from different perspectives.

Note that despite the fact that a review has to have a focus, it is necessary to address the other perspectives as discussed in the preceding paragraph. For instance, a review can focus on research findings but can deal with the methodology to find the flaw in the methodology that likely affected the research findings. Research findings oriented review can also deal with theories that relate to the study. Subsequently, it introduces the practical application of the knowledge gained from the study (Randolph 2009).

From a CS perspective: A review conducted by Mubarak *et al* (2022) focuses on the findings on the detection of elderly behavior based on deep learning algorithms for healthcare support. The review addressed the algorithms behind each of the study and went further to introduce the real-world practical applications of the deep learning algorithms in developing a device for detecting elderly behavior for healthcare support.

From the perspective of information systems: Sabi *et al* (2016) conducted a theoretical review to find insufficiency in existing theories and models as regards cloud computing. The study proposed a cloud computing model that takes account of different constructs for adoption in Universities.

We propose researchers within the computing ecosystem explain the focus of the review they intend to conduct with reasonable justification in a dedicated section as per the title of this section. The explanation of the review focus will easily reveal to readers, reviewers and editors the focus of the review to know exactly where to focus on assessment of the manuscript or dissertation. Readers intending to conduct a review on the same topic can easily identify the focus, establish the gap and propose a new focus for review on the same topic.

Selection of research topic for SLR

The choice of the research topic for a literature review is critical, the topic should be of interest to the researcher and currently trending in the literature. The topic or research area to be chosen for the review has to be justified. The topic will depend on the computing discipline as discussed in chapter 1 and interest. The research areas considered for the review should be a hot research area that is attracting unprecedented attention from the research community and it is well established in the literature. To understand the hot research area, the researcher can conduct a preliminary search for publication trends in any of the academic search engines and bibliographical databases discussed in chapter 2 to view the trends before choosing the topic for review.

For example, on the 1 July 2022 a search with the keyword 'artificial intelligence' in ScienceDirect returned the search results as depicted in figure 3.3. Careful observation of figure 3.3 indicates that the research trend in artificial intelligence is growing steadily with enough materials supporting it, therefore, it can be chosen as a research area for conducting a review.

If the topic doesn't return enough material or indicates that the area is outdated by showing a declining number of publications, it should not be chosen for conducting SLR because it may not be of interest to the research community, thus, lacking potential for high impact.

3.4.2 Motivation

The motivation for the SLR should be adequately discussed to show the reader motivation for the SLR. Before conducting SLR the researcher should conduct a preliminary search in the academic search engine and bibliographical database listed in chapter 2 to find out if SLR on the same topic has already been conducted. If the search indicated that no SLR on the topic has already been conducted, the researcher can go ahead to conduct the SLR as the first SLR on the topic. When SLR is found on a similar topic to the topic the researcher intended to conduct the

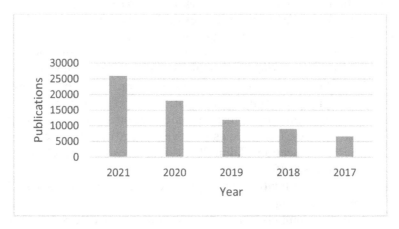

Figure 3.3. Research trends on artificial intelligence for the previous five years in ScienceDirect.

SLR, the researcher can propose a different focus for the SLR on the same topic to avoid repeating what has been published. For example, if the SLR already published focuses on the application of robotics in combating COVID-19, the focus can be tailored to findings or methodology.

For example, Chiroma *et al* (2020) published SLR on the applications of machine learning in controlling COVID-19. Already, there are existing published SRLs on the similar topic. However, a lack of comprehensive taxonomy, ignoring bibliometric analysis in the previous published works and the use of mostly preprint papers to conduct the SLR motivated Chiroma *et al* (2020) to conduct SLR on a similar topic with different focus to fill the existing gap. In another example, Jauro a lack of published SLR on the adoption of deep learning algorithms in solving problems in the emerging cloud computing environment motivated Jauro *et al* (2020) to conduct SLR.

3.4.3 Keywords

Our approach adopted the keywords convention in Liberati *et al* (2009). The searched keywords are critical in querying databases to retrieve papers for inclusion in the SLR. The keywords should be formulated in line with the objectives of the SLR. The keywords selection typically starts from general terms before narrowing down to the specific terms based on the study objectives. Preliminary keywords need to be formulated before evaluating them to arrive at the final search keywords. The keywords finally used to query the academic search engines and bibliographical databases for the identification or exclusion of records for the SLR should be reported. The keywords indicate the scope or limitation of the SLR. For example, the keywords used for searching all the relevant academic search engines and bibliographical databases (refer to chapter 2) are as follows: federated learning*, smart city*, deep learning* and sustainability*.

3.4.4 Research questions

A research question in SLR is critical because it gives researchers a guide on what to look for in each study to be reviewed. For example, what are the techniques used in solving problems in software engineering or computer graphics (Weidt and Silva 2016)? It has been suggested that the formulation of research question should be guided by five elements, as follows: population: this is the group involved in the research such as human, software, etc; intervention: area of interest to the researchers such as pair programming; comparison: aspect of the research involving evaluation by comparisons; outcome: the intervention effect such as prediction accuracy; context: the research settings or environment used for the investigation, such as CS in higher education (Salim 2015). Examples of research questions are outlined in Jauro *et al* (2020):

    i. What are the investigations that applied deep learning to tackle problems in emerging cloud computing?

    ii. What are the domains where deep learning is used to solve problems in emerging cloud computing?

iii. Where is the emerging cloud computing research source for datasets?

iv. What are the limitations of the previous studies?

3.4.5 Literature search and data sources

The literature search strategy in computing should adopt the review based on the work of Kitchenham *et al* (2009). The primary search terms should carefully be selected to ascertain the most appropriate search terms. For example, using the review set objectives, the following terms should be applied to search the relevant literature in reputable academic archives: 'multi-agent in smart city'; 'multi-agent in transportation'; 'multi-agent in energy'; 'multi-agent in real estate'; 'multi-agent in industry'; 'multi-agent in healthcare'; 'multi-agent in waste management' etc. Table 2.3 in chapter 2, section 2.4 presents the academic database used for the literature search.

3.4.6 Study selection procedure

The papers retrieved from the academic databases should pass through different stages for selecting the relevant papers. In the first stage, the papers should be screened based on the title, abstract, conclusion and the full content of the paper. The study selection method is represented as shown in figure 3.1, the search procedure should carefully be designed to ensure a comprehensive review is conducted.

3.4.7 Exclusion and inclusion criteria

To screen the relevant literature, the inclusion and exclusion criteria were used. Based on the set environments, the main study articles were picked based on the criteria in figure 3.4. Therefore, the inclusion and exclusion environments applied in this present review are presented in table 3.1.

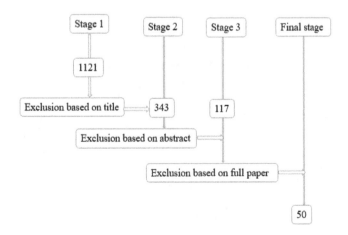

Figure 3.4. Study selection procedure.

Table 3.1. Criteria for full paper selection.

Inclusion criteria	Exclusion criteria
The SLR focuses on multi-agent in smart city.	The other application of internet of things in other areas aside from smart city were out of the scope of the SLR.
The review process focuses on different aspect of the applications of multi-agents in smart city only.	The review process does not focus on other multi-agent methods aside from smart city.
The review considered papers that are written in English only.	The review does not considered papers that were written in other languages other than English.
The review considers published peer reviewed articles only.	Non-peer review publications such as workshop, short communication, editorial, descriptions and technical reports were not included.
The SLR selected only articles in a reputable forum like journals or conferences or edited books.	The articles in the form of books, editorial, abstracts or keynotes speech were out of the scope of the paper selection criteria.

3.4.8 Inclusion and exclusion of papers

The analysis of the paper at this stage mainly focuses on title and abstract, it is suggested that the data for the papers should be exported to a CVS file when the duplicate is removed before importing it into the worksheet. It is only the title and the abstract that is analysed at this stage. A column indicating the status of each paper can be added to the worksheet in view of the fact that the any researcher involved in the screening at this stage can assign status to each of the papers such as 'include', 'exclude' or 'doubtful' based on the criteria defined for exclusion and inclusion. Each of the researchers should put their own outcome of the analysis (typically, this stage is subjective). The articles in the analysis that were marked doubtful should be discussed rigorously by the team members and disagreements settled. In the case where the disagreement is not settled, it is suggested that diagonal reading of the paper should be adopted to settle the disagreement about the doubtfulness of the paper. The first screening should be conducted by the first author before other co-authors perform it. The selected papers should be downloaded and made available to each team member via a cloud platform such as Dropbox (Weidt and Silva 2016). For example, the primary search returns 1121 articles, which were reduced to 343 articles on the bases of titles checked, and 117 studies based on abstract checked. After that, 117 selected studies were revised comprehensively to obtain a final list of 50 articles based on the full content of the papers. The pictorial representation of the exclusion and inclusion process is depicted in figure 3.4.

Figure 3.5 shows the article search results returned from the academic databases sources.

Figure 3.5 is the visual representation of the articles returned indicating that the ISI WoS has the longest bar. This is showing that the highest number of articles

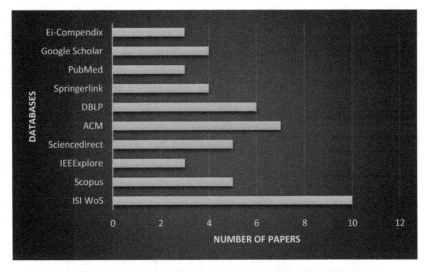

Figure 3.5. Number of articles obtained from the queried search engines.

selected for the SLR are from the ISI WoS. This is followed by ACM and DBLP academic databases, respectively. On the other hand, Ei-Compendix, PubMed and IEEE Xplore have the shortest bar compared to the bars of other academic databases. This indicates that the Ei-Compendix, PubMed and IEEE Xplore have the lowest number of manuscripts selected for inclusion in the SLR.

3.4.9 Screening based on introduction and conclusion (optional)

The introduction and conclusion analysis of the paper is required to refine the selection of the papers, though this stage is optional. At this point, the papers are selected based on the analysis of the paper introduction and conclusions. The selection criteria are the same as those described in the preceding section. A spreadsheet should be created for listing the articles for the researchers to re-mark the papers as excluded, included or doubtful. At this stage a quality criteria checklist and cut-off point for a paper to be included is expected to be prepared for the verification of the suitability of each paper analyzed. The papers that fall short of the cut-off point can be deleted. The initial works such as reading all the papers retrieved, deleting article below the cut-off points, applying the checklist are expected to be performed by the first author and guided by the supervisors (Weidt and Silva 2016).

3.4.10 Stopping the search and the number of articles required for the SLR

At what stage is it require to stop the search? There is no universally accepted answer to the appropriate time to stop the search and determine the comprehensiveness of the search. For instance, a researcher can consider 30 articles sufficient for the SLR, whereas others may consider that too few to conduct comprehensive SLR. However, there are suggestions by scholars in the literature on when to stop the literature search. For example, Levy and Ellis (2006) argued that the search should be stopped when searching using the same keywords in the different academic search engines and abstract databases returned no new result, while Kastner *et al* (2009) practiced capture–mark–recapture technique to approximate the comprehensiveness of the articles in the literature with confidence interval (Mohamed Shaffril *et al* 2021).

3.4.11 Data extraction and synthesis

At this stage, data can be extracted for the purpose of extracting information from the published empirical studies and eliminating redundant studies. The extracted data should be tabulated. Hartling *et al* (2010) suggested that two independent reviewers should evaluate the data extracted to ensure that the criteria initially set for screening the selected articles were actually met. Additional reviewers should be given the data for review. The review comments from independent reviewers should be compared for evaluation to find out if discrepancies exist or not. In case of any discrepancies, it should be settled by all the parties. To avoid the possibility of bias and preserved integrity two independent reviewers should be invited to evaluate the extracted data side by side with the objectives of the study to comment on the suitability of the data and the study objectives.

3.4.12 Answers to research questions

It is in this stage that the research questions already set at the beginning of the SLR should be answered by analyzing the selected papers that passed the screening criteria. To make the work easy, a spreadsheet should be created populated with the papers' titles or IDs in the rows and questions for querying in the columns. Subsequently, one should read each of the articles carefully, extract the possible answer to the research question and post directly to the spreadsheet. A different format or form can be used for the synthesis of the extracted data such as tables, graphs and any other artifacts that can facilitate information visualization (Weidt and Silva 2016).

3.4.13 Systematic literature review quality assessment

The proposed approach suggests that researchers in computing always assess the quality of the SLR conducted to give confidence to readers that the SRL passed the quality assessment criteria. Therefore, SLR is expected to be evaluated to ensure that it has the quality. There are different approaches to assess the quality of SLR. However, this book adopted the York University, Centre for Reviews and Dissemination (CDR) Database of Abstracts of Reviews of Effects (DARE) criteria because of its acceptability. Kitchenham *et al* (2009) evaluated SLR using the York University, CDR DARE criteria based on the following four quality assessment questions (Kitchenham *et al* 2009):

    QA1: Is the SLR inclusion and exclusion criteria appropriately described?

    QA2: Does the study search comprehensively and rigorously cover all the relevant studies?

    QA3: Does the quality/validity of the studies include assessment by reviewers?

QA4: Were the rudimentary data/studies described sufficiently?

The four questions outlined the preceding section were scored as follows:

QA1: Yes (Y)—The criteria for inclusion were comprehensively outlined in the SLR. Partly (P)—it is considered partial in the case that the inclusion criteria were implicit, while it is No (N) if the inclusion criteria definition were unavailable.

QA2: Y—If the researchers search at least four academic search engines and abstract databases, add other strategies for searching or identify all journals relevant to the topic of interest, search them and reference. It is P when researchers search for three or four academic search engines and abstract databases without any additional search strategy or search for journals and conference proceedings that are restricted. Lastly, it is N when the authors search at most two academic search engines and abstract databases or set of journals that are extremely restricted.

QA3: Y—The quality criteria were defined by the authors explicitly and extracted from each of the primary study. P—The research question reflects the issue of quality that is addressed in the study. N—The study ignore to involved the issue quality assessment for each of the primary studies.

QA4: Y—Adequate information concerning each of the study is presented. P— The information about the primary study is presented in summary. N—Each primary study results are not identified.

The scores assigned are as follows: Y = 1, P = 0.5, N = 0, or Unknown (i.e. unspecified information). The first author assessed each of the papers as the coordinator of the quality evaluation extraction process. The co-authors were assigned four papers each to assess independently. The disagreement that arose was discussed until it was settled (Kitchenham *et al* 2009).

Table 3.2 presents an example for the evaluation of SLR using the DARE criteria assigning score to each of the study. The quality evaluation of the studies indicated that none of the studies scored less than 1, three studies scored 3.5, two studies scored 2 and two studies scored 3 while only one scored 4 points. Figure 3.6 presents the stages involved in the proposed SLR method for computing.

Table 3.2. Systematic literature review quality evaluation.

Study ID	Type of article	QA1	QA2	QA3	QA4	Score	Initial rate agreement
SLR1	SLR0	Partial	Yes	Partial	Partial	2.5	4
SLR2	SLR0	Yes	Partial	Yes	Yes	3.5	4
SLR3	SLR0	Partial	No	Yes	Partial	2	4
SLR4	SLR0	Yes	Yes	Partial	Partial	3	4
SLR5	SLR0	Yes	Partial	No	No	1.5	4
SLR6	SLR0	Yes	Yes	Yes	Yes	4	4
SLR7	SLR0	Partial	Yes	Yes	Yes	3.5	4
SLR8	SLR0	Yes	No	Partial	Partial	2	4
SLR9	SLR0	Yes	Yes	Yes	No	3	4
SLR10	SLR0	Yes	Yes	Partial	Yes	3.5	4

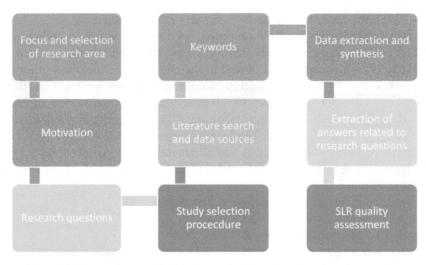

Figure 3.6. Proposed systematic literature review from the perspective of computing.

3.4.14 Discussion

This is the section where the main findings in the SLR should be summarized including the strength of the evidence found in each of the main outcomes. The relevance of the findings to stakeholders such as the healthcare providers, users and policy makers should be considered (Liberati *et al* 2009). For example, Jauro *et al* (2020) argued that the SLR conducted shows that deep learning has started making inroads into data analytics for the emerging cloud computing paradigm. It is found in the SLR that deep learning was able to solve machine learning problems such as clustering, classification and prediction. The analysis conducted captured the publication trend, frequency of adopting deep learning in emerging cloud computing and different architectures of emerging cloud computing. It is found that researchers started giving attention to the research area in 2017 before it stimulated interest in the research community to conduct more researches. This is indicated by the steady increase in number of publications.

3.4.15 Limitations

The limitations of SLR should be outlined in SLR to help other researchers working in similar areas easily identify the limitations of SLR to work on it. Liberati *et al* (2009) explained that limitations can be at the study and outcome level. At the study level, there is the possibility of incomplete retrieval of the research and bias in the reporting. At the outcome level, risk of bias exists. That is an example to demonstrate the discussion of limitations in an SLR. The study has a number of limitations: our search for documents is limited to manual and restricted to international journals and conference proceedings (Kitchenham *et al* 2009).

3.4.16 Challenges and future research opportunities

It is expected to discuss incisive critique that can trigger future progress in testing and building theory, spark a new upsurge in empirical studies and advance methodology by mapping out future research directions and accompanying critique of the surveyed works (Hodgkinson and Ford 2014). This is a dedicated section to outline and discuss the limitations of the already published studies, open research problems and suggest new perspectives for solving research problems in the future. This can provide research opportunities to both novice and expert researchers. An example is the challenge in the dataset for Internet-of-Vehicles: data analytics in the Internet-of-Vehicle environment needs very large data.

Internet-of-Vehicle dataset problem. Performing data analysis in the Internet-of-Vehicles requires datasets generated from the Internet-of-Vehicle environment. However, the Internet-of-Vehicles is still a new concept in pilot testing by different organizations. There is a scarcity of sufficient data to perform data analytics for the Internet-of-Vehicles using deep learning algorithms within the context of big data. It found that most of the Internet-of-Vehicles is in the trial period, therefore, getting the data released to a third party is challenging despite the fact that data provides a major stake in dealing with deep learning. Without data there is no machine learning no matter how excellent is the algorithm. In the future, we recommend the development of a public Internet-of-Vehicles repository for data for the research community to have access to sufficient Internet-of-Vehicles data. Free access to Internet-of-Vehicles data will spark waves of empirical studies using deep learning within the Internet-of-Vehicles environment (Chiroma *et al* 2021).

3.5 The brief structure of systematic literature review

To SRL structure simple for understanding by readers, we provide a summary of the proposed SLR method together with the other vital components for a complete SLR in computing. Table 3.3 presents the brief structure of the SLR.

3.6 Common mistakes in conducting systematic literature review

There are common mistakes typically committed by researchers in conducting SLR. To assist readers in avoiding committing such common mistakes in the future, we outline the mistakes as follows (Gall *et al* 1996):

1. In many cases the researcher does not relate the outcome of the SLR to the study conducted by the researcher.
2. Lack of sufficient time taken by the researcher to define the best descriptors and identify the best literature sources to be used for SLR relevant to the topic.
3. In reviewing the literature, researchers often rely on secondary sources instead of the primary sources.
4. SLR methodology not reported in the literature review.
5. Instead of reporting statistical results in isolation they are reported in syntheses by meta-analysis or chi-square.
6. Contrary findings and perspectives in interpretation are often ignored in synthesizing quantitative literature.

Table 3.3. Summary of the SLR main components with brief description.

Component	Sub-component	Brief description
Introduction	• General introduction on the SLR research topic. • Reason/s why the research question is important. • Why SLR is significant. • Objectives, contributions to knowledge.	Provide introductory remarks in the research context and significance of SLR.
Proposed SLR method for computing	• Focus and selection of research area. • Motivation. • Keywords. • Research questions. • Literature search and data sources. • Study selection procedure. • Data extraction and synthesis. • Extraction of answers related to research questions. • SLR quality assessment.	Provide brief description on the procedure and stages involved in conducting SLR.
Discussion	• Results—findings from the SLR. • Analysis and synthesis—restructuring/ reorganization in analytic framework. • Evaluation—similarities and differences. • Evaluation—strengths and weaknesses. • Implication of the SLR to stakeholders, research and practice.	Provide a summary of the findings, analysis and synthesis, evaluation and implications.
Limitations	• Bias. • Incomplete study.	Discussed the limitations of SLR.
Challenges and future research opportunities	• Incisive critique. • Future progress.	Challenges and future research direction should be outlined and discussed.
Conclusions	• Re-state main objective of the SLR. • Indicate that the objective of the SLR was achieved. • Significance of the SLR. • Generalized concluding remarks, relevance of SLR to the research community.	Elaborate summary supporting the data provided in SLR.

3.7 Research problem formulation

In summary, formulation is the transformation and translating of research problems into research questions that are answerable scientifically. Problem formulation is the situation whereby a problem to be solved for research is established from the literature, observations, or any other source and a framework proposed detailing the stages required to solve the research problem already established before developing the plan for solving the problem. It is expected that problem formulation should provide an unambiguous statement of purpose and scope of the research. Different sources of research problems for postgraduate students exist. For example, the most grounded source is to conduct extensive SLR in the research area or read an already published SLR. The supervisory committee/scientific adviser can suggest new ideas and developments in the research area. News coming from the industry can be a source of research problems. Established scientists occasionally publish their views on future developments in the research area. It tackled contradiction and ambiguity. There is the application of already established techniques in a new domain. Also, there is replication of research outcomes with modifications. A good research problem is expected to be interesting to the researcher and worth tackling within a reasonable period of time and the researcher should be ready to commit sufficient resources such as time, fund, efforts, etc. The researcher has the belief that he/she can make significant scientific contributions in tackling the research problem by improving the understanding of CS. It has no potential risk of harming the society or the researchers themselves. The researcher feels the level of expertise required to tackle the problem is adequate because the work is expected to be done by the researcher. The processes of problem formulation are as follows: explore the research topic; conduct SLR; coin the problem statement; and develop research questions (optional) and objectives before defining the scope of the research (Salim 2015). Figure 3.7 depicts the stages involved in research problem formulation.

3.7.1 Developing problem statement

After identifying the research problem from the SLR or any other source, the problem formulated is represented as a statement, it can be in a single statement or a small number of paragraphs running into more than a page. The problem statement

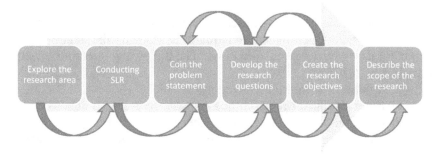

Figure 3.7. Stages involved in research problem formulation.

declares the summary of the proposed research from the point of view of the researcher justifying the research problem. The opening statement should be written in such a way that it simulates the interest of a large readership to relate. The problem must be specified leading to the proposed study indicating why the research problem is important. The use of a quotation is strongly discouraged in the leading sentence. Numerical information and short sentences can be considered for great impact. The problem statement is the statement that clearly shows the need for further research. Where the proposed study can extend the current body of knowledge or how the proposed study differs from what is already in existence should be outlined and discussed. The problem statement identifies the gap between the current study already published and the proposed study. A research question can be posed for addressing the research problem (Salim 2015).

3.7.2 The problem statement–computer science perspective

The most significant challenge in the forecasting of time series is the development of a model with the capability to produce forecasting results that is accurate. However, academicians and practitioners view it as a big challenge in view of the fact that it is associated with many limitations. Dynamic factors in the real world make time series forecasting a complex problem because insufficient, incomplete and uncertainties in the historical dataset are influenced by the multiple dynamic factors. Least and most significant factors influence the performance of the system, as such, getting such information is very important. Nevertheless, the relationship that exists in factors affecting the forecasting are not clear and quantifying it is difficult, especially as the information is unclear, incomplete and uncertain. To worsen the situation, getting practical and experimental data is difficult. The hybrid model combining ARIMA and artificial neural network already discussed in the literature is yet to solve the limitations outlined in the preceding paragraph. A multivariate model is required for forecasting in place of the univariate model. Feature selection in already published works is not of concern because only one feature is used at a time in univariate time series data. Therefore, an alternative hybrid forecasting model should be proposed to solve the problem typically promptly and tackle time series data uncertainties. The best forecasting model should be accurate and robust to gain the confidence of users in adopting it for use frequently (Salim 2015).

3.7.3 Research questions

Developing research questions is required in the stages involved in research problem formulation. Before formulating research questions, here are the stages involved for the formulation of the research questions. The following questions need to be answered (Salim 2015):

    i. Am I familiar with the literature in the field?
    ii. What are significant research questions in the research area?
    iii. What are the areas that require further investigation?
    iv. Can the proposed study fill the research gap or enhance better understanding?

v. Has the literature already suggested similar study?

vi. Has the proposed study been conducted by previous researchers? If yes, is there any gap to fill?

vii. Is the research question attracting attention from the research community? Or it is becoming outdated?

viii. Is the proposed study going to have significant impact in the research area?

If the questions were answered, then one can go ahead to formulate the research questions. For example, research questions can be formulated as follows:

i. How can a novel hybridized linear and nonlinear model be designed?

ii. How can the linear and nonlinear models be hybridized to minimize over-fitting to enhance the prediction performance of the model?

iii. How can the local minimum problem typically found in previous hybrid models be minimized?

iv. Can the hybrid model perform better than the constituent models and the models already discussed in the literature?

In simple terms, research questions are derived from the statement of the problem. Converting the research problem statement into question form gives the research questions. Consider the following two statements as stated in Salim (2015):

Statement of the problem: The design of the study is to measure the effectiveness of introducing the awareness of information security course on students of CS.

Research question: What is the effect of introducing the awareness of information security course on students of CS?

3.7.4 Aim and objectives of the research

The aim of the research describes the broad goal/purpose of the research in general terms of what is intended to be achieved. The objectives of the research are formulated in specific terms describing what is expected to be achieved within the scope of the research after the research work is conducted. The objectives inform the reader what the research proposes to achieve and it is listed as the specific topic to be investigated within the core framework of the research. The objectives should be complete, clear and specific in communicating to the reader the intention of the research. Each of the research objectives is expected to contain one aspect of the research. The objective should start with action oriented words or verbs such as 'to determine', 'to find out', 'to explore', 'to measure', 'to ascertain' etc. An example of the aim and objective of a research project are provided in the following (Salim 2015).

3.7.4.1 Aim of the research

The aim of this research is to develop a hybrid of linear and nonlinear model with minimal over-fitting and local minima problem capable of improving the prediction performance of the model. In addition, the hybrid can have the capacity to tackle insufficient and incomplete data.

3.7.4.2 Objectives of the research–computer science perspective
Examples of objectives of the research are listed as follows:
    i. To develop a hybrid model by combining a linear and nonlinear model that is accurate and robust with the sequence for tackling incomplete and different sizes.
    ii. To propose a novel cooperative feature selection method that selects the optimum number of features significant as input factors.
    iii. To investigate the influence of a cooperative feature selection method, hybrid of particle swarm optimization algorithm based backpropagation neural network and dynamic sequence on the prediction performance of time series.
    iv. To evaluate and validate the proposed hybrid linear–nonlinear model performance by comparing it with classical models on four different time series data with varying behavior and scale.

3.7.4.3 Objectives of the research–cyber security perspective
Examples of objectives of research are listed as follows:
    i. To design and develop adaptive intrusion detection system with capability to learn dynamic situation in network traffic and regularly adapt to reflect the changing situation.
    ii. To improve the discriminative nature of an intrusion detection system to tackle vague boundaries between the suspected traffic and genuine traffic pattern on imbalance data.
    iii. To investigate the design of ensemble classifiers.
    iv. To design an improved new lightweight layer security and analyze for countering blackhole attacks.
    v. To design an improved security framework for countering heavy attacks from wormhole.

3.7.4.4 Objectives of the research–software engineering perspective
Examples of objectives of research are listed as follows:
    i. To investigate the adoption of scaling agile framework practices in addressing global software development (Beecham *et al* 2021).
    ii. To design and develop improved automation of software product line based on a multi-product lines approach for exploiting the split between managed and managing sub-systems (Abbas *et al* 2020).
    ii. To investigate group mode coordination problems in global software engineering projects for better understanding of global software development (Stray and Moe 2020).
    iv. To develop a non-homogeneous Poisson process model for open source software for understanding the fixing of problems in subsequent releases (Singh *et al* 2017).
    v. To investigate a release update based on entropy and maximizing of user's level of satisfaction subject to bug fixing to the level of satisfaction (Singh *et al* 2017).

vi To investigate the adoption of a quality model by practitioners for integration into software analytics tools within the context of agile software development (Martínez-Fernández *et al* 2019).

3.7.5 Significance of the research

It is necessary to explain how the proposed work contributes to the body of knowledge in the research field. The important of the research and benefits should be clearly discussed. Commercial benefits, current practice changes as a result of the research, new perspectives on the current way of doing things or benefits to the community should all be discussed in this section (Salim 2015).

3.7.6 Research scope

Any reasonable research should have scope because a research work cannot solve everything without boundaries. The limit of the research has to be specified in clear terms. Scope of the research indicates the study boundary, time frame and domain where the data is collected. The attributes and type of data should be clearly defined within the scope of the research as well as the study area. The technique/algorithm for processing the data has to be specified to fit the scope. An example of scope is research that adopted a quantitative prediction method with four different sets of multivariate data, namely: KLSE closing price; China crop yield; total export earning of natural rubber products; and composite index used for the validation of a proposed hybrid model. At least 50 data samples will be used because a linear model like ARIMA requires at least 50 data samples categorized as simple and complex time series for forecasting. The ARIMA and artificial neural networks are adopted as the linear and nonlinear model for hybridization for improvement of the proposed hybrid model. Nonlinear parameters were excluded; only nonlinear time series data were considered (Salim 2015). A summary of good research in computing is presented in table 3.4.

3.8 Summary

This chapter presented SLR and research problem formulation. A clear explanation of what constitutes a literature review and its benefits to researchers were outlined and discussed. Different types of literature reviews such as narrative, metadata analysis and SLR were discussed. The chapter attempted to propose the procedure for SLR from the perspective of computing. Nine stages including focus and selection of research area, motivation, keywords, research questions, literature search and data sources, study selection procedure, data extraction and synthesis, extraction of answers related to research questions and SLR quality assessment were proposed for SLR from the perspective of computing. Research problem formulation is discussed in the chapter. Formulation is the transformation of a research problem into a research question that is answerable scientifically. Problem formulation is the situation whereby a problem to be solved by research is established and proposes a detailed framework on the procedures required to solve the research problem before developing the plan for solving the problem. The stages involved in

Table 3.4. Characteristics of good research in computing.

Characteristics	Description
Novelty.	The idea can be new or build on existing work or modify it. It can be proven from extensive SLR.
Interesting to the research community.	Ensure that the research problem to be solved should be of interest to the research community.
Originality.	A work not derived from the idea of someone else or built on existing work or modification. It is totally new with a unique solution. It can be proven from rigorous SLR.
Tackling a new and complex problem.	The problem should be new and complex that has not been solved by any researcher in the past. This can be proven by conducting extensive SLR.
Adaptability.	The proposed method should have the ability to work with different sizes of datasets and robust enough to handle distorted data with noise. It can be proven by experimenting with varying data sizes and distorted data.
General application.	Ability of the proposed method to solve varieties of problem with little adaptation. The documented approach should be easily to understand and implement.
Real-world application.	Identify specific area of application in the real-world environment.
Publishable.	The research work should have the potential for publication in a reputable journal.
Produced research problem.	Good research always produces another research problem for a future research opportunity. The weaknesses of the research should be outlined for expanding the scope of the work in the future.

research problem formulation include exploring the research area, conducting SLR, coining of the problem statement, developing the research question, developing research objectives and describing the scope of the research. Lastly, the characteristics required for good research in computing were outlined in tabular form.

References

Abbas N, Andersson J and Weyns D 2020 ASPLe: a methodology to develop self-adaptive software systems with systematic reuse *J. Syst. Softw.* **167** 110626

Almutari M, Gabralla L A, Abubakar S and Chiroma H 2022 Detecting elderly behaviors based on deep learning for healthcare: recent advances, methods, real-world applications and challenges *IEEE Access* **10** 69802–21

Beecham S, Clear T, Lal R and Noll J 2021 Do scaling agile frameworks address global software development risks? An empirical study *J. Syst. Softw.* **171** 110823

Centre for Reviews and Dissemination 2022 What are the criteria for the inclusion of reviews on DARE? https://york.ac.uk/crd/ (accessed 1 September 2022)

Chalmers I and Glasziou P 2009 Avoidable waste in the production and reporting of research evidence *Lancet* **374** 86–9

Chiroma H, Ezugwu A E, Jauro F, Al-Garadi M A, Abdullahi I N and Shuib L 2020 Early survey with bibliometric analysis on machine learning approaches in controlling COVID-19 outbreaks *PeerJ Comput. Sci.* **6** e313

Chiroma H, Abdulhamid S I M, Hashem I A, Adewole K S, Ezugwu A E, Abubakar S and Shuib L 2021 Deep learning-based big data analytics for internet of vehicles: taxonomy, challenges, and research directions *Math. Probl. Eng.* **2021** 9022558

Chiroma H, Shuib N L M, Abubakar A I, Zeki A M, Gital A Y U, Herawan T and Abawajy J H 2016 Advances in teaching and learning on Facebook in higher institutions *IEEE access* **5** 480–500

Clarke M and Chalmers I 2018 Reflections on the history of systematic reviews *BMJ Evid.-Based Med.* **23** 121–2

Eagly A H and Wood W 1994 *Using Research Syntheses to Plan Future Research* (New York: Russell Sage Foundation)

Gall M D, Borg W R and Gall J P 1996 *Educational Research: An Introduction* 6th edn (White Plains, NY: Longman)

Gilbody S, Wilson P and Watt I 2005 Benefits and harms of direct to consumer advertising: a systematic review *BMJ Qual. Saf.* **14** 246–50

Hartling L, Spooner C, Tjosvold L and Oswald A 2010 Problem-based learning in pre-clinical medical education: 22 years of outcome research *Med. Teach.* **32** 28–35

Hodgkinson G P and Ford J K 2014 Narrative, meta-analytic, and systematic reviews: what are the differences and why do they matter? *J. Organ. Behav.* **35** S1–5

Jauro F, Chiroma H, Gital A Y, Almutairi M, Shafi'i M A and Abawajy J H 2020 Deep learning architectures in emerging cloud computing architectures: recent development, challenges and next research trend *Appl. Softw. Comput.* **96** 106582

Kastner M, Straus S E, McKibbon K A and Goldsmith C H 2009 The capture–mark–recapture technique can be used as a stopping rule when searching in systematic reviews *J. Clin. Epidemiol.* **62** 149–57

Kitchenham B, Brereton O P, Budgen D, Turner M, Bailey J and Linkman S 2009 Systematic literature reviews in software engineering—a systematic literature review *Inf. Softw. Technol.* **51** 7–15

Liberati A, Altman D G, Tetzlaff J, Mulrow C, Gøtzsche P C, Ioannidis J P, Clarke M, Devereaux P J, Kleijnen J and Moher D 2009 The PRISMA statement for reporting systematic reviews and meta-analyses of studies that evaluate health care interventions: explanation and elaboration *J. Clin. Epidemiol.* **62** e1–e34

LeCompte M D, Klinger J K, Campbell S A and Menke D W 2003 Editor's introduction *Rev. Educ. Res.* **73** 123–4

Levy Y and Ellis T J 2006 A systems approach to conduct an effective literature review in support of information systems research *Informing Sci.* **9** 182–212

Martínez-Fernández S *et al* 2019 Continuously assessing and improving software quality with software analytics tools: a case study *IEEE Access* **7** 68219–39

Meerpohl J J, Herrle F, Antes G and von Elm E 2012 Scientific value of systematic reviews: survey of editors of core clinical journals *PLoS One* **7** e35732

Mohamed Shaffril H A, Samsuddin S F and Abu Samah A 2021 The ABC of systematic literature review: the basic methodological guidance for beginners *Qual. Quant.* **55** 1319–46

Musa N *et al* 2022 A systematic review and Meta-data analysis on the applications of Deep Learning in Electrocardiogram *J. Ambient Intell. Human Comput.* **14** 9677–750

Pati D and Lorusso L N 2018 How to write a systematic review of the literature *HERD: Health Environ. Res. Des. J.* **11** 15–30

Peričić P T and Tanveer S 2019 Why Systematic Reviews Matter: A Brief History, Overview and Practical Guide for Authors www.Elsevier.com/connect/authors-update/why-systematic-reviews-matter/ (Accessed: 15 July 2021)

Petticrew M and Roberts H 2006 *Systematic Reviews in the Social Sciences: A Practical Guide* (New York: Wiley)

Randolph J 2009 A guide to writing the dissertation literature review *Pract. Assess. Res. Eval.* **11** 13

Robinson K A, Saldanha I J and Mckoy N A 2011 Development of a framework to identify research gaps from systematic reviews *J. Clin. Epidemiol.* **64** 1325–30

Sabi H M, Uzoka F M E, Langmia K and Njeh F N 2016 Conceptualizing a model for adoption of cloud computing in education *Int. J. Inf. Manage.* **36** 183–91

Stray V and Moe N B 2020 Understanding coordination in global software engineering: a mixed-methods study on the use of meetings and Slack. *J. Syst. Softw.* **170** 110717

Singh V B, Sharma M and Pham H 2017 Entropy based software reliability analysis of multi-version open source software *IEEE Trans. Softw. Eng.* **44** 1207–23

Salim N 2015 UCP 0010 – research methodology (slides) (Department of Information Systems, Faculty of Computing, Universiti Teknologi Malaysia)

Weidt F and Silva R 2016 Systematic literature review in computer science—a practical guide *Relatórios Técnicos Do DCC/UFJF* **1**

Chapter 4

Computing research tools and resources

Research tools and resources are required for practical implementation of computing ideas. The research tools differ depending on the nature of the research. The choice of the suitable research tool and resources is a prerequisite for successful research. Many tools and resources exist for computing research. In this chapter, we discuss different computing research tools and resources to ease the work of researchers in locating suitable tools and resources to conduct research. Simulators, frameworks and libraries related to different disciplines in computing ecosystems are outlined and discussed. In addition, to improve the productivity of a researcher, the chapter outlines productivity software that can help improve the researcher's productivity while focusing on the core technical aspects of the research. We believe that after reading this chapter, the reader will understand different research tools and resources required to conduct research in different computing disciplines.

4.1 Introduction

Research tools and resources in computing research comprise both the software and hardware required to successfully accomplish research. Typically, when a researcher conducts a rigorous literature review, they formulate the research problem, develop a conceptual framework and collect the required research data. What comes to the researcher's mind is the software and hardware needed to practically solve the research problem. A lot of the research tools and resources exist out there and it is not feasible to cover all research tools and resources in a single chapter. However, every research problem has a suitable research tool and resources needed for the execution of the research project. For example, the research tool and resources needed to solve a research problem in information systems on the perception of students on e-learning differ from those of cybersecurity addressing an issue on network security. In the case of hardware, it also differs depending on the computing discipline and nature of the research because of the size of data varying across the

doi:10.1088/978-0-7503-5017-4ch4

research domain. For example, research in data science (DS) that typically deals with a very large amount of data ranging into TB or PB in some cases, will definitely require high performance computing systems to process the data as opposed to particular research in software engineering dealing with data in MB. In the case of software, it also varies depending on the computing discipline and nature of the research. For example, research in information systems or information technology might require SPSS running on a personal computer for data analysis, whereas research in DS might require Hadoop running on a cluster system or super computer for data analysis.

On the other hand, there are other non-technical issues that are not a core technical aspect of the research but are required in the research to give it an appealing appearance and allow the researcher to manage the whole research report with ease, thereby improving the productivity of the researcher. We refer to those tools as productivity tools in view of the fact that the tools improve the productivity of a researcher. For example, a researcher needs to manage references, write a report free of grammatical errors, back up files, collaborate, etc. The productivity tools take care of all these activities automatically allowing the researcher to focus on the core technical aspect of the research. Many of the research tools and resources are open source developed from both academia and industry to keep pace with the growing interest in computing research. Therefore, the research tools have the approval of both academia and industry.

In this chapter, we present different type of research tools and resources required in conducting research in computing to ease the work of researchers in locating suitable research tools and resources. In addition, the chapter outlines productivity tools that can help improve the productivity of the researcher by allowing the researcher to focus on the core research while the productivity software manages other aspects. We only focus on the main research tools and resources to give the beginner initial reading material, as it is not feasible to exhaust the complete collection of research tools and resources that are available.

4.2 Research productivity tools

In this section, the chapter outlines and discusses research productivity tools, as depicted in figure 4.1, required by researchers to improve the productivity of the research team working on a project. The tools are not compulsory for use in research but necessary to improve the productivity of the research team/researcher. The list of existing research tools cannot be exhausted in the chapter but we select the major tools as initial productivity working tools for researchers, especially graduate students and early career researchers.

4.2.1 Reference management software

Typically, a researcher has to manage a lot of references because many references are consulted during research activities. Those references are typically listed at the end of the research report/journal paper/conference paper/thesis/dissertation and cited in the text in a particular format such as APA, MLA, Chicago, Harvard, etc.

Figure 4.1. Research tools for improving researcher productivity.

In some cases, the references run into the hundreds. Those references need to be properly managed to keep track of the justification for the research for any reader willing to do further work on the reference or verify the justification provided by the research and locate where the research established the gap from the existing body of literature. Manually managing those references can undoubtedly distract the attention of the researcher from the core technical research activities, especially if the references run into the hundreds. Therefore, different references management software were developed to automatically manage the references while the researcher concentrates on the core aspect of the research. For the purpose of this book, we discuss EndNote as the reference management software of choice because of its wide acceptance within the research community and popularity in general. Other than EndNote, reference management software such as the Mendeley, Zotero, MyBib, Refbase, Citavi, ReadCupe, etc exists.

4.2.2 EndNote

Lehigh University's information resources developed EndNote as reference management software for the students and faculty members of the University. Librarians supported and actively promoted EndNote in view of the fact that it enhanced the maximum utilization of the library resources, improving the visibility of services rendered by the library to both graduate students and faculty members (Siegler and Simboli 2002). EndNote is now the product of Clarivate Analytics as bibliographic citation management software. EndNote has gone through a series of modifications for improvement by adding new features. EndNote makes it possible for citations to be accessible online, via iPad applications and desktop. Members of research teams located in different geographical locations collaborating on a project can compile, format, share resources and bibliographies. The collaborating tool in EndNote allows collaborators to share references selectively simultaneously monitoring updates, and to control the team members' access. It is integrated with the Web of Science to allow the selection of references and identify a suitable journal for possible publication. The updates in EndNote include improved group sharing, electronic reference type, manuscript matcher, and allow the creation of a citation report. Electronic media resources include multimedia applications, social media, episodes for television, discussion forums and blogs. This gives the researcher the opportunity to include all the information extracted from the electronic resources in the reference type (Hupe 2019). A detailed explanation of the different aspects of EndNote is provided below (Hupe 2019).

4.2.2.1 Group sharing

This has the ability for imposing privileges to members of a research group. The members of the shared references and bibliographies can impose privileges, for example, members can be given the privilege for reading only or writing only or read–write. The activities of the research group members can be tracked for the users to see the updates performed by different members in the bibliography and references. The custom group sharing function of EndNote allows the sharing of some particular portions of the library shared with users that are online but not members of the research group/team. The research group members have the privilege to view the group shared with them through the online EndNote on the library desktop. In group sharing, members of the research group don't need to search for the complete collaborative library trying to locate materials, only the selected portions can be shared and the level of the access privilege (Hupe 2019).

4.2.2.2 Citation report creation

EndNote allows users that subscribed to Web of Science to generate a citation report for a group of selected references in the EndNote library because EndNote is integrated with Web of Science. The report generated can give the analysis of the aggregate statistics of the publications such as the number of citations for each published paper, yearly contributions, etc. Other analysis can be conducted based on the articles indexed in Web of Science.

4.2.2.3 Manuscript matcher

This feature of EndNote is very useful for a beginner or early career researcher who is developing a manuscript for submission to a journal. EndNote can help the user find a suitable reputable journal reducing the risk of making a submission to a bogus journal. The manuscript matcher is very helpful in finding the journal that matches the scope of the manuscript developed by the researcher. The researcher is only required to supply a major component of the manuscript for the relevant journal to be searched. For example, a major component that defines a journal paper includes title and abstract. The author is required to enter the title and the abstract of the paper to the manuscript matcher. Subsequently, the manuscript matcher generates ranking of the relevant journals and analysis of the journals. The journal generated for a possible submission provides the submission link for each of the journals on the search result. That makes it convenient to the user to have access to the journal submission page to start the submission process. The advantages of EndNote in summary are provided in table 4.1 as extracted from the EndNote blog.

4.2.3 Plagiarism detection tool

The burning issue before a teacher, editor or publisher is how best to detect plagiarism in a submitted work. The stakeholders in the academic publishing world really want to detect plagiarism with ease because of the high volume of manuscripts received. The traditional way of detecting similarity in a submitted work is to copy any portion of the work submitted and paste it into a search engine to search for any document online that matches the text. The process is manual, tedious and time consuming for voluminous works to go through such a process. As such, plagiarism detection software packages such as Turnitin, iThenticate among many others, have sprung up to eliminate the limitations of the manual process of detecting plagiarism.

Table 4.1. Summary of the EndNote advantages.

Feature	Function
Writing fast	EndNote allows the user to automatically place a citation in the text (intext-citation) while creating a bibliography at the end of the report using the MS Word feature.
Better research	EndNote uses tools that find a PDF for the user throughout the entire search period for easy reading, reviewing, annotating and search for the PDF in the library resources.
Organized and focused	EndNote gives the researcher a sense of organization to remain focused on the core research component by allow the researcher to create rules to automatically organize references while working. The Tabs in EndNote allow easy multitasking and provide convenience in working with multiple windows.
Enhanced collaboration	EndNote provides a platform for easy collaboration among the research team separated by geographical location. The research team can share a library with a set of permissions access.
Published in reputable journal	EndNote has the feature for matching a manuscript with reputable journals using the manuscript matcher. As such, it provides an excellent guide to beginners and reduces the chances of submitting a manuscript to a bogus or fake journal.
Ubiquitous	The user can have access to the research in progress from any location and at any time from the cloud platform. The user can work across different platforms such as moving between online and desktop and iPad applications.

It is imperative to note that it is the responsibility of the author to ensure that work submitted for assessment or publication is free from any form of plagiarism. In addition, the journal editorial board is saddled with the responsibility to ensure that the journal publishes materials free from plagiarism. As a result of web-based plagiarism detection tools, checking for plagiarism in a submitted manuscript is easy, if the editorial system is integrated with a plagiarism detection tool, unlike in the era of hardcopy where detecting plagiarism is extremely difficult. Therefore, this makes the work of the editorial board easier in screening manuscripts for plagiarism. Submitted manuscripts to journals are screened through a plagiarism detection tool for the editor to assess the manuscript before proceeding for peer review. With such a screen method, the journal can significantly reduce the chances of publishing a plagiarized manuscript (Debnath 2016).

4.2.3.1 Turnitin

Turnitin is a web-based software package for promoting originality by researchers, early career researchers, instructors and students. Turnitin is used as a deterrent for preventing plagiarism in academic publications. Students typically submit an e-version of the form through the Turnitin software online for checking originality of the text submitted for matching the material in the database of Turnitin and creating an originality report. Typically, students can view the reports of the work submitted but cannot view the Turnitin report of others. Recently, Turnin has gained an unprecedented popularity and become the choice of many institutions, publishers and organizations across the world in combatting plagiarism. Turnitin had been developed in 1997, and is tried and tested across institutions globally (Batane 2010). It has a database that archives millions of papers that were submitted previously to Turnitin, billions of web page contents, publications, encyclopedias available online, news agencies and other sources (iParadigms 2011).

Turnitin compares the content of a submitted document to the content of the documents in the database to generate a report on the score—the percentage of non-originality linked to the identified source in the database. The originality report generated with the material reproduced by Turnitin is studied by the investigator to ascertain the level of the originality of the submitted document or otherwise. Turnitin not only focuses on student-to-student work collusion but uses external sources to compare the student work submitted (Heckler *et al* 2013). This makes it simple for the investigator to identify if the student submitted work that is not original (Marsh 2004).

In addition, Turnitin compares submitted work to top premier content journals such as open access journals and top publishers like but not limited to Elsevier, Springer, Taylor and Francis, IEEE, and Wiley Blackwell. Turnitin exposes the manipulation of text content with the intention of bypassing the Turnitin integrity checks. It identifies code plagiarism in the case of programming assignments submitted by students verifying for source code originality checks (Turnitin 2013). However, it is critical to understand that the similarity report generated by Turnitin is not an index for plagiarism. A good or bad score doesn't exist, scoring 0% similarity index doesn't necessarily indicate that the work is 100% original. On the other hand, 75% (see figure 4.3) doesn't mean that the work has failed to reach the required standard. The report needs to be subjected to human judgment to decide what is going on in the work.

Turnitin typically generates an originality report, as shown in figure 4.2, of any submitted work indicating with highlighted text, as shown in figure 4.3, that matches with the source found in the Turnitin database. When the report is generated it is the

ORIGINALITY REPORT

75%	75%	14%	63%
SIMILARITY INDEX	INTERNET SOURCES	PUBLICATIONS	STUDENT PAPERS

PRIMARY SOURCES

1	dspace.mah.se Internet Source	47%
2	Submitted to University of Greenwich Student Paper	10%
3	www.ajtmh.org Internet Source	7%
4	Submitted to The University of Manchester Student Paper	1%
5	cs.uef.fi Internet Source	1%

Figure 4.2. Originality report generated by Turnitin.

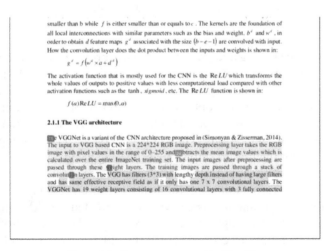

Figure 4.3. Document screened by Turnitin.

individual that will look at the report alongside the highlighted text in the content to take a decision based on the author's intention. Turnitin gives educators and students an easy way to take critical decisions on the originality of the work submitted by students for further instructions, corrections or legal action (Turnitin 2013). Self-evaluation is equally important for students/authors to check their work by themselves before submitting it formally to the instructor, journal, conference or any other venue for publication or assessment in the case of students submitting assignments. This is just to be sure of what the student/author is submitting to avoid avoidable embarrassment and save time.

4.2.4 Spelling and grammar checkers: Ginger Software spelling and grammar checker

Typically, researchers need to write reports in different forms such as PhD thesis, MSc thesis, technical report, journal paper, conference paper, edited book chapter or standalone book. These reports are generated from the research activities. Writing that is free of grammatical error typically gives a very good impression about the work and it will allow the evaluators to concentrate on the technical aspect of the work instead of correcting the grammar. Many evaluators don't like to read a manuscript/thesis with a lot of grammatical errors, sometimes it is frustrating to the extent of provoking the evaluator to give negative comments about the work. Many journal chief-editors reject papers from the desk without allowing them to pass through the peer review process because of grammatical errors. This shows the importance of a thorough proofreading of a manuscript. A carefully proofread manuscript makes the reader follow the work easily with the possibility of impressing the reader to keep on reading the work. Many tools were developed to help in conducting a thorough proofreading of the report generated from the research activities to allow researchers to focus on the technical aspects of the work while the tool proofreads the manuscript. This chapter discusses Ginger Software spelling and grammar checker because of it is popularity and acceptability. However, other proofreading software packages exist.

4.2.4.1 Ginger Software spelling and grammar checker
The Ginger Software spelling and grammar checker provides the opportunity for the user to correct grammatical errors with very high accuracy and speed, thereby improving the standard of the English language. The Ginger Software proofreading tool works by providing several options to the user about the grammar mistakes detected by the Ginger Software proofreading tool. It is the user that will choose from the best available suggestions. The Ginger Software proofreading tool has the capability of allowing the user to skip some of the suggestions where they are not in line with the context of the idea in the manuscript. As a result, users are advised to study the suggestions before adapting the text to ensure accuracy of the grammar. Even the most severe grammar mistake can be corrected by the Ginger Software proofreading tool with very high degree of accuracy. The Ginger Software proof-reading tool has the ability to correct severe spelling errors, typos, phonetic errors

and words that were misused based on the sentence context. The issue of spelling checking has not always been easy, but with the help of the Ginger Software proofreading tool, a single click can correct multiple number of grammatical errors. Spelling in English language can be tricky as often the pronunciation of a word has not much to do with the spelling. This makes many people wrongly spell words that native speakers would not. It is very unfortunate that wrong spelling can give a bad impression about the author, mostly attributed to carelessness in handling the spellings. It very important to know how to do correct spelling because wrong spelling makes writing difficult to understand. An author writes for readers and wrong spelling sends a bad impression about the author. But with the Ginger Software proofreading tool the checking of the writing for spelling and grammar errors is fast and easy. The author may not require anyone to review the manuscript text for grammar issues. The user can employ the Ginger Software proofreading tool online for the purpose of checking spelling or the full version of the Ginger Software proofreading tool that includes checking grammar, misuse of words and an audio version of the text that can be downloaded (Spell Checker 2022).

4.2.5 Google documents

Google documents mostly refers to Google Docs, which allow the user to create a document online for easy collaboration while working on the document online in real time ubiquitously from any device. A document created using Google Docs can be edited among the collaborators in real time, making it easy for sharing, comments and suggestions. It has the facility for using @mentions to extract relevant users, files and attract rich online collaboration to work on the docs. Google Docs has a module called Smart Compose that helps the user to write very fast, focusing on ideas while the errors in the writing can be corrected by the spelling and grammar suggestions. It can perform voice typing and it provides a fast document translator. Another advantage of Google Docs is that it is connected to Google applications for use with the document created using Google Docs thereby saving a lot of time. Comments can be replied to directly from Gmail, while embedding of charts from Google Sheets and the document can easily be shared through Google Meet. Relevant content and images can be searched in the web and Google Drive from the document directly. An MS Word file can easily be edited online without necessarily converting the MS files. The layers on the document improve collaborative and assistive features such as the Smart Compose and action items. A PDF file can be imported and promptly edited. In terms of security, Google Doc enforces security measures like advanced malware protection to keep data of the user safe. The document is cloud-based, thereby eliminating the need for local files on physical systems, and minimizes exposure to risk on the device (Google Document 2020).

4.2.6 ShareLaTeX

Many authors/writers prefer to process words with a LaTex word processing software package instead of the commonly used MS Word. LaTex software can be available online or standalone for the user to use to create a document for the purpose of developing a manuscript generated from research activities. ShareLaTeX is one of the platforms available online as a LaTex editor that give users the opportunity to collaborate in real time with team members working on a project to compile the project in a PDF. As opposed to WriteLaTeX, ShareLaTeX requires the user to register and all the projects are privately inherent. The online ShareLaTeX has advanced features that enable collaboration, synchronization with Dropbox and change of history but is only available to subscription users (ShareLaTex 2020).

4.2.7 Backup tools

Backup of research documents is critical in today's research world. It is frustrating to lose a completed project or a project in progress as a result of computer damage, fire outbreak, cyber or virus attacks. This will result in wasted work hours, causing delay to the project completion time period and loss of resources already committed to the project. For postgraduate students, imagine an MSc or PhD student preparing for a viva say in a month's time and suddenly the whole project is damaged by a virus that attacks the systems causing the student lose the work that was done over 3 or 4 years without any trace of a copy. In another example, a researcher generates data spending a lot of resources, only to wake up in the morning and find that the data has been lost as a result of system breakdown. The manuscript prepared for submitting to a journal, conference or edited book is corrupted by a virus or the hardware is damaged or stolen; this will be highly devastating to the authors/ scholars because the energy invested to accomplish the work has been wasted without any other copy to fall back on. In view of the aforementioned issues regarding the loss of projects, authors/students are advised to have a backup of all the materials involved in the project activities, especially soft copies. The backup can be on standalone devices such as a pen drive, external disk, printed copies, etc. However, these backups also have the possibility of being damaged, stolen or misplaced. In addition, these take up physical space, as such, requiring additional hardware resources to use for the backup. This chapter recommends cloud-based backup platforms like but not limited to Google Drive, iCloud, OneDrive and Dropbox. These cloud storage platforms only require the user to open an account to store documents free for a small amount of storage space. However, if the space required is large, the user will have to pay for the services to have additional storage space. These are frequently used storage platforms excellent for backups of research documents and datasets.

4.2.8 Finding a suitable journal for submitting a paper

For new researchers, finding a credible and suitable venue for the submission of a manuscript may be difficult. In the internet era, many bogus journals have infiltrated the academic community where fake journals and publishers are rampant on the internet. Those kinds of journals accept any manuscript submitted without any peer review. As long as the author pays the publication fees, such journals are willing to publish any manuscript submitted by an author without peer review. In many cases, they mimic the characteristics of a legitimate journal website with fake impact factor and other metrics associated with credible journals. Many academics/researchers have fallen victim, especially early career researchers. To avoid falling into the trap of such journals, we suggest researchers especially early career researchers, use the well-known credible tools for finding credible and suitable journals such as Elsevier JournalFinder and Springer Journal Suggester. These two journal search engines only require the user to enter title, abstract, subject area and keywords of the manuscript. Then, the journals search tool returns suggested journals with a submission link to the user to submit the manuscript.

4.3 Computing research tools

In this section, the chapter discusses computing research tools and frameworks (see figure 4.4) needed by researchers to implement a proposed conceptual framework or research idea in computing. The research tools are necessary for practical work. Many computing research tools exist but cannot all be covered in this chapter. However, we have selected some major tools from different computing disciplines as initial working tools for researchers, especially graduate students and early career researchers.

Figure 4.4. Computing research tools.

4.3.1 Software engineering

The tools required for software engineering research are many, though not covered here because this is beyond the scope of the chapter. However, one of the major tools in software engineering research is discussed to avail the reader with an initial tool for starting research in software engineering. We selected Visual Paradigm because it is widely accepted in the research community and has the ability to model different aspects of software engineering including automatic code generation in different programming languages.

4.3.1.1 Visual Paradigm

Visual Paradigm is an award-winning software engineering tool widely accepted for software development and management. It provides different features required for the development of software such as enterprise architecture, project management, software development and collaboration platform. Visual Paradigm allows team members to collaborate for managing transformation complexity for accommodating the dynamic nature of the markets, technology and requirement for regulations. It is found in Visual Paradigm that it is a typical single point solution for business transformation, project management, enterprise architecture planning and agile software development to enable an organization to stay competitive and maintain steady growth. Visual Paradigm fosters innovations through open standards. Universities, the private sector, consultants, and government enterprises globally have accepted Visual Paradigm as a software engineering tool that fosters innovations (Visual Paradigm 2022a). Visual Paradigm integrates software design and project management tools in a central environment, encompassing all that is required by team members to effectively build a software project. Formal and notational modeling are contained in Visual Paradigm for modeling and casual drawing. The diagrams that are considered under the modeling classification such as the unified modeling language, BPMN and others typically comes with the data model for more manipulation, that is, generation of code, syntax, checking of consistency, etc. Visual Paradigm comprises more than 150 different charts and graphs for business under the casual drawing category accessible from both the desktop and cloud platform. The user must have access to the internet to get access to the charts and business graphs in the cloud platform and enjoy the web compatibility diagram features, as shown in figure 4.5 (Visual Paradigm 2022b).

The features of Visual Paradigm such as database engineering, user experience design, enterprise architecture, code generation, system modeling, project management and team collaboration are depicted in figure 4.5 and a summary of major features extracted from Visual Paradigm (2022a) with a corresponding description is presented in table 4.2.

4.3.2 Information systems and information technology

Research in information systems and information technology heavily makes use of Statistical Package for the Social Sciences (SPSS) for data analysis as the research area deals with both qualitative and quantitative data mostly gathered through

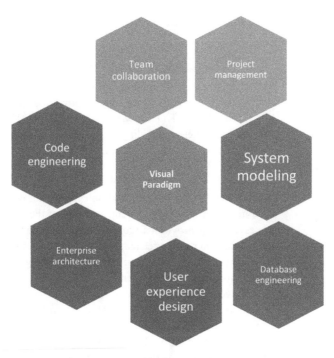

Figure 4.5. Visual Paradigm features.

questionnaire and interview. Although the IBM statistical package for the social sciences (SPSS) is highly used in the Information systems and information technology research, it extends to other research areas in the computing ecosystem, especially software engineering and human computer interaction, but is not as heavy as the information systems and information technology. SPSS is not the only research tool for data analysis, others exist such as R. However, we selected SPSS because it is well established, enjoys popularity in the research community and offers easy availability of materials for learning the IBM SPSS statistical package. On the other hand, qualitative data collected at the course of information systems, information technology and software engineering can be analyzed using NVivo. Therefore, IBM SPSS statistical package and NVivo are discussed in the following subsections.

4.3.2.1 Statistical Package for the Social Sciences

SPSS is well established, having been launched in 1968 and acquired by IBM in 2009. Officially, the package is known as IBM SPSS statistics, however, users mostly refer to it as SPSS. The IBM SPSS statistical package is established statistical software manly for analyzing different types of data and editing. IBM SPSS is a comprehensive statistical package that comprises multiple features design for executing varieties of statistical analysis. The data for analyzing in the IBM SPSS statistical package can be from any source such as scientific research, Google

Table 4.2. Summary of the description of Visual Paradigm features.

Feature	Description
Visual modeling	This feature contains powerful tools for modeling and it assists the researcher/developer in building and managing diagrams including models such as drag and drop editor, unified modeling language, ArchiMate, DFD, ERD, SoaML, SysML and CMMN. It provides the tools for reusing elements, diagram, syntax validation, transformation of element and costume properties.
Business analysis and design	This is a tool for improving productivity and efficiency in business such as strategic planning that helps in discovering and defining the goals of the business. Process design for visualizing workflow with BPMN, generation of a quality report and activities of the working procedure. Process analysis provides a tool for simulating the process and animation. The process reengineering tool provides capability for documentation of the plan, gap identification, designing of new process and monitoring of improvement.
Project management	With effective project management, a better software project outcome is ensured. It provides a built-in project management tool for maintaining the project management life cycle from the planning, execution and activities for the control of the project. It can generate a report very fast. It organizes management activities using a 2D configuration process map. Management tools such PERT, roadmap, spider charts, WBS, Fishbone, implementation plan and a lot of others are available for keeping pace with managing the project.
Agile and Scrum development	It provides the set of tools for making agile backlog and management process effective. It contains user story mapping that has drag and drop objects for creating the user story, a tool for estimating the story and spring backlog management. The scrum process canvas allows the development team to manage all the project activities in a single page, including the scrum roles, events, artifacts, and generates the scrum report very fast.
Code and database engineering	Typically, this feature bridges the gap between design and implementation with the help of the code and database engineering support tool. It has the capability of generating and reversal of source code in more than ten programming languages. For example, Java source code can be generated from unified modeling language and allows the changes made in the source code to reflect on the unified modeling language. The Java source code generated and the software design are synchronized using round trip engineering in such a way that an update in the unified modeling language will be reflected in the Java source code. It can form a sequence diagram from the Java source code, hibernate ORM, generate and reverse state machine code. In the case of a database, it can export the database from ERD and generate ERD from the database/DDL.

Online diagrams	It provides the cloud platform for easy creation of diagrams and team collaboration without the need for the user to set up and configure a physical computer system. It provides convenient drag and drop diagram editors with more than 100 different types of diagram covering technical, business and general diagrams. It has over 1000 diagram templates for quick-start drawing of diagrams. It is compatible with different web browsers and platforms.
User experience design	It simplifies the design of the user interface. The tool provides the features for crating wireframes for visualizing the flow of the screen and layout. It gives the visualization of the wireframes as a flowchart. The animation embedded in the wireframe makes the wireflow alive via the animation components and a prototyping tool is available for demonstrating the entire work.
Team collaboration	This component allows the research/development team to work on the same project concurrently, collaboratively, and smoothly. The cloud platform stores the work safely with security, and the work can be accessed ubiquitously by any team member.

Analytics, customer database or website server log files. The IBM SPSS statistical package is compatible with varieties of file format that are commonly used for structural data such as MS Excel, text files including, .txt or .csv and relational database. The IBM SPSS statistical package contains statistical tests and multi-variate analyses as follows: t-tests, chi-square, analysis of variant (ANOVA), ANCOVA, correlation, regression, nonparametric like the Mann–Whitney U, Kruskal–Wallis, factor analysis, cluster analysis, reliability and validity test and construct validity. The use of the statistical tools to predict a variety of data for the identification of groups such as clustering analysis and factor analysis. On the other hand, the IBM SPSS statistical package performs descriptive statistics such as frequencies, means, mode, median, cross-tabulation, descriptive ratio statistics.

4.3.2.2 IBM SPSS Amos for structural equation modeling

IBM SPSS Amos is a software package for the development of structural equation modeling (SEM) that provides support to research and theories. It extends standard multivariate analysis methods such as regression, factor analysis, ANOVA and correlation. IBM SPSS Amos builds attitudinal and behavioral models that capture a relationship that is complex better than the conventional multivariate statistic tools. It uses the user interface or intuitive graphical interface for interaction between IBM SPSS Amos and the user. Typically, IBM SPSS Amos is included in the IBM SPSS statistical package premium edition. However, IBM SPSS Amos can be purchased separately as a standalone software package without the IBM SPSS statistical package. In IBM SPSS Amos, estimate, assessment, specification and model can be presented in an intuitive path diagram to visualize hypothesized relationships that exist in variables. A user-defined estimate can be specified by the user using simplified technique. Models can be built using non-graphical, programmatic methods, and ways for non-programmers to build models without drawing the path diagram are provided in IBM SPSS Amos. In creating SEM that includes special cases as path analysis and longitudinal data models with observed and latent variables, the candidate model is specified using SEM in an exploratory way or IBM SPSS Amos compared with several models using Akaike information and Bayes information statistics to suggest the best candidate model. It fits the model confirmatory factor analysis, variance of the component, errors in the variables and the latent variable in general. Mean structures and multiple group datasets are analyzed. Data from different populations are analyzed at the same time. Factor and regression models are integrated together into a single model before fitting them simultaneously. Multiple models are analyzed simultaneously before IBM SPSS Amos determines the nested models to automatically compute the test statistics. The path diagram is translated into a Visual Basic program. Automatically generated parameter constraints are used to fit linear growth curve models.

4.3.2.3 NVivo

NVivo is a software package developed by QSR International. NVivo is for conducting analysis for qualitative and mixed method data. It is an analytical tool that facilitates researcher in discovering new knowledge from qualitative data and mixed methods—qualitative and quantitative data. NVivo can assist the researcher in organizing, analyzing and discovering meaningful insights from data to produce a clear articulated finding backed by evidence from rigorous analysis. The interface of NVivo allows the user to import different varieties of data such as text, audio, interview, focus group, images, video, spreadsheet, survey, journal articles, social media sources, web content and online surveys. NVivo has a feature for collecting data centrally from multiple sources for conducting in-depth data analysis. The themes and trends of data are identified based on the way the data are coded. Cases can be organized as people, places and core metrics of the analysis. The cases can be linked to age and gender of a group for comparing different groups in the data. Meaning can be discovered in data through asking complex questions. In NVivo, word frequency chart, word cloud, comparison diagrams can be used for data visualization. Specific queries can be used in NVivo to detect emerging topics and sentiments for the identification of themes to reach conclusions. The NVivo integration add-in allows the importation of notes and data directly from MS Excel and Word. NVivo is compatible with frequently used applications such as the surveyMonkey, EndNotes, etc. Table 4.3 is a summary of the benefits of NVivo as listed by the Kent State University Library.

4.3.3 Data science

There are resources required to conduct research in DS. In terms of programming language, Python with DS libraries such as visualization, statistics and machine

Table 4.3. Summary of the benefits of using NVivo.

Feature	Description
Analysis	It has the ability to organize and analyse unstructured text, audio, video and image data.
Importing	NVivo can import citations from bibliographic management, notes and captures from Evernote.
Capturing	It has the capability of capturing data from social media such as Facebook and Twitter using the NCapture plug-in in a web browser.
Multi-lingual	It can conduct simple text analysis queries like text search or word frequencies in different languages such as English, French, German, simple Chinese, Portuguese, Spanish and Japanese.
Trial	NVivo has a free trial version to use before taking a decision on an NVivo subscription.

learning aspects are very important in DS research. However, Python is not the only language of choice for DS; other platforms such as Scala or Java are considered because Python alone is not effective in big data analytics. Multi-server cluster resources such as the Apache Spark, Apache Hadoop cluster and facilities such as cluster resources for the storage and processing of big data are required for smooth big data analytics. The cluster system can be mounted in the institution or public, private or hybrid cloud. Typically, just one server is not enough for the processing of big data. Therefore, the tools for visualization, machine learning and others required for dealing with big data need to be running in a distributed environment in view of the fact that running a single server is not sufficient. A Linux-based system is required because most of the cluster systems are Linux-based. A cluster administrator is needed for the maintenance of the cluster hardware and software as well as supporting the user community for smooth operations. Students need to have access to different online services that are highly relevant to DS and datasets with varying sizes (see chapter 5 for details on datasets) (ACM 2021).

4.3.4 Libraries and frameworks

The tools discussed in this section can be used for research in computer sicence (CS), DS and cyber security (CyS) especially where data analytics is required to perform prediction, association rule miming, classification or clustering. The tools discussed here comprise both hardware and software platforms suitable for conducting research in the aforementioned computing disciplines. Many machine learning libraries and frameworks exist that help in solving machine learning/data mining problems such as prediction, classification, etc, but only the major ones are discussed in this section.

4.3.4.1 RapidMiner

RapidMiner is a software platform for DS research mainly focusing on data preparation, machine learning, text mining, deep learning and data analytics. It was developed and launched in 2001 at the Technical University of Dortmund artificial intelligence unit. RapidMiner is considered a general purpose DS platform. An open core model is used for the development of the cross-platform written in Java. Graphical user interface (GPU), Java API and command-line interface are supported by RapidMiner. The architecture of RapidMiner is based on the client/server model that is provided as on-premise, public or private cloud infrastructure. It supports large-scale data analytics such as the unsupervised learning in Hadoop, supervised learning and native algorithms with scoring in the SparkRM and cluster, respectively. Many machine learning algorithms including k-means, fuzzy k-means, support vector machine, linear regression, decision tree, random forest, logistic regression, Naïve Bayes, are covered in the RapidMiner. RapidMiner was an open access platform before it metamorphosed into commercial license with trial version having limitations of using only one logical processor and limited to 10 000 rows of data (Nguyen *et al* 2019).

4.3.4.2 WeKa

Weka is well established in the research community as a platform for conducting data mining research. The machine learning algorithms in Weka are implemented in Java. Weka was developed by the University of Waikato, New Zealand. It was released to the public as a non-commercial platform under the GNU GPLvs-license. The functionality of Weka can be extended using both the official and non-official package system available that increases the approaches of data mining implementation. Weka has four options for data mining, listed as follows: command-line interface, explorer, experimenter, and knowledge flow. The latest version of Weka supports Hadoop and deep learning algorithms. On the other hand, MapReduce is supported by Weka but Apache Spark is yet to be supported by the platform (Nguyen *et al* 2019).

4.3.4.3 TensorFlow and TensorFlow Federated

TensorFlow is an open source software platform that uses graphs to represent mathematical operations in the node for numerical computation design for solving large-scale distributed problems. The multidimensional data arrays called the tensors are represented by edge of the graph developed by the Google Brain Team in Google machine intelligence research. TensorFlow comprises two hundred basic operations written in C++ such as mathematics, manipulation of array, flow control and management of operations. The TensorFlow is used under the Apache 2.0 open access designed for research, development and system production. TensorFlow can run on a system with a single CPU, GPU, large-scale distributed system that runs on hundreds of nodes, embedded devices and mobile devices. Hardware acceleration with Android neural network API, Google and Amazon cloud environment are supported by TensorFlow. Python and C++ provide the programming interface of TensorFlow. Other machine learning libraries that support machine learning research exist in the literature such as Keras, Deeplearning4j, etc (Nguyen *et al* 2019). On the other hand, there is an open source framework called TensorFlow federated for processing distributed datasets to enhance experiment and open research in computing.

4.3.4.4 CloudSim

Readers interested in conducting research in cloud computing need to be conversant with available platforms required for conducting the research. Many cloud computing platforms exist but the most popular and well established platform for cloud computing research is CloudSim.CloudSim is a platform equipped with the toolkit for the modeling and simulation of cloud environment functions such as job/task queue, creating datacenter, events processing, communications between entities, implementing policies, etc. The CloudSim toolkit provides the functionality for conducting experiments with varying workload and performance measures for resources simulated for the development of infrastructure, providing a control environment for the tuning of bottlenecks before deploying in the real-world cloud environment, CloudSim provides a repeatable and control environment for testing application services. It provides the platform for modeling service brokers and allocation of policies. System elements with network connections are simulated in the CloudSim. The interconnection of private and public resources in a federated cloud environment can be simulated. Running CloudSim doesn't require a high performance computing system and it is developed based on Java; any system with dual core 2 GB RAM and 1 GB HDD is sufficient to run the CloudSim. However, the hardware requirement may differ based on the IDE the user is using for the Java CloudSim (2019).

4.3.4.5 Cybersecurity simulators

Research in cybersecurity requires a platform for simulation of ideas for the development of cybersecurity solutions. Like any other computing discipline, cybersecurity solutions start from abstract ideas before experiment is conducted to ascertain the feasibility of the solution for practical application in the real-world environment. In cybersecurity, there is no fit-all simulator for cybersecurity research because cybersecurity is broad and involves different aspects of the computing cyberspace. The areas in the cybersecurity include but are not limited to digital forensics, network monitoring, intrusion detection, penetration testing and network auditing. It is extremely difficult to have a single simulator to simulate all the aspects of cybersecurity. For example, conducting research in digital forensics requires an autopsy platform for conducting analysis. Autopsy is an open source platform for digital forensic analysis, it is user friendly with capability for the analysis of all kinds of digital devices and media. Autopsy has different modules performing different functions. Other simulators with corresponding cybersecurity area include: network monitoring: PRTG; intrusion detection: Nessus; penetrating testing: metasploit; and network auditing: Nmap. The use of the simulator depends on the cybersecurity area the researcher is interested in working on.

4.4 Computer engineering

Many tools for conducting research in computer engineering (CE) are available but cannot be exhaustively discussed in this section. Therefore, two popular tools Gem5 and Webots will be discussed in the next subsections to serve as an initial tool for beginners before exploring other alternatives.

4.4.1 Gem5 simulator

CE research deals with the hardware component of the computer system, especially the processor. Researchers need a simulator to simulate scenarios or components before deploying them for real design and development in the real world. In this subsection, we introduce a simulator for computer system research called gem5 simulator (Gem5 2022). The gem5 simulator is a simulator that provides a platform for computer-system architecture research incorporating system architecture and processor microarchitecture. The gem5 simulator is an open source software platform for the simulation of computer architecture commonly used in both academia and industry, and was developed in the University of Michigan with support from National science foundation, Hewlett-Packard, AMD, Sun, ARM, IBM, Intel and MIPS. It has received attention from CE researchers citing it in over 2900 publications, and the following labs use the gem5 simulator: Google, AMD Research, ARM Research, Metempsy, Micron, HP, Samsung, among many others. The gem5 simulator presents the following interpretation-based CPUs (Gem5 2022):
  i. Simple one-CPI CPU;
  ii. Detailed model of an in-order CPU;
  iii. Detailed model of an out-of-order CPU.

4.4.2 Webots

Research in robotics can be conducted from different computing perspectives. For example, it can be from the perspective of CE, CS or software engineering. Research related to robotics is costly, especially when it involves conducting the research with physical components. Therefore, to reduce the cost of conducting research in robotics, save development time and ease of developing robot prototype, simulation platforms were designed and developed for researchers to use. In this subsection, we selected Webots out of many of the robotics platforms because of it is robust, open source, well established and has acceptability in industry, education and research.

Webots is a platform with GUI for editing simulation and robot controllers, developed by Cyberbotics Ltd in 1998, with continuous updates for the simulation of robots; it is an open source platform. Webots provides the environment for the modeling, programming and simulation of robots. It is designed and developed mainly for professionals and accepted for use by industry, education and research. The Webots library contains sensors, actuators, robots, materials and objects for easy design of robots and simulation. Different type of robot prototypes can be created, developed, tested and validated using Webots such as tracked robots, flying drones, autonomous underwater vehicles, modular robots, multi-legs robots, industrial arms, aerospace vehicles, two-wheeled table robots, bipeds, automobiles, etc. Webots allows the importation of computer aided design models from Blender or OpenStreetMap. A robot can be programmed using C, Python, C++, Java, MATLAB or ROS with API covering robotics basic needs (Cyberbotics 2021).

4.5 Hardware and software platforms

Running simulations in computing requires a hardware platform to conduct experiment in the laboratory. This section discusses some suitable hardware platforms for executing research conceptual ideas.

The GPU is massive parallel architecture specialized hardware that provides an environment for the acceleration of computing. The GPU is used as a general purpose processor. For large-scale data mining problems, the GPU can provide massive parallelization to speed up the processing of the large-scale data mining problem. The algorithm for solving the problem is scaled up vertically for data volumes that are beyond traditional techniques. The system that requires high speed processing to solve real-world and real-time problems to aid the decision making process will certainly require the services of the GPU, especially the application of a deep learning algorithm to process images. GPU operations involve the computation of matrix-based operations that help in speeding up computational speed. The manufacturers of GPUs always strive to improve the configuration of the GPU by configuring many core accelerators capable of improving the performance of the machine or cluster system by having access to the GPU's power of computation (Nguyen *et al* 2019).

Many accelerated libraries exist but the frequently discussed accelerated libraries are as follows (Nguyen *et al* 2019):

Compute Unified Device Architecture: The Compute Unified Device Architecture is a parallel platform for computing that involves programming models designed and developed by NVIDIA the GPU general computing capabilities. The Compute Unified Device Architecture libraries drop-in acceleration across linear algebra, video processing, deep learning, image processing and analysis. The Compute Unified Device Architecture provides the platform for the creation of high performance GPU applications.

Compute Unified Device Architecture deep neural network library: This is the library that houses the primitive deep neural networks, it provides the platform for tuning the implementation for the standard routines like forward and backward convolution, pooling, normalization and activation layers. The Compute Unified Device Architecture gives room to deep learning implementers to concentrate on the training of artificial neural networks instead of spending much time on low speed GPU tuning. The Compute Unified Device Architecture deep neural network library is used for the running of other deep learning frameworks including Theano, Caffe2, MatLab, CNTK, TensorFlow and PyTorch.

Intel Math Kernel Library: is a ready-to-use mathematical library that optimizes source code with minimal amount of effort for the generation of Intel processors. The *Intel Math Kernel Library* is compatible with many operating systems, compilers, programming languages, threading models and linking. It reduces development time, improves the performance of applications, and accelerates mathematical processing routines. The Intel Math Kernel Library includes the deep neural network, linear algebra, data fitting, sparse solvers, fast Fourier transforms, vector statistics, vector mathematics and miscellaneous others.

AMD Radeon Open Compute platform: The AMD Radeon Open Compute platform is an alternative to the commonly used Compute Unified Device Architecture. It has a programming language dependent open source HPC providing an environment for computing equipped with GPU. Peer-to-peer multi-GPU operations with remote DirectMemory access is featured in the AMD Radeon Open Compute platform. The heterogeneous system architecture runtime API gives the platform for the execution of HHC, Heterogeneous-compute Interface for Portability, C++, Python and OpenCL. The Heterogeneous-compute Interface for Portability has the capability to convert the Compute Unified Device Architecture source code to C++ source code and it has no performance impact over the coding directly in the Compute Unified Device Architecture. It is easier to import Compute Unified Device Architecture to Heterogeneous-compute Interface for Portability because both Heterogeneous-compute Interface for Portability and Compute Unified Device Architecture are in C++ programming language (Nguyen *et al* 2019).

4.6 Summary

Research tools are required for the successful implementation of research ideas emanating from the computing discipline ecosystem. Different research tools and resources were discussed in this chapter to help students and early career researchers to be conversant with research tools in computing. The research tools are classified into two main categories: productivity tools and computing research tools. Simulators, frameworks and libraries related to different disciplines in computing ecosystems were outlined and discussed. In addition, to improve the productivity of a researcher, the chapter outlined productivity software that can help improve the researcher's productivity while focusing on the core technical aspect of the research.

The productivity tools discussed in the chapter include EndNote, plagiarism, proofreading software, Springer Journal Suggester, Elsevier Journal Finder, ShareLaTeX, Google Docs. On the other hand, computing research platforms discussed include Webot, IBM SPSS, Visual Paradigm, CloudSim, MATLAB, TensorFlow, gem5 simulator, cybersecurity simulators, etc. A summary of the research tools is presented in table 4.4, some of which were discussed in the chapter, while many of the tools were not discussed because, as pointed out in the introduction, a lot of tools exist but we discussed only the major ones as a starting point for new researchers to begin with.

Table 4.4. Summary of the research tools.

Productivity tools	Software tools	Remarks
Reference management	EndNote, Mendeley and Zotero	Manages references while the researchers focus on the core technical aspect of the writing.
Proofreading	Ginger Software, spell checker and Springer Exemplar	Automatically detecting and correcting grammatical errors in a manuscript.
Finding journal	Elsevier Journal Finder and Springer Journal Suggester	Help in finding suitable journals for submission.
Backups	Google Drive, Dropbox, iCloud and OneDrive	They provide a platform for backup of research in progress to avoid losing it in case the local machine crashes.
Plagiarism	Turnitin, iThenticate and paper rater	For the detection of similarity and possible plagiarism.
Writing manuscript	ShareLatex, MS Word, Smmry and Text2mindmap	These tools help in writing manuscripts including automatic summarization and visualization.
Research tools		
Discipline	Tool	
DS	Tensorflow and MATLAB	Data analytics using algorithms
CS	TensorFlow, TensorFlow federated, MATLAB, CloudSim and Webot	These different simulators for use in computing research. For example, Webot is for simulating robots before building the robot and CloudSim is for simulating a cloud environment.
CE	gem5, MATLAB and Webot	Robotics and processor.
CyS	Digital forensic—autopsyNetwork monitoring—PRTGIntrusion detection—Nessus Penetrating testing—metasploit Network auditing—Nmap	Developing cybersecurity solution.
IS	NVivo, IBM SPSS and R	Qualitative and quantitative data analysis.
IT	IBM SPSS, R and NVivo	Qualitative and quantitative data analysis.
SE	VP Paradigm, IBM SPSS, R and NVivo	Modeling, qualitative and quantitative data analysis.

References

ACM 2021 *Computing Competencies for Undergraduate Data Science Curricula: ACM Data Science Task Force* (New York: ACM)

Batane T 2010 Turning to Turnitin to fight plagiarism among university students *J. Educ. Technol. Soc.* **13** 1–12

Cloudsim 2019 *Cloudsim tutorials* https://cloudsimtutorials.online/cloudsim/ (accessed 1 November 2022)

Cyberbotics 2021 *Open source robot simulator* https://cyberbotics.com (accessed 1 November 2022)

Debnath J 2016 Plagiarism: a silent epidemic in scientific writing—reasons, recognition and remedies *Med. J. Armed Forces India* **72** 164–7

Gem5 2022 *About gem5* https://gem5.org/about/ (accessed on 1 November 2022)

Google Document 2020 *Google Docs* https://www.google.com/docs/about/ (Accessed: 8 November 2021)

Heckler N C, Rice M and Hobson Bryan C 2013 Turnitin systems: a deterrent to plagiarism in college classrooms *J. Res. Technol. Educ.* **45** 229–48

Hupe M 2019 EndNote X9 *J. Electron. Resour. Med. Libr.* **16** 117–9

iParadigms, LLC 2011 White paper: The ethics of self-plagiarism iThen-ticate. Professional Plagiarism Prevention https://www.ithenticate.com/resources/papers/ethics-of-self-plagiarism

IBM Software *IBM SPSS Amos* https://ibm.com/downloads/cas/K8V9RWB2 (accessed 1 November 2022)

Kent State University Library *NVivo* https://libguides.library.kent.edu/statconsulting/NVivo (accessed 1 November 2022)

Marsh B 2004 Turnitin.com and the scriptural enterprise of plagiarism detection *Comput. Compos.* **21** 427–38

Nguyen G, Dlugolinsky S, Bobák M, Tran V, García Á L, Heredia I, Malík P and Hluchý L 2019 Machine learning and deep learning frameworks and libraries for large-scale data mining: a survey *Artif. Intell. Rev.* **52** 77–124

ShareLaTex 2020 *ShareLaTeX is now part of Overleaf* https://sharelatex.com/ (accessed 1 October 2022)

Siegler S and Simboli B 2002 EndNote at Lehigh *Issues Sci. Technol. Librariansh.* **34** 149

Spell Checker 2022 *Spell checker* https://gingersoftware.com/spellcheck (accessed 1 November 2022)

Turnitin 2013 *Does Turnitin detect plagiarism?* https://turnitin.com/blog/does-turnitin-detect-plagiarism (accessed 1 November 2022)

Visual Paradigm 2022a *Introduction and system requirement* https://circle.visual-paradigm.com/docs/introduction-and-system-requirements/ (accessed on 1 October 2022)

Visual Paradigm 2022b *Exploring all the powerful features visual paradigm has to offer* https://visual-paradigm.com/features/ (accessed 1 October 2022)

Chapter 5

Computing datasets and data engineering

It is believed that in the future, data will be the new crude oil. In computing research, data is the backbone of the research, without data no critical research will be conducted in computing. Considering the critical nature of data in research, we have dedicated this chapter to discussing datasets and data engineering: qualitative and quantitative. Researchers always consider where to get data for the research before embarking on the research if it is feasible to get the required data. This chapter vividly discusses datasets, sources of datasets for researchers conducting research in computing—computer science, computer engineering, information systems, data science, cyber security, information technology and software engineering—to easily have access to available data. Data engineering methods and different types of datasets are outlined and discussed. The weaknesses and strengths of benchmark, real-world and synthesis data were pointed out as well as the technique/procedure for managing research data, especially large-scale datasets while maintaining the integrity of the data.

5.1 Introduction

Before the chapter delves into a broad explanation about datasets, let us provide a proper definition of what the data is all about. Data is information being converted for economical form for processing. The data comes in different forms such as videos, images, text and sound. The data is represented in the form of 0's and 1's, meaning binary numbers. The 0's and 1's are used in the computer memory for pattern generation for storing different types of data. In the computer memory, the smallest unit of data is referred to as a bit and the bit represents a single value while bytes represent eight binary digits. Data is transmitted through the transmission media in the form of binary numbers. In the last decade, the amount of data being generated has increased significantly because of the dramatic increase of computer users (JavaPoint 2022).

doi:10.1088/978-0-7503-5017-4ch5

Data is the solid foundation for any meaningful research. A lot of data exists on the internet and offline, it is not possible to discuss all the datasets that exist. With this in the researcher's mind, the chapter intends to discuss some major datasets and sources where the reader can easily have access to credible data for beginning research in computing before exploring more as they get into the world of research. In view of the fact that the book is dedicated to disciplines within computing, only datasets related to different disciplines within computing were considered. For example, datasets relevant to cyber security, computer science and data science were discussed, especially the nature and sources of the dataset. Research is conducted within the context of datasets, for example research on cyber security requires data from the domain of computer security.

The datasets for the research require management. Any serious research must define the procedure for managing the research data. All the data collected during the research should be managed properly to maintain the integrity of the data from the beginning until after the research.

The datasets for the research in most cases require data engineering to properly prepare them for processing. Data collected from a real-world scenario comes with a lot of challenges such as a large number of features/inputs that are relevant and irrelevant that need to be addressed before analyzing the data. High quality data is required to produce quality results. No matter the excellence of the methodology used for the processing of the data, if the data quality is poor, the output will also be poor. Therefore, quality data produces quality output.

In view of the significant role played by data in computing research, this chapter is dedicated to discussing sources of datasets relevant to each discipline within computing, today's reality of large-scale data, type and nature of the datasets, data engineering and research data management. This will provide reader with essential tips and a broad view on datasets relevant to different disciplines in computing before narrowing down to the researcher's area of interest.

5.2 Large-scale datasets as today's reality compared to small-size datasets

It is approximated that every day, 2.5 quintillion bytes of data are generated (Wu *et al* 2014) and 1.8 PB of data is generated every day on the internet (Zhang *et al* 2018), this has brought the world to the big data arena and data continues growing at exponential speed. Recently, big data has become a hot research area for academia and industry. A voluminous amount of data is being collected by organizations continuously. The sources of these data are from different platforms such as websites, sensors and social networks (Chiroma *et al* 2018, Hashem *et al* 2016). Big data is beyond the capacity of the conventional database, computers and software. Big data requires the power of high performance computing for parallel processing. The processing of big data is based on nonlinearity with unpredicted behavior in some cases. (Cheng *et al* 2016). Typically, the commonly used software cannot process big data for curating, capturing and management of the data (Yu *et al* 2016).

The large-scale data discussed shows that there is a dramatic increase in data because of the technological advancement and massive usage. The commonly used data for the evaluation of algorithms is the UCI repository benchmark dataset. The datasets in the UCI repository are small-size datasets that do not represent the reality of today's volume of datasets generated from different sources. The large-scale data sizes ranges from GB, TB, PB, etc, for example, a large-scale data with a 1000 genomes project that contains human genetic variations is 200 TB in size, the Kafka cluster contains 100 TB of LinkedIn activities data and Walmart houses 2.5 PB of data. Compare this to the small-size dataset in the UCI repository, mostly measured in K, KB, M, etc, for example, the size of letter recognition data is 696K, BCW is 121K, dermatology dataset is 25k and KDD 1.3M (Chiroma *et al* 2018). The difference is clear between small-size and the large-scale datasets. An algorithm that works perfectly on small datasets may not even run on large-scale datasets, posing challenges for algorithms. For example, shallow artificial neural network (ANN) works perfectly at speed on small datasets, but as the size of the data keeps increasing, the performance of the ANN keeps decreasing and becomes slow in processing the data. This has motivated the emergence of a new generation of ANNs referred to as deep learning algorithms. Deep learning algorithms work perfectly on very large datasets, as the data increases the performance of the deep learning algorithms increase.

5.2.1 Definition of big data

Big data is a dataset that the traditional database management system cannot process and manage. The traditional database management system is not capable of handling a large magnitude of dataset feeds rapidly. There is no universally accepted definition of big data. However, Gandomi and Haider (2015) explained that the TechAmerica Foundation's Federal Big data commission defined big data as the description of a voluminous amount of data generated at a high velocity, complex and variant data requiring technology and techniques that are advanced to enable capturing, storing, distributing, managing and data analytics.

5.2.2 Characteristics of big data

The characteristics of big data as extracted from Hashem *et al* (2015), Gandomi and Haider (2015), Liu *et al* (2015), and Wu *et al* (2016) are as follows and depicted in figure 5.1 for better understanding:

Volume: The volume of the dataset is very large, e.g. gigabyte (GB), terabyte (TB), petabyte (PB), etc. Examples: 1024 MB = 1 gigabyte (GB), 1024 GB = 1 terabyte (TB), 1024 TB = 1 petabyte (PB), exabyte (EB), zetabyte (ZB), yottabyte (YB), brotobyte (BB), etc. 1 terabyte of data can be stored on 1500 CDs or 220 DVDs, which is sufficient to store 1 million Facebook pictures. Facebook stores 260 billion pictures on over 20 petabytes of storage space, and it processes 1 million pictures per second.

Variety: The data comes in different types of format, i.e. structural heterogeneity, e.g. the data can be structured, semi-structured and unstructured. Structure data is a

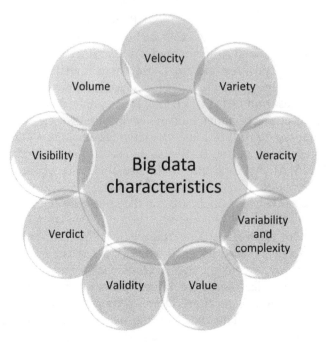

Figure 5.1. The characteristics of big data.

dataset in tables of Excel sheets or a relational database. Unstructured data is a dataset that lacks structure to be processed by a computer, e.g. text, audio, image and video. Semi-structured data is data that is in between structured and unstructured that does not conform to strict standards, e.g. text language for exchanging data on the web.

Velocity: This is the rate at which the data is being generated from the source, internally (e.g. sensor) or externally (e.g. social media), this causes the content of the dataset to be constantly changing.

Veracity: Some sources of data have unreliable characteristics. For example, the sentiment of a customer on social media is uncertain in view of the fact that it entails human judgement, yet it contains valuable information.

Variability and complexity: Variability is the variation in the rate of the data flow, the rate at which the data is flowing is not consistent, the rate of the flow can be low or high. Complexity refers to the fact that big data is generated from many different sources, as such, analyzing big data becomes very difficult and a challenge.

Value: The value of the generated data is very low relative to its density. That is, the data received in its original form is typically very low with high density.

Validity: Emphasis is on the verification of the data quality to ensure its logicality, correct data collection without any form of bias.

Visibility: Emphasis is on having a full picture of the data so as to make a useful decision.

Verdict: The decision by the key stakeholders based on the available choices within the scope of the problem, resources availability and capacity for computation.

5.2.3 Case studies

There are case studies in the world where big data is experienced. Table 5.1 summarizes a few among the organizations that deal with the big data phenomenon as an example.

5.2.4 Content large-scale data format

The content format of datasets typically differs depending on the nature of the content, basically three content formats exist, as discussed by Hashem *et al* (2015) and JavaPoint (2022).

Table 5.1. Summary of case studies for big data.

Case study	Description	Big data processing	Domain
Facebook	This is the most popular social network that connect billions of people across the globe.	Stored 260 billion photographs on over 20 PB storage space. 1 million pictures are processed per second (Gandomi and Haider 2015).	Social Media
Nokia	Nokia is a communication company that produces mobile phones for people around the world. Globally, many people use the Nokia phone to communicate, capture pictures and share experiences.	Nokia has over 100 terabytes of structured data and petabytes of multi-structured data (Hashem *et al* 2015).	Communication
Amazon	Amazon is the largest internet-based retailer in the world according to sales and capitalization.	Amazon handles between over 500 000 and over 1 million transactions per second. This may require PB of storage space to store the transaction records.	Commerce
Flicker	Application for sharing and managing pictures and videos online.	Generates almost 3.6 TB data (Zhang *et al* 2018).	Social Media
Google	Search engine that gives information about web page, images, videos and lots more.	Every day Google processes 20 000TB of data (Zhang *et al* 2018).	Technology

5.2.4.1 Structured data

This is information that is quantitative, predefined for easy searching and well organized. Typically, it is stored in a relational database and managed by structured query language developed by IBM in the 1970s and continues to be modified. Structured data are defined by static framework limiting machine or humans to access the data within the confines of a rigid framework. The structured data can easily be query, input, store and analyze. Examples of structured data include numbers, dates, hotel databases, student database systems, excel sheets with numbers organized into rows and columns.

5.2.4.2 Semi-structured data

Semi-structured data does not have a table organization with a corresponding relational database. However, tags or other markers are used for the separation of semantic elements and enforcement of hierarchies of records and data fields. In semi-structured data, the same class entities can have different characteristics despite the fact that the grouping is done side by side with each other, and the order in which the attributes appear doesn't matter, it has no significance. The era of the internet makes semi-structured data common because data types are not limited to only full text documents and databases. Examples of semi-structured data include emails; it is categorized as semi-structured data because it contains structured data such as name, date, time and email address. These email attributes are organized into folders like inbox, trash, sent, draft, etc. Despite email applications allowing findings by keywords, the message in the email is unstructured. As such, emails contain both structured and unstructured data making them semi-structured.

5.2.4.3 Unstructured data

Unstructured data is open text, videos, location information, social media data, images and any other data without a predefined organization or without following a particular pattern in the content. Data from online reviews, documents, expressing opinions and feelings are qualitative data that do not follow a predefined pattern, typically such type of data are difficult to analyze. However, such data can be structured for the purpose of extracting new knowledge using a technique called machine learning.

5.2.5 Challenges regarding big data

Large-scale data comes with challenges, the good issue about big data is that research can be conducted on it from different perspectives. For example, research on big data can be conducted from the perspective of information systems (IS), information technology (IT), software engineering (SE), computer engineering (CE), data science (DS), cyber security (CyS) and computer science (CS). There are many challenges facing the industry in dealing with big data, and a few are listed below for researchers to explore from different computing perspectives (Chen *et al* 2014):

Network: Transferring big data over the network is a challenge because of very high demand for bandwidth, so industries are increasing their bandwidth in order to handle the transfer of the data which means an increase in expenses.

Storage: There is a challenge in storing the data in a central location because of the increasing magnitude of the big data at very high speed. The data are stored in a different storage device instead of central storage to avoid the challenges of central storage. However, it increases the cost of hardware.

Security: Many security threats exist such as privacy, confidentiality etc. Such threats are increasing because of the volume, velocity and variety features of big data.

Analytics: Analyzing big data requires high computing resources, high volume of memory, high energy consumption and it emits carbon dioxide.

5.3 Benchmark, real-world and synthesis datasets

Real-world data or experimental data are collected from the real-world environment using devices such as sensors, cameras, equipment operations, etc from a population in a particular location. Or it can be collected from experiment within a confined environment. A real-world dataset captures real-world dynamics and it requires data engineering to improve the quality of the dataset because real-world datasets typically come with many irrelevant attributes and missing points. On the other hand, benchmark datasets are typically clean data deposited in a public repository for researchers to have access to it. Mostly, such benchmark datasets are publicly available for use by researchers, for example, the UCI machine learning repository. Such datasets can easily be collected without the need for any specialized equipment, they are clean which makes them free from data engineering and typically not expensive to collect. Typically, algorithms work smoothly on benchmark datasets unlike real-world datasets. Algorithms can exhibit excellent performance on benchmark datasets but perform otherwise in real-world datasets because of the different characteristics that exist in the two different datasets. It is advisable that algorithms that model for real-world applications should be modeled based on real- world datasets to capture the reality of real-world dynamics, so not just the hypothesis of their performance on the dataset is a benchmark (Muhammad *et al* 2021). Synthesis data are datasets collected from simulated environments in the computer that mimic a real-world environment. Typically, the simulated environment models the scenario of the real world. It is simple to collect the data without the need for physical equipment to be mounted in the physical world. However, the simulated environment may not capture unexpected events that can possibly be prompted by some events in the real-world environment. So, the data collected from such an environment can't capture those scenarios. As such, an algorithm that works on synthesis datasets is not guaranteed to work in the real-world environment when deployed (Gidado *et al* 2020). A summary of the comparison among the different types of datasets is presented in table 5.2.

Table 5.2. The summary of the strengths and weaknesses for the different types of datasets.

	Real-world data	Benchmark data	Synthetic data
Strength	Captures real-world dynamics	No specialized equipment required	Simple to collect
	Ability to capture unexpected events	Doesn't require data engineering	Doesn't require data engineering
		Freely available	Not expensive
		High quality	High quality
		Does not require equipment	
Weakness	Expensive to collect	Bias	Inability to capture unexpected events
	Tedious and time consuming	Can't capture real-world dynamics	Can't capture real-world dynamics
	Requires data engineering	Outdated as time passes	Outdated as time passes
	Requires physical equipment		
	Low quality		

5.4 Characteristic of real-world datasets

The characteristics of real-world data, as shown in figure 5.2, are discussed in the next subsections to prepare the minds of students and early career researchers on what to expect when collecting data from the real-world environment and the tips to tackle the issues.

5.4.1 Missing values

In practice, it is extremely difficult to collect real-world data without missing values. In a dataset with missing values, the missing values are represented by values that are out of range, for instance negative value in datasets that has positive values as the dominant values or represents it with 0 or blank or dash. The values are missing for some reasons likely because of malfunction resulting from equipment measurement, changes in the procedure for experimental data collection and similar data collection from multiple sources. Therefore, the importance of the missing values should be taken into consideration. Responding to a questionnaire during a survey is vulnerable to missing values because the respondent may likely not respond to a particular question on the questionnaire, for example issue of age or income. Many of the methods in machine learning assume that missing values are not significant, assuming that the values are unknown. It is a researcher that is familiar with the data that will make a decision on why the values are missing and find out the significance of the value or whether they can afford to code them as missing values. In some cases, the missing value can motivate research to investigate reasons for the missing values (Witten *et al* 2011).

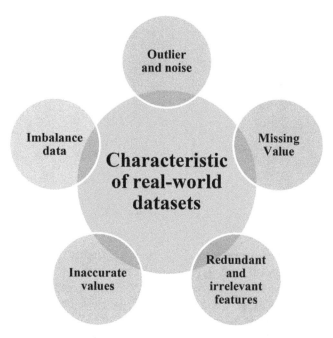

Figure 5.2. Real-world dataset characteristics.

5.4.2 Inaccurate values

When dealing with datasets for analysis, it is important to check datasets carefully to find attributes that are rogue and check the values of the attributes for correctness. In most cases, the data gathered were not purposely meant for data mining. Therefore, when the data were collected, many of the fields did not really matter, so were left unchecked or blank. If they did not affect the value of the data there was no need for correcting the values. Errors and omissions in databases have great importance when the data is to be used for data mining activities. For example, banks can view customer age as insignificant, so the database of the bank may not contain the age of the customer. However, age of the customer can be an important attribute in mining rules. Incorrect values are triggered by typographical error committed during data entry in the database like the misspelling of attributes which can create additional values for the attributes. In some instances, it is having different names for the same entity, just like having Pepsi as well as Pepsi Cola. The original data that contains the error is preserved through the process of converting the file to be used for the purpose of data mining. Therefore, examining the possible values of the attributes in the data is sacrosanct (Witten *et al* 2011).

5.4.3 Imbalanced data

Naturally, many real-world data contain imbalanced classes. Imbalanced data means the situation where the normal classes are much more than the number of abnormal classes in datasets. The interest is normally on the minority classes as

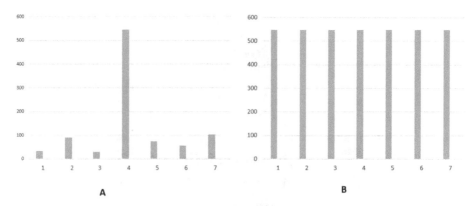

Figure 5.3. (A) Unbalanced class distribution and (B) balanced class distribution.

opposed to the majority normal classes because it is highly costly to misclassify the abnormal class. It is very difficult in real-world applications to gather a high number of abnormal classes as a result of operations in the real-world environment. Several imbalanced applications exist in the real-word scenario such as intrusion detection, fraud detection and medical diagnosis. In the case of cyberbullying, it is extremely difficult to get the number of cyberbullying posts to be higher than the number of non-cyberbullying posts, thus creating a situation of imbalanced classes distribution in the dataset. In this case, the classification model finds it difficult to perform classification with a high level of accuracy. Therefore, many proposals have been devised to solve the problem of imbalanced datasets (Liu and Zhou 2006). For example, rescaling or rebalancing of the classes distribution is one of the commonly used methods for solving the problem of imbalanced datasets. The rebalancing influences the classes on the learning process to be in proportion to the cost (Zhou and Liu 2010). Zerkouk and Chikhaoui (2020) used oversampling technique to solve the problem of an imbalanced dataset. Data for daily living activities of elderly people were collected and it was found that there was imbalanced class distribution in the data with the abnormal behavior as the minority because abnormal behavior was rarely compared to the overwhelming normal behavior leading to imbalance data. The oversampling technique was used to augment the minority samples to be on a par with the majority class, thus balanced classes distribution was obtained. Figure 5.3 was created to illustrate oversampling technique, (A) is showing the class distribution before the oversampling technique is applied while (B) is showing the class distribution after the oversampling technique was applied to get a balanced class distribution.

5.4.4 Outliers and noise

Observations or the subset of observations that appear extremely different from the normal observations are referred to as outliers (Titouna *et al* 2015). These observations are typically dissimilar, inconsistent and exceptional from the normal observations. Example of outliers include suspected fraudulent credit card transactions and inconsistent brain signal (Zhang 2013). In addition, unreliability and uncertainty characterized datasets collected from wireless sensor networks. The uncertainty in a wireless sensor network can cause serious damage, especially in health-related applications, thus the applications of a wireless sensor network demand precise reading. Therefore, an efficient distributed algorithm for processing the data is required to ensure precise and reliable data extraction from the noisy measurement and detect outliers from the sensors in wireless sensor networks (Safaei et al 2020). The different categories of outliers are as follows: vector-line, collective outliers, sequences, trajectories and graphs (Zhang 2013). However, the outliers can be detected in datasets. Methods of detecting outliers include but are not limited to: density-based methods; statistical methods; example-based methods; clustering-based methods; and sparse cube methods (Zhang 2013). In recent times, advanced methods such as hybrid unsupervised approach (Savić et al 2022), ensemble method (Jayanthi et al 2021), clustering for semi-supervised method (Zhao et al 2022) are proposed for the outlier's detection.

5.4.5 Redundant and irrelevant features

In a real-world scenario, there is a problem with a very large amount of data; dealing with a large amount of data becomes a complex task because the number of attributes (features) contained in the data is typically very large. Not all the features in most cases are relevant for giving useful information to the researcher. As a result of that, some of the features in the data are irrelevant and redundant, and capable of reducing the performance of the algorithm (Agrawal et al 2021). The datasets can have millions of records with hundreds of thousands features (Krishnaveni and Radha 2019). Therefore, discarding the irrelevant and redundant features of the data while simultaneously retaining the quality of the data becomes the vital role of feature engineering (Agrawal et al 2021).

5.5 Case study: collecting data from a real physical environment—smart city

In this section, we take the smart city as a case study to show the generation of data in a real physical environment (see figure 5.4). This section discusses the generation of the data from a smart city environment. Video detection devices are embedded in the smart city environment for capturing videos. It captures the vehicles at the rate of 30 frames/second and gives information about the speed of a vehicle as well as the density of the traffic. Image data are collected from the smart city, the image data are generated from different sources such as surveillance satellite and unmanned aerial vehicles with cameras to collect images. In regard to video capturing, video technology like surveillance cameras, CCTV, drones, unmanned aerial vehicles and vehicle detection videos are used in the smart city to capture video data. The video data are used to secure the city and control traffic flow. Apart from videos and images captured in the smart city, text data are also collected from the smart city. The text data are generated from different sources within the smart city. Sources of the text data in the smart city include Twitter, online customer conversation, online

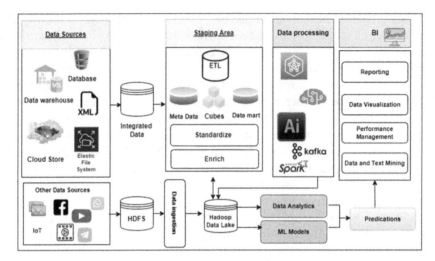

Figure 5.4. Smart city environment integrating urban computing. Reproduced from Hashem *et al* (2023), CC BY 4.0.

forum, emails, SMS from mobile phone (Muhammad *et al* 2021). As shown in the preceding paragraph, data with different content format are generated ranging from structured, semi-structured and unstructured data. Those data can be collected, stored and analyzed to get new insights that will assist decision makers in taking appropriate decisions.

5.6 Knowing your dataset

It is highly required for a researcher to get to know the data meant for the purpose of conducting the research. Tools as simple as histograms can get the job done. The histogram can be used by the researcher to view the distribution of the nominal attribute values. The values of the numerical attributes can be plotted as a graph, sorted or plotted against the samples, all these associations with the data are very important and helpful. Identification of outliers from graphical visualization of data is easy. The outliers may be representing as an error in the data or some hidden notation for coding situations that are unusual like writing 9999 as missing year or missing of weight to be represented with – 1. In this situation, experts in the domain should be consulted to provide a clear explanation of the anomalies, missing values, identified in the data file. Explanation regarding the use of integers not numerical to represent certain categories can be solicited from the domain experts. The use of correlations to plot attributes against each other or plotting the attributes against the class distribution can reveal important information about the data. It is necessary to perform data cleaning on the research data despite the fact that is time consuming and tedious. Some researchers feel with very large-scale data is it not feasible to check the data. But instead of ignoring the checking of the data completely, it is advisable to extract a sample of the data to perform checking carefully (Witten *et al* 2011).

5.7 Cross-datasets

There are situations where generating a large amount of data is difficult, challenging, costly and time consuming. To circumvent the problems of limited data, cross-datasets approach is adopted to rescue the situation. For example, research in electroencephalogram (EEG) applications need a very large amount of data for rigorous analysis. In the case where such a large volume of data is not available for EEG application research, the cross-datasets methods can be used. Different high quality data from the research community can be collected to use for analysis. For example, the data collected from different machines with human subjects coming from different countries, cultures and age groups can be used for the cross-datasets method of modelling. One research used cross-datasets approach to develop an EEG-based device for detecting emotion using distinct datasets for modelling the algorithms. The database for analyzing the emotion used physiological signals for the training, whereas the SJTU Emotion EEG Dataset is used for testing the EEG-based emotion recognition device. It was found that the accuracy of the EEG-based emotion detection device was improved by 8.2% (Joshi *et al* 2022).

5.8 Dark datasets

Dark data is the data gathered from the operations of different computer networks but is unable to be processed to get new knowledge that can help decision makers take appropriate decisions from the data acquired as the result of the computer network operations. Organizations collect data from computer network operations beyond what is required by the organization to process and be analyzed. In some instances, the organization may not be aware of the data collected from its operations. Sensors and other devices in the industry are responsible for generating dark data. Despite the fact that companies knew the existence of the dark data coupled with incurring additional expenses for storage and securing the dark data, they still retain the dark data believing that it may be needed in the future. However, DeepDive can be used to process dark data. Structured data can be extracted from unstructured dark data with the use of DeepDive, which has very high precision, accuracy, and recall compared to other information extraction systems with affordable data engineering cost. Its processing speed is faster than humans. DeepDive was developed in 2011 as an open source project and continues undergoing development since its inception (Zhang *et al* 2016).

5.9 Research data management

The data generated during research activities is expected to be managed very well to preserved its credibility, privacy and sanctity. Before now, the cycle of research data involved generating, analyzing and publications. However, the pattern has changed over time and it now includes several additional cycles like sharing, access, reuse and preservation. Seven cycles for managing research data are identified as follows: planning, collection, analysis, preservation, reuse, sharing and publication. Research data management is the process that involves the guiding principles for researchers

Figure 5.5. Major factors to consider in managing research data.

and stakeholders to make optimum usage of the data generated during the research activities (Blog 2021). However, policy on managing research data can differ depending on the policy of the institution regarding research data management. Figure 5.5 depicts different components of data management.

We propose the management of research data based on the guiding principles provided by Australian Research Council and Universities. The stages involved in managing research data are outlined and discussed as follows (National Health and Medical Research Council, Australian Research Council and Universities Australia 2019):

5.9.1 Storing, preservation and discarding

The storage, retention and discarding of research data depends on the policy of the institution. The data can be stored in the institutional repository or an external repository. Retaining research is very important in view of the fact that it may be the only asset left for researchers after the research project has been completed. The following should be considered when storing, preserving and discarding research data:

  i. Copyright policy and arrangement for a license that is already in place.
  ii. It should adhere to the guiding principle of the discipline global best practice depending on the discipline.
  iii. It should comply with the requirement for privacy, ethics and publications.
  iv. The period for retaining research data is a minimum of 5 years after publication but it may differ based on legislation (state, territory or

national) or specific type of the research, for example, student assessment, 12 months after the project. For clinical trials, 15 or more year's period is required for retaining the research data.

v. For gene therapy research or research that has community, cultural or historical value, the data should be retained permanently, preferably in national collections.

vi. Procedure for discarding of the data and information should be spelled out clearly and recorded.

5.9.2 Safety, security and confidentiality

The policies regarding the enforcement of the data ownership, database access, and archiving in agreement with confidentiality, privacy and legislation must be put in place by institutions to give researchers guiding principles. The policies should require that the researchers be aware of data access restriction and agreement regarding the confidentiality, and ensure the security of the computer system housing the research data. The personnel controlling information technology should be competent in handling network security and control access to the system. The personnel managing electronic material and other primary materials should have adequate awareness of information security and access control.

5.9.3 Third party access

How to make available to a third party within or outside the institution interested in the research data and output should be described clearly. The policy should involve open access sharing of the data through a control medium. Facilities for secured access, storage, managing data, records, primary materials and granting requests for reference purposes should be put in place by the institution. They should provide license standards to the researchers and institution for sharing the data and principles governing the use of the data, for which Creative Commons Attribution licence2 is suggested to be adopted. In cases where research data is requested and access denied, the reason for the denial should be explicitly explained with justification in a transparent manner. Intellectual property should be enforced based on the institution policy guiding intellectual property matters.

5.9.4 Data storage facilities

Data owned by researchers or the institution should be stored in the facilities provided by the institution or the institution should approve the facility for the purpose of storing the research data. The facility is expected to comply with the relevant privacy criteria, regulations, laws, guidance and discipline specific standards regarding safety and security. The control or ownership of the facilities for data storage and archiving should be addressed by the policy. In addition to the facilities provided by the institution for data storage, the data can be published in an external repository such as the national, international, discipline specific or regional repositories.

5.9.5 Data retention and publication

Justifying research outcomes and data sharing motivate the retention of research data. It is the researchers that determine the research materials to be retained for long-term and wide accessibility. The following items need to be considered when deciding the research material and data to retain:

    i. Non-replicability and uniqueness of the material and data;
    ii. Reliability, usability and integrity;
    iii. Relevancy to the research collection;
    iv. Economic benefit to be derived.

Apart from the requirement for typical publication, researchers have an option to make the data available to a data center, national and international collections or institution and research community data repositories.

5.9.6 Confidentiality management

The sensitive information or confidentiality generated at the course of executing the research project must be handled with utmost care by the researchers. Research data that typically contains sensitive or confidential information falls into the following categories: data provided in confidence such as secret and sacred cultural practice, religion or location information; data or information subjected to privacy law such as user personal data; data or information regarding national security.

5.9.7 Responsibilities of researchers on data and developing a data management plan

The responsibilities of researchers pertaining to the management of research data should be outlined at the beginning of the research and they should abide with all the relevant institution policy concerning data management. As such, it is encouraged to develop a research data management plan for proper guidance. The data management plan should include but not be limited to the following: devise proper measures to ensure security of the systems, network, physical and technological; license, contractual and confidentiality agreements; write down the policies and procedures; provide adequate training to the project team members on data management; create a form for storing the data or information; disclose the purpose for which the data or information will be used; criteria for making the data or information available to a third party interested in the data should be spelled out; respect any agreements signed regarding confidentiality and consent obligations. In the case of loss of data or inappropriate access or use of the data, it should be reported to the appropriate authority. There should be agreement on the data with researchers in case of the researchers leaving the project or switching institution before the completion period. Good data management practice should be put in place to avoid loss of data by ensuring regular backup of the data to external storage and avoiding data duplication by ensuring stable storage format. Requesting the data based on a freedom of information request should be respected and the data should be provided in a format that can be easily understandable.

5.10 Research data repositories and sources

As already discussed in section 5.1 of this chapter, it is not possible to exhaust the entire available data existing out there, especially that on the internet. However, this chapter discusses major repositories and sources of data, as depicted in figure 5.6 whose credibility is highly recognize by the research community from the perspective of computing disciplines. A repository is the location or platform where data and information are stored for different purposes such as research, marketing, analysis, etc. The data or information can be about users, computers, products, people, culture, etc. Different data repositories are discussed below.

5.10.1 IEEE DataPort

The IEEE DataPort is a data repository platform developed and maintained by IEEE. It is easily accessible by users to store research data, access, search and manage the data. It provides capabilities for data download and accessing from the cloud. The IEEE DataPort is designed in such a way that it is robust in accepting data in different formats up to 2 TB of size. The features of the IEEE DataPort as extracted from the DataPort website are presented in table 5.3.

The IEEE DataPort contains different categories of data from different disciplines within the computing ecosystem (chapter 1). The different categories together with corresponding number of available datasets, examples and remarks are presented in table 5.4 (IEEE 2021).

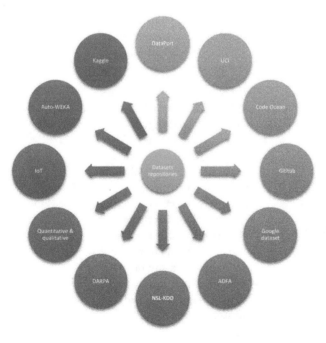

Figure 5.6. Dataset repositories for research in computing.

Table 5.3. Summary of the features of IEEE DataPort.

Feature	Description
Storage	Users and institutions are allowed to stored data indefinitely for researchers, industry and engineers to access the data.
Access	Accessing the datasets by researchers, industry and engineers for analysis for the advancement of technology is allowed.
Analysis	The platform facilitates data analytics by allowing access to the data to be downloaded and used.
Research	It supports research in such a way that the platform provides support for reproducing research outcomes.

Table 5.4. The datasets related to computing available in IEEE DataPort.

Category	Datasets available	Sample and description of the dataset	Remarks
Artificial intelligence	493	**Brain MIR data:** The data contains 3985 (training) + 667 (testing) devoted for the OpenBHB challenge. In addition, 628 images without label are available. *Opportunity++* is for supporting research in artificial intelligence with emphasis on multimodal perception and learning of activities for human beings e.g. actions, gestures, behavior, etc.	It will be interesting to propose novel deep learning architecture.
Cloud computing	38	**Cloud attack dataset:** It is created from CIC-IDS2017 Dataset. The data was in .csv originally but converted into images of 9×9 pixels to develop a distributed denial of service convolutional neural network model to effectively detect the attacks on network. **SDN Distributed denial of service attack images:** It was also in .csv before being converted to image with a size of 5×5 pixel. It is effective for evaluating deep learning algorithm-based intrusion detection.	The data can be utilized for developing cloud computing cyber security solutions.

Computational intelligence	169	**VIG track dataset:** It comprises 124 samples of visual intention extracted from unique features of eye motion collected from 31 human subjects. It is labeled as TEXT or IMAGE.	The data can be increased.
Computer vision	250	**3D hand pose data RGB:** The dataset is for hand pose gesture.	It can be used for developing assistive technology.
COVID-19	56	**COVID-19 and normal chest x-ray:** This comprises COVID-19 data with two classes infected and uninfected chest x-ray images. **COVID-19 fake news:** The fake news on COVID-19 was collected from websites containing satire or fake news about COVID-19. On the other hand, authentic news regarding COVID-19 was extracted from reliable news outlets like BBC News, CNN, *The Atlantic*, etc.	Developing diagnoses or tool for filtering fake news about COVID-19.
Internet of Things	155	**Architecture of 60 IoT computing board:** The data comprises 60 IoT computing boards from the prototype industry. The data was extracted from the datasheets of the manufacturers.	The dataset when properly analyzed can pave the way for future IoT computing board architecture.
Image processing	360	**Data for power transmission line:** This contains both the image of the real power transmission line and synthetic images of power transmission lines.	It can be used to develop a model for monitoring.
Machine learning	579	All datasets can be used for machine learning. The datasets can be applied to solve machine learning problems such clustering, prediction, association rule and classification.	Machine learning algorithms.
Security	114	**Malware analysis dataset:** The data comprises grayscale images, static and dynamic analysis data. The raw data was collected on Android malware.	Cyber security.

(Continued)

Table 5.4. (*Continued*)

Category	Datasets available	Sample and description of the dataset	Remarks
Sensors and education and learning technologies	111	**Dataset for online learning queries:** The data gathered information about online learning searches in Google by people from different countries across the world.	Education dataset that can be used in information systems research.
Communication	252	**Channel state information for 5G:** The data is for channel state based on the 5G NR standard that is published by 3GPP generated by the CDL channel model. **Path loss measurement:** This is a path loss dataset collected from path loss measurement conducted by LoRa —868 MHz transmitting radio and receivers numbering 5. It covers both the outdoor and indoor area.	Helpful in communication systems.
Transportation	88	**Travel time datasets:** Road network information including weekday peak, weekend peak, weekend off-peak and weekday off peak. **Car hacking data:** Data collected on hacking cars for security researchers.	Cyber security.
Biomedical and health sciences	198	**Cell images:** Ultrafast image system called asymmetric detection time stretch microscopy is used for the collection of cell images containing human arm motion for daily living activities.	Computer vision.
Social sciences	57	***Intention for blockchain technology adoption***: The dataset is used for blockchain technology adoption by financial institutions.	Information systems.
Power and energy	242	***Electrical power distribution:*** The dataset has 240 images of the electrical power network: 120 are of damaged structures and 120 are in normal conditions.	Monitoring power facilities.

Image fusion	33	***Drone distribution Inspection image data:*** The dataset comprises approximately 30 000 images of overhead distribution infrastructure to support artificial intelligence innovations.	Facilitates innovations.
Environment	39	**Smart city water consumption dataset:** Smart water meters were used for the data collection indicating the consumption of water by different users in a smart city. **Wireless sensor network for monitoring:** The dataset collected is from the sensor nodes embedded in the environment.	Improves innovations in a smart city.

5.10.2 University of California Irvine machine learning repository

This is a data platform comprising multiple databases collections, data generators, domain theories mainly utilized for conducting machine learning research by the research community to evaluate the effectiveness and efficiency of intelligent algorithms. David Aha and fellow graduate students created the archives in 1987 at the University of California Irvine (UCI). The UCI machine learning data repository is widely accepted as a source of machine learning datasets from across the world among educators, students and researchers right from its inception. The archive has generated impact in the research community with over 1000 citations placing it among the top 100 computer science most cited papers. The repository funding is from National Science Foundation (Asuncion 2007).

5.10.3 Kaggle and Code Ocean

Kaggle houses a huge amount of community published data repository. It offers free access to GPU, customization, not requiring setup, Jupyter notebooks environment and source code. For DS research, Kaggle offers the source code and data required for the DS work. The platform has over 50 000 datasets and public notebooks over 400 000 for analysis. The Kaggle notebook can be used for running machine learning source code and exploring the code. It is equipped with a cloud computational environment for reproducing research outcome and collaborative analysis. The notebook in Kaggle is of two types, namely, Script and Jupyter. Script executes sequentially everything as a source code, and can be created in R or Python through a user interface. The second notebook is Jupyter comprising cells sequence in which each cell is formatted as Markdown or in a programming language of the user's choice. Kaggle has search and filter features that allow searching for datasets, notebooks, users and competition across the Kaggle. It is integrated with newsfeed to give an overview of the activities of users on the platform, especially when new datasets are uploaded. The notebook tab allows quick access to the notebook listing (Kaggle). Code Ocean is the platform where researchers share source code and research data for the research community to reuse/re-run or reproduce research results. The platform provides an avenue for researchers to collaborate, organize, develop, publish, secure and share source code without requiring any special software. Code Ocean is an asset for computational research projects in terms of research data and source code. The platform is freely available and open to individual researchers for uploading discoveries from the computational research community (Code Ocean). Code Ocean and Kaggle are similar as both of them share research data and source code.

5.10.4 GitHub platform

On 19 October 2007 the development of GitHub started. By April 2008, GitHub site was launched by Tom Preston-Werner, Chris Wanstrath, P J Hyett and Scott Chacon, after the beta release. GitHub headquarter is domiciled in California and it has been a subsidiary of Microsoft since 2018. Git is open source version control systems s its role in GitHub. GitHub publishes datasets, stores and collaborates on open datasets. Arguably, GitHub is a repository of large ready-to-use machine learning datasets for modelling with fast, user friendly and with data that is efficient. The high-quality datasets in GitHub are organized based on topics for easy identification by researchers working in different disciplines to locate relevant datasets. GitHub offers a platform for hosting the development of software, open source projects and the control of versions using Git. In addition, Git has the functionality for distributed version control and managing source code. Every project has GitHub features for tracking, requesting, managing tasks, continuous integration and wikis. As of November 2021, it was reported that GitHub has over 73 million developers and over 200 million (28 million public) repositories (GitHub 2021).

5.10.5 Google Dataset Search

The dataset search developed by Google is a search engine for datasets. It has indexed almost 25 million datasets providing a single platform for searching datasets and access to data links. Querying the database with a simple keyword a user can discover a lot of repositories available online. Dataset Search aims to: share data with the aim of encouraging the storage and publication of data following global best practice; and improve the impact of scientists' work through the citation of datasets. The search engine has a feature for filtering the datasets based on the type of the data, for example, image, text, tables, etc and access mode freely available or subscription from the providers of the data. Any researcher willing to publish data in Dataset Search for discovery by users can publish it through the open standard schema.org and researchers, students, business analysts and data scientists are constantly finding data through Dataset Search relevant to their area of interest. Dataset Search provides a snapshot of the datasets on the web. With over 2 million open government datasets provided by US government, the US has become the leading publisher of open government data. The datasets on Dataset Search have grown over time and continue to grow. Finding of datasets is easy when the required information about the data is provided such as the name of the data, creator, and the format of distribution. The dataset discovery approach for Google is based on schema.org which improves the discovery of datasets from diverse disciplines such as science, machine learning, government data, social science, etc. When a researcher describes the data on a web page using schema.org it can be discovered through Dataset Search. Google Data Search has over 20 cancer datasets (Wen *et al* 2021).

5.10.6 Quantitative and qualitative means of data collection

There are some research areas in the computing ecosystem that require question-naires and interviews for the purpose of collecting data to conduct research. For example, information systems and information technology require these depending on the nature and objective of the research. Some specific areas in CS and SE also require questionnaires or interviews to collect data for analysis. For instance, human–computer interaction requires them to collect data about a particular interactive system that has been developed. As a result of that, questionnaires and interviews are discussed in this section.

Questionnaires play the role of providing an interview that is standard in different subjects and it is a critical part of a survey. The respondents respond based on the itemized questions asked on the questionnaire. The questions differ because of the peculiarities of different research areas. The means of communication between the researchers and human subjects is the questionnaire. Questionnaires are administered to the subject for response by the researchers or recruited research assistants to administer on behalf of the researchers. Researchers articulate questions on the questionnaire requiring answer from the respondents. The answers to the questions on the question-naire are conveyed back to the researchers through the questionnaire responded to by the human subjects. Therefore, to ensure that the correct data are collected, the questionnaire must be handled with utmost care as it forms the core of the survey process. On the other hand, a poorly developed questionnaire provides poor or incorrect data not suitable for the research. In developing the questionnaire, the first item is to properly define the objectives of the study. Typically, clients or administrators of the questionnaires need the questionnaire that can collect the relevant information to answer the questions requiring the answer leading to answering the objectives of the research. A straightforward questionnaire that is easily understood and can easily be respond to by the respondents is required for collecting the correct answers. Respondents typically want questions that do not take a long time, have uncomplicated data entry procedure, minimize effort to respond and capture their interest. The data processor wants an uncomplicated questionnaire layout that is simple for the production of tables. The researcher has to make all efforts to meet the requirement of the people while working within a stipulated budget (Brace 2018).

An example related to SE where a questionnaire and interview is used for the purpose of data collection is when a user interface prototype is created for operation that has to be evaluated to ascertain the requirement of the user. The evaluation can be performed informally by test driving, and feedback is provided immediately by the user verbally on the efficacy of the interface such as with an interview response or formally designed study where the user is required to respond to a questionnaire and the response analyzed using statistical methods. Modification is done on the design based on the feedback received from the user or outcome of the analysis conducted. Once the first prototype is developed, different qualitative and quantitative data are collected to help in improving the interface design. In collecting qualitative data: a questionnaire about the prototype can be designed, developed and administered to the end users of the prototype to respond. The questions on the questionnaire can be as simple as Likert scales, open ended, percentage, numeric response, yes/no, etc. In the case where quantitative data is required for the analysis, users are commissioned to interact with the system while observing the interaction to find out the time taken to look for display, number of errors occurring, type of the errors, robustness to error recovery, how easy it is to locate help and references per time standard. All these data are collected, analyzed and the outcome used for modification of the interface prototype (Pressman 2010).

5.10.7 Knowledge discovery in database 99—DARPA, ADFA Linux and NSL-KDD

The pioneer cyber security benchmark datasets—Knowledge Discovery in Database (KDD99) created for the public for the purpose of evaluating the performance of intrusion detection systems was developed by Defense Advanced Research Projects Agency (DARPA) in conjunction with other institutions interested in the project to respond to the lack of standard benchmark datasets for evaluating cyber security systems. The research community accepted the benchmark datasets as standard data for evaluating proposed security systems. However, with the advance in technology, the KDD99 no longer represents the reality of current architecture for attack protocols, inconsistencies and corruption in the data. Therefore, evaluating recently developed intrusion detection systems will not provide adequate performance metrics (Creech and Hu 2013). In response to that, ADFA Linux (ADFA-LD) cyber security benchmarks datasets have been developed to capture the current architecture for the attack protocols (Abubakar *et al* 2015). The NSL-KDD is a reaction to solving the challenges of KDD99. NSL-KDD still suffers from some challenges but it is better than KDD99, as it is believed to be a better benchmark dataset for the evaluation of multiple IDS methods because it has better representation of the current real networks. Other datasets on IoT, dark web, DNS, malware, IDS, and ISCX are available in the repository (University of New Brunswick n.d.).

5.11 Features engineering

In the situation where there are very high features containing relevant, irrelevant and redundant features in a dataset, dimension reduction is employed to reduce the features to get only the highly relevant features. The main purpose of feature reduction is to improve performance, especially accuracy, visualization and understand the knowledge acquired. Different approaches for the reduction of the features exist in the literature, however, one of the easy ways of reducing the features is referred to as feature selection. In this method, only the important relevant features with the relevant information are selected to solve the problem.

The second approach is feature extraction; feature extraction developes the transformation of the input space to a small number of subspaces that preserve the most relevant input features. Feature selection or feature extraction can be used separately, or the two methods can be applied to reduce dimension in a combination manner. In feature selection, the subset of the features available in the dataset with the relevant information with the ability to contribute to the learning accuracy are selected for the learning algorithm. The two approaches each have their limitations and strengths: critical information related to a particular feature is preserved without loss; reduces the size of features to minimize memory space and improve algorithm efficiency; enhances the quality of data; saves resources in subsequent data collection or usage. Feature selection has comprehension of the data to acquire knowledge on the process of generating the data. However, it has the chance of losing or omitting some original important features in a dataset with very high features diversity. On the other hand, feature extraction doesn't lose information in the original features despite reducing the size of the features. However, it has the limitation of lack of information about the degree to which the original feature contributes and the linear combination of the original features lacks interpretability. A typical example of feature extraction method is principal component analysis widely used in the literature. It is a nonparametric tool for extracting the most relevant features from a set of redundant or noisy data (Khalid *et al* 2014).

With regards to feature selection, techniques such as exhaustive search, random search, greedy search were applied to solve the feature selection problems in finding the best feature subsets. However, most the techniques have the challenge of premature convergence, high computational cost and huge computational cost. To deviate from the limitations of the traditional techniques, Nature-inspired meta-heuristic algorithms such as genetic algorithm, bat algorithm, cuckoo search optimization algorithm, Grey wolf algorithm, firefly algorithm, flower pollination algorithm, etc were applied because they can find the best feature subsets while maintaining accuracy of the algorithm. In most cases, Nature-inspired meta-heuristic algorithms are effective and efficient (Agrawal *et al* 2021). In summary, feature extraction creates new features combination with some transformation, whereas feature selection excludes irrelevant features and includes relevant features without altering the original features (AlNuaimi *et al* 2020). Reducing the number of features in datasets has been attracting attention because of a large number of features collected from the following types of problems: application requiring the fusing of data from multiple number of sensors; integration of multiple models with different parameters for solving classification problem; and association rule mining from large features (Zongker and Jain 1996). A study reported a comprehensive review of Nature-inspired meta-heuristic algorithms covering 64 different algorithms for feature selection classified into eight major taxonomic structures. A unified Nature-inspired meta-heuristic algorithms framework was developed for the explanation of various techniques for feature selection (Brezočnik *et al* 2018). Feature selection method is mainly categorized into three, namely, filter, wrapper and embedded methods. The wrapper method is sub-categorized into exponential (search strategy), sequential (selection strategy), and randomized algorithms where Nature-inspired meta-heuristic algorithms fall (Agrawal *et al* 2021). The filter-based feature selection method is independent of the model proposed when evaluating the importance of features in data. In the wrapper-based method, computation of the features score considers the accuracy of the prediction. Prediction accuracy and feature selection are combined in wrapper-based feature selection method while the embedded method is a hybrid of both the wrapper and the filter methods (Han *et al* 2016).

5.12 Summary

The chapter discusses datasets, sources of datasets for researchers conducting research in computing—CS, IS, CE, IT, SE, CS and DS—to easily have access to freely available and subscribed data. Data engineering methods such as dealing with incorrect data, imbalanced data, missing values, outliers and noise and irrelevant features were discussed in the chapter. In addition, different types of datasets including content format were outlined and discussed. Datasets from different computing disciplines and research areas can be found in the repositories.

Feature engineering methods: feature selection and extraction along with their respective advantages and disadvantages were discussed. The weaknesses and strengths of benchmark, real-world and synthesis data were pointed out as well as the technique/procedure for managing research data, especially large-scale datasets while maintaining the integrity of the data. Table 5.5 lists the datasets and links to the sources.

Table 5.5. The summary of datasets and sources.

Data repository	Web link
UCI Machine Learning	http://archive.ics.uci.edu/ml/datasets.php
IEEE DataPort	https://www.ieee.org/about/ieee-dataport.html
GitHub	https://github.com/
Kaggle	https://www.kaggle.com/
Chiroma *et al* (2019)	https://ieeexplore.ieee.org/stamp/stamp.jsp? tp=&arnumber=8531611
DARPA	https://www.darpa.mil/
ADFA Linux	https://research.unsw.edu.au/projects/adfa-ids-datasets
Google Dataset Search	https://datasetsearch.research.google.com/
Code Ocean	https://codeocean.com
NSL-KDD	https://www.unb.ca/cic/datasets/nsl.html
IoT, dark web, DNS, malware, IDS, and ISCX	https://www.unb.ca/cic/datasets/index.html
Auto-WEKA sample datasets	https://www.cs.ubc.ca/labs/algorithms/Projects/ autoweka/datasets/

References

Abubakar A I, Chiroma H, Muaz S A and Ila L B 2015 A review of the advances in cyber security benchmark datasets for evaluating data-driven based intrusion detection systems *Procedia Comput. Sci.* **62** 221–7

Agrawal P, Abutarboush H F, Ganesh T and Mohamed A W 2021 Metaheuristic algorithms on feature selection: a survey of one decade of research (2009–2019) *IEEE Access* **9** 26766–91

AlNuaimi N, Masud M M, Serhani M A and Zaki N 2020 Streaming feature selection algorithms for big data: a survey *Appl. Comput. Inform.* **18** 113–35

Asuncion A 2007 *UCI machine learning repository, University of California, Irvine, School of Information and Computer Sciences* http://ics.uci.edu/~mlearn/MLRepository.html

Brezočnik L, Fister I and Podgorelec V 2018 Swarm intelligence algorithms for feature selection: a review *Appl. Sci.* **8** 1521

Blog 2021 *Guide to research data management* https://labfolder.com/guide-research-data-management/ (accessed December 2019, 2021)

Brace I 2018 *Questionnaire Design: How to Plan, Structure and Write Survey Material for Effective Market Research* (London: Kogan Page Publishers)

Cheng S, Zhang Q and Qin Q 2016 Big data analytics with swarm intelligence *Ind. Manag. Data Syst.* **116** 646–66

Chen M, Mao S and Liu Y 2014 Big data: a survey *Mob. Netw. Appl.* **19** 171–209

Chiroma H *et al* 2018 Progress on artificial neural networks for big data analytics: a survey *IEEE Access* **7** 70535–51

Creech G and Hu J 2013 Generation of a new IDS test dataset: time to retire the KDD collection *2013 IEEE Wireless Communications and Networking Conf. (WCNC) (April 2013)* (Piscataway, NJ: IEEE) 4487–92

Dataset search: Google Dataset Search https://datasetsearch.research.google.com/ (accessed 16 December 2021)

Gandomi A and Haider M 2015 Beyond the hype: big data concepts, methods, and analytics *Int. J. Inf. Manage.* **35** 137–44

GitHub 2021 *Where the world build software* https://github.com/ (accessed 12 December 2021)

Gidado U M, Chiroma H, Aljojo N, Abubakar S, Popoola S I and Al-Garadi M A 2020 A survey on deep learning for steering angle prediction in autonomous vehicles *IEEE Access* **8** 163797–3817

Han H, Guo X and Yu H 2016 Variable selection using mean decrease accuracy and mean decrease gini based on random forest *2016 7th IEEE Int. Conf. on Software Engineering and Service Science (ICSESS) (2016, August)* (Piscataway, NJ: IEEE) 219–24

Hashem I A T, Chang V, Anuar N B, Adewole K, Yaqoob I, Gani A, Ahmed E and Chiroma H 2016 The role of big data in smart city *Int. J. Inf. Manage.* **36** 748–58

Hashem I A T, Yaqoob I, Anuar N B, Mokhtar S, Gani A and Khan S U 2015 The rise of 'big data' on cloud computing: review and open research issues *Inf. Syst.* **47** 98–115

Hashem I A T, Usmani R S A, Almutairi M S, Ibrahim A O, Zakari A, Alotaibi F, Alhashmi S M and Chiroma H 2023 Urban computing for sustainable smart cities: recent advances, taxonomy, and open research challenges *Sustainability* **15** 3916

IEEE 2021 *IEEE DataPort* https://ieee-dataport.org/datasets (accessed 15 December 2021)

Joshi V M, Ghongade R B, Joshi A M and Kulkarni R V 2022 Deep BiLSTM neural network model for emotion detection using cross-dataset approach *Biomed. Signal Process. Control* **73** 103407

Jayanthi J, Lydia E L, Krishnaraj N, Jayasankar T, Babu R L and Suji R A 2021 An effective deep learning features based integrated framework for iris detection and recognition *J. Ambient Intell. Human Comput.* **12** 3271–81

Krishnaveni N and Radha V 2019 Feature selection algorithms for data mining classification: a survey *Indian J. Sci. Technol.* **12** 2–11

Muhammad A N, Aseere A M, Chiroma H, Shah H, Gital A Y and Hashem I A T 2021 Deep learning application in smart cities: recent development, taxonomy, challenges and research prospects *Neural Comput. Appl.* **33** 2973–3009

National Health and Medical Research Council, Australian Research Council and Universities Australia 2019 *Management of Data and Information in Research: A Guide Supporting the Australian Code for the Responsible Conduct of Research* (Canberra: NHMRC)

JavaPoint 2022 *Unstructured data* https://javatpoint.com/semi-structured-data (accessed 12 December 2021)

Ma X, Qian F, Zhang S, Wu L and Liu L 2022 Adaptive dual control with online outlier detection for uncertain systems *ISA Trans.* **129** 157–68

Liu Y, Yang J, Huang Y, Xu L, Li S and Qi M 2015 MapReduce based parallel neural networks in enabling large scale machine learning *Comput. Intell. Neurosci.* **501** 297672

Liu X Y and Zhou Z H 2006 The influence of class imbalance on cost-sensitive learning: An empirical study *6th Int. Conf. on Data Mining (ICDM'06)* (Piscataway, NJ: IEEE) 970–4

Khalid S, Khalil T and Nasreen S 2014 A survey of feature selection and feature extraction techniques in machine learning *2014 Science and Information Conf. (2014, August)* (Piscataway, NJ: IEEE) 372–8

Pressman R S 2010 *Software Engineering: A practitioner's approach* (New York: McGraw-Hill), pp 41–2

Safaei M, Asadi S, Driss M, Boulila W, Alsaeedi A, Chizari H, Abdullah R and Safaei M 2020 A systematic literature review on outlier detection in wireless sensor networks *Symmetry* **12** 328

Savić M, Atanasijević J, Jakovetić D and Krejić N 2022 Tax evasion risk management using a Hybrid Unsupervised Outlier Detection method *Expert Syst. Appl.* **193** 116409

Titouna C, Aliouat M and Gueroui M 2015 Outlier detection approach using bayes classifiers in wireless sensor networks *Wirel. Pers. Commun.* **85** 1009–23

University of New Brunswick n.d. Canadian Institute of Cybersecurity https://unb.ca/cic/datasets/nsl.html (accessed 15 January 2023)

Witten I H, Frank E and Hall A M 2011 *Data Mining: Practical Machine Learning Tools and Techniques* 3rd edn (San Mateo, CA: Morgan Kaufmann Publishers)

Wu X, Zhu X, Wu G Q and Ding W 2014 Data mining with big data *IEEE Trans. Knowl. Data Eng.* **26** 97–107

Wu C, Buyya R and Ramamohanarao K 2016 Big data analytics = machine learning + cloud computing *arXiv preprint* arXiv:1601.03115

Wen D *et al* 2021 Characteristics of publicly available skin cancer image datasets: a systematic review *Lancet Digit. Health* **4** E64–74

Yu S, Liu M, Dou W, Liu X and Zhou S 2016 Networking for big data: A survey *IEEE Commun. Surv. Tutor.* **19** 531–49

Zhao Y, Li H, Yu X, Ma N, Yang T and Zhou J 2022 An independent central point OPTICS clustering algorithm for semi-supervised outlier detection of continuous glucose measurements *Biomed. Signal Process. Control* **71** 103196

Zerkouk M and Chikhaoui B 2020 Spatio-temporal abnormal behavior prediction in elderly persons using deep learning models *Sensors* **20** 2359

Zhang J 2013 Advancements of outlier detection: a survey *ICST Trans. Scalable Inf. Syst.* **13** 1–26

Zhang Q, Yang L T, Chen Z and Li P 2018 A survey on deep learning for big data *Inf. Fusion* **42** 146–57

Zhang C, Shin J, Ré C, Cafarella M and Niu F 2016 Extracting databases from dark data with deepdive *Proc. 2016 Int. Conf. on Management of Data* 847–59

Zhou Z H and Liu X Y 2010 On multi-class cost-sensitive learning *Comput. Intell.* **26** 232–57

Zongker D and Jain A 1996 Algorithms for feature selection: an evaluation *Proc. 13th Int. Conf. on Pattern Recognition 2(1996, August)* (Piscataway, NJ: IEEE) 18–22

Chapter 6

Methodology from a computing perspective

Research methodology is the core component of any valid research. However, there is no consensus on research methodology for computing but this chapter intends to provide a guide on research methodology from the perspective of computing instead of the commonly written general research methodology. Deciding on which computing methodology to apply in research is often a challenge to researchers, especially early career researchers, post-graduate students and novices. This chapter is the heart of the book that discusses methodology from the perspective of different computing discipline in the ecosystem—computer science (CS), computer engineering (CE), information systems (IS), data science (DS), cyber security (CyS), information technology (IT) and software engineering (SE). For easy understanding, the chapter presents case studies to demonstrate methodology from different aspects of the computing disciplines ecosystem. We believe that after reading this chapter, the reader will clearly understand the methodology in each of the computing disciplines and can avoid adopting the wrong methodology for a particular discipline or research area.

6.1 Introduction

Methodology is the analysis that is applied to the methods in a research area or to any application. The methodology explores the systematic and theoretical processes involved in the methods and principles that are associated with the research field. Typically, it involves the process of collecting information and data about the subject for exploration, conducting analysis and the methods for finding the solution to the problem is established. The methodology details the procedure on how it is conducted so that the reader can understand the complete process of establishing the outcome of the research. The process to get the result is as significant as the result of the research itself (Pedamkar 2022). Methodology differs from discipline to discipline because of the peculiarity or nature of the research area. Different

doi:10.1088/978-0-7503-5017-4ch6

disciplines and research fields exist in computing with some unique differences. Therefore, the methodology to adopt across the computing disciplines or research fields can have some variance depending on the research area or discipline. For example, Pressman and Maxim (2015) explained that the software development life cycle that defines the principles for successfully executing a software project is referred to as software development methodology. The chosen methodology depends on the time frame and requirement of the software development project.

Choosing the correct methodology for the appropriate discipline or research area is critical for the success of the research outcome. Adopting the correct methodology to apply it in the research area or discipline not suitable for the methodology can invalidate the outcome or even ruin the entire research project. Therefore, the correct research methodology should be adopted for the appropriate discipline or research area. The methodology should always be described in detail to the extent that other researchers in the research field can reproduce it. If not, the quality of the methodology can be doubted by other scientists and once methodology is invalidated it means that the entire research will be rejected. Research methodology is the core component of any valid research. However, there is no consensus on research methodology for computing but this chapter intends to provide a guide on conducting research methodology from the perspective of computing instead of the commonly written books on general research methodology or niche areas within the computing discipline itself.

Post graduate candidates, novices and early-stage researchers in industry as well as academics are often challenged with identifying and deciding on which computing methodology to apply for solving a particular problem in a specific computing discipline, e.g. SE or CS. After determining the methodology, then comes the issue of how to apply it. In all, having a deep grasp of these remains essential for post graduate candidates, novice and early-stage researchers.

This chapter intends to present details of research methodology from different perspectives of computing disciplines: CS, SE, IS, DS, CyS, CE and IT. This chapter can be of great importance to postgraduate students, novices and early-stage researchers as it comprises the procedure for research methodology from different perspectives of computing discipline. The chapter seeks to equip readers with an understanding of the different research methodologies for different computing disciplines and how to overcome potential challenges in deciding the appropriate methodology.

6.2 Research methodology in computing

Research methodology gives details of the particular approaches employed. The analyzed research methods include laboratory experimentation, case study, conceptual analysis, simulation, field experimentation, and data analysis (Glass *et al* 2004). The methodologies in the different computing disciplines of the ecosystem are related to CS in view of the fact that CS is the origin of most of the computing disciplines and the legacy discipline (see chapter 1). Before delving into the discussion about each of the research methodologies for each of the computing

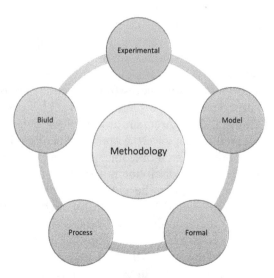

Figure 6.1. Research methodology in computing.

disciplines, we present the different types of research methodology in CS. It is good for the reader to see the relationship connecting methodology in CS with methodology in other computing disciplines. Figure 6.1 presents a pictorial representation of the methodologies. The different research methodologies in CS are categorized in the following (Amaral 2011).

6.2.1 Process

Process methodology enables the understanding of the procedures applied in achieving computing tasks. The application of this methodology is mostly seen in the fields of man–machine interface and software engineering which involve the building and usage of computer systems by humans. The process methodology could be useful in understanding cognition from the perspective of artificial intelligence.

6.2.2 Modeling

Modeling focuses mainly on describing an abstract concept to represent a real system. The abstract model is expected to be as simple as possible to enable researchers to have much better understanding of the system by allowing the usage of the model in conducting experiments that may not be possible to be conducted on the actual system due to accessibility or cost constraint. In most cases, the model method is applied in combination with the four previously discussed methodologies. Model-based experiments are referred to as simulations. The act of creating formal description of a model to authenticate the functionalities or precision of a system is known as model checking.

The experiment, formal and build methods were already discussed in section 1.5.1, chapter 1.

6.3 Relating the methodology to the computing disciplines

The different types of the methodologies described in the preceding section has connection with the computing disciplines. For example, CyS that is involved in the development of CyS solutions to protect enterprise systems falls into experiment, build and modeling. In CyS, intrusion detection systems can be evaluated to determine its vulnerabilities. A new CyS system can build on or modify an existing CyS system for effectiveness and efficiency. An abstract idea of CyS systems can be modeled to save the cost of a real system before its development and deployment in the real-world environment. An information system can adopt the build methodology as it involves the development of an enterprise system that helps an organization improve efficiency and compete effectively with competitors. CE adopts the build and experiment methodology because it involves the design, construction and evaluation of computer hardware. When a new component is constructed or an existing one is modified it has to be evaluated to ascertain its strengths and weaknesses. Formal methodology can be applied in DS as it encompassed data analytics based on algorithms. IT can adopt the build and process methodology.

6.4 Algorithms

An algorithm is the backbone of computing because it plays a critical role in the overall efficiency and effectiveness of a system. Regardless of the performance of a system, without an efficient algorithm the system can experience low performance. Therefore, an algorithm is the core of computing.

The Human Genome Project has shown much improvement with regards to achieving its aim of recognizing the complete one hundred thousand genes found in human DNA, establishing the order of the chemical base pairs (around three billion) that form human DNA, storage of the information in a database and development of data analysis tools. Good algorithms are needed to perform each of these tasks. The internet has become a necessity for people around the world to efficiently access useful information. Management of a huge volume of information on websites is aided by algorithms. Another application of algorithms is in e-commerce where goods and service are exchanged via electronic means. This mostly requires personal information, privacy relating to credit card numbers, bank statements and PIN/ passwords. Numerical algorithms and number theory have enabled the development of digital signatures and public-key cryptography which are the fundamental technologies for ensuring information privacy. There is a need for commercial companies and manufacturers to efficiently allocate scarce resources. Many algorithms developed to perform the same task mostly differ in terms of efficiency. The divergence in efficiency can be much more substantial than that of hardware or software. The overall performance of a system not only depends on having fast hardware but also on choosing an efficient algorithm. As huge progress is seen in other aspects of computing, advances are being made by researchers/developers in the area of algorithms as well (Cormen *et al* 2009).

6.4.1 Algorithm performance analysis

There is no any standard method of comparing different classifiers on multiple datasets. Researchers apply various mathematical and intuitive procedures to establish whether the disparity of the algorithms is random or real. At the initial stage, training two or more learning algorithms on appropriate datasets is considered. The algorithms are evaluated based on classification accuracy, area under the curve (AUC) and other measures of evaluation. No assumptions about a sampling scheme can be made as the variance of the results across multiple samples has not been recorded. The major requirement is for the accumulated results to present reliable evaluation on the performance of the algorithms on each dataset. Such numbers usually come from a repeated and stratified random split or cross-validation on the training and testing data. Significant difference exists between the analysis used to compare different classifiers on one dataset and those used on multiple datasets. When comparing performance on a single dataset, iterative training and testing over arbitrary data samples is conducted, after which the average and variance of the performance is computed. It is important to note that the statistical procedures and tests must be designed carefully in order to prevent biased variance estimation since the data samples are related. Multiple resampling from each set of data is applied particularly not for variance but for performance score evaluation. The variances are computed by taking the differences in performance over independent datasets but not dependent data samples, therefore, the elevated type 1 error will not be a problem. Because score computation is not biased by multiple resampling, several kinds of cross-validation or leave-one-out methods can be employed having no any risk. Additionally, the issue on precise statistical tests for the comparison of classification algorithms on a single dataset does not have any link with the comparison on several datasets since the former has to be handled first to tackle the latter. Training algorithms on multiple datasets certainly produces a sample of independent variables hence making such comparisons even easier than the comparison conducted on a single dataset (Demšar 2006).

The well-known t-test is found to be unsafe statistically and inappropriate conceptually, therefore, caution against its application should be taken. The Wilcoxon signed-rank test is recommended as a better alternative. The sign test is another test that is less commonly used and weaker than the Wilcoxon test but has some distinct advantages. It is important to note that the statistics described determines the divergence among classifiers from various aspects, hence, the choice of test type should focus on both the statistical correctness and the target outcome. Other researchers compute the mean classification accuracies of classifiers on various types of test data. An incomparable result on various datasets would present meaningless averages. In other case studies, algorithms are evaluated based on some related problems, for instance, medical datasets for a particular ailment from various healthcare centers or different text mining problems with related features. Averages are vulnerable to outliers as they allow the excellent performance of a classifier on one dataset to compensate the overall poor performance, or the reverse in some cases. A complete failure on one domain can prevail over the fair results on most others. This behaviour may be required in some situations, however, classifiers that present good performance on many tasks as possible are generally preferred. This renders the averaging across multiple datasets to be improper. Since only a few researches present such averages, it can be assumed that the general community finds them insignificant. Accordingly, averages are unworthy when performing statistical inference using the t-test or the z-test (Demšar 2006).

6.5 Solving real-world problems using algorithms

6.5.1 Existing algorithm

An algorithm can be used to solve different problems; it can be selected from the pool of existing algorithms to solve a problem without any modification. The solution produced by the existing algorithm must be evaluated to show that it is the most effective algorithm for solving the problem. The evaluation is performed by comparing the existing algorithm results with state-of-the-art algorithms to ensure that it is the best algorithm to tackle the problematic issue at hand. In the case where the result indicates that another algorithm performs better than the proposed one, it must be discarded to adopt the algorithm with the superior result in solving the problem. In whatever case, the algorithm must always be compared with other algorithms for evaluation purposes to determine its strengths and weaknesses.

For example, timely COVID-19 diagnosis of patients is crucial in order to prevent the communication of the disease to other individuals. A deep learning algorithm that can distinguish between COVID-19, pneumonia, viral pneumonia, and patients that are healthy was considered. The approach adopted transfer learning strategy. Binary and multiple class datasets were used, grouped in four categories for the purpose of experiments: (i) COVID-19 dataset having chest x-ray images with the mix of images with confirmed cases and the remaining images found to be healthy; (ii) chest x-ray images where 224 of the images were confirmed positive for COVID-19 while 700 of the images were normal bacterial pneumonia, and the remaining images were healthy; (iii) the dataset of x-ray images with confirmed cases of COVID-19, over 700 images with both viral and bacterial pneumonia, the remaining over 500 images were healthy; (iv) dataset with over 5200 x-ray images with bacterial pneumonia confirmed cases, 1345 images with viral pneumonia, and the remaining images were in healthy conditions. In the study, nine variants of convoluted neural network (CNN) were used for the classification problems. Results show that the ResNeXt-50 outperformed other variants of the CNN (Hira *et al* 2021).

6.5.2 Modified algorithm

On the other hand, there are situations whereby the algorithm needs to be modified to solve an existing problem. It is believed that all intelligent algorithms have limitations that hinder performance or robustness in solving real-world problems. Thus, it motivated researchers to modify some of the algorithm for enhancing its performance, especially, to suit solving a particular problem. If an algorithm is modified, the performance must be evaluated to show its effectiveness and efficiency over the classical algorithms. The modified version, original version and other algorithm variants should be compared to measure the performance of the modified version of the algorithms. For example, a proposed modified CNN-based model to track pedestrians named Matching-Siamese network (MSN). The model, using Faster-R-CNN first identifies pedestrians from surveillance videos and numbers them sequentially. The MSN is designed by adjusting the Siamese network structure to compute the similarity between two of the inputs. The computed similarity of the image establishes if there is identity match or not between the queried image of the target pedestrian. Finally, the pedestrian images and character of the probe image are used in all videos to track the target pedestrian. The results obtained in this study indicated that the modified CNN outperformed the most popular algorithms in both computational efficiency, accuracy and overlap rate especially in contexts of disappearing and reappearing objects. Additionally, a recent probe image could be used by the method to achieve its tracking aim in videos within a range of randomly selected regions and time (Luo *et al* 2018).

6.5.3 New algorithm

Though it is very rare, a new algorithm can be designed to solve a problem in the case where there is no algorithm sufficient to solve the existing problem. The procedure for the design of the new algorithm should follow the stages in algorithm design and analysis: problem understanding, considering the capabilities of the computational device, selecting exact or approximate problem solving, algorithm design technique, designing the algorithm and data structure, specifying the algorithm, proving the algorithm correctness, analysing the algorithm, coding the algorithm and testing (Levitin 2007).

6.6 Conceptual framework

The conceptual framework is the researcher's model based on the concept of the study variables showing the main components and stages involved in solving a statement of the problem specifying pattern and direction of flow. The conceptual framework is the researcher's own constructive framework that explain links and various components that exist in the proposed study, it is better represented with a visual diagram and text explaining it than with text only. The design of the conceptual framework is typically not accepted because it is a proposal of the researcher for solving the research problem within a narrow scope.

In most computing research, researchers mostly provide a visual representation of the stages involved in the conceptual framework. It is highly encouraged to draw a flowchart, block diagram or activity diagram showing the flow of the complete step-by-step procedure of the study. It makes it easy for evaluators to follow and understand the conceptual framework. If the researcher is able to draw a comprehensive diagram of the conceptual framework, it can make it easy for the researcher to reduce it to text and analyze it. Any missing component in the conceptual framework can easily be traced and amended appropriately. The visualization can make it easy for the reviewer or evaluator to identify the new component added to the study. When designing the visual representation of the conceptual framework,

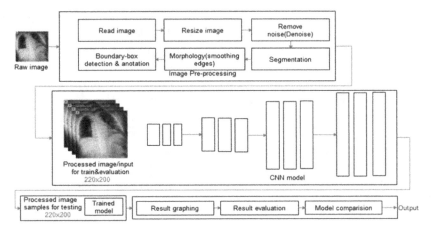

Figure 6.2. A conceptual framework showing complete methodology for image processing. Reproduced from Oyelade *et al* 2021), CC BY 4.0.

the researcher must ensure that it captures the component required to solve the problem identified from the systematic literature review (SLR). They should resist the temptation of re-drawing the already existing conceptual framework, of course some of the components that are already existing should be part of the proposed flow diagram but always be innovative in drawing the conceptual framework by including new components to come up with a new flow diagram. For example, figure 6.2 depicts a flow diagram of a conceptual framework for detecting COVID-19 from x-ray images using CNN.

6.7 Comparative study: hardware and software

In computing research, it is mostly required to evaluate output by comparing what has been proposed with the existing one to show the strengths and weaknesses of the proposal and the existing ones before reaching a conclusion about the proposal. It is required that the evaluation should be done in a fair manner to ensure that none has an advantage over another. Readers should be aware that evaluation is a core component in computing research methodology. For example, comparing algorithm performance must be performed in the same computing environment and the same datasets. The speed of algorithms cannot be compared on two different systems with varying system configurations because the hardware has an effect on the speed of the algorithm. Thus, comparing algorithms has to be performed on the same computer system and the same datasets for fair comparison. For instance, when an algorithm is run on a system with high configuration, the speed will not be compared with another algorithm that runs on a system with lower configuration, as this amounts to unfair comparisons because of the different configurations of the two systems. The system with the higher configuration has advantage of speed over the system with lower configuration, as such, automatically the algorithm that runs on the high configuration system will have better speed.

There are cases whereby researchers compare results with already published results especially on accuracy. In this case, it should be done carefully to avoid unfair comparison. caution should be applied in selecting the result to compare with. The published study to be selected for the comparison must have run the algorithm on the same datasets as the new study, as it is not reasonable to compare an algorithm that was run on different datasets in view of the fact that algorithm behavior and performance varies across datasets. It is expected that only the accuracy should be compared but certainly not the speed of the algorithms because of the differences in the hardware platforms used by the different studies.

In the methodology section, it is expected that researchers should report the hardware and software used to carry out the study. This will help in reproducing the results by another group of researchers. The system configurations can motivate other researchers to conduct similar research with different hardware to find new results. For example, Zhao *et al* (2019) reported the software and hardware used to conduct their research as Python, 64-bit operating system, Ubuntu 14.04, 2 micro-processors system dual Intel Xeon E5-2630V4 2.2 GHz CPUs, Intel Xeon, 128 GB RAM, GPU: Nvidia Titan 12G.

In the case of CE, when a microprocessor speed has been improved by adding new features to the microprocessor, the speed of the modified microprocessor is typically evaluated by comparing the speed of the two microprocessors to measure the effectiveness and efficiency.

6.8 Case studies

In view of the differences in the methodology in computing disciplines, a case study from each discipline is presented for the reader to easily understand the differences that exist in the methodologies. However, the methodologies discussed in this section are not exhaustive for each of the disciplines but can show the main differences and the appropriate methodology for each discipline.

6.8.1 Case study 1: software engineering

The study presented in this section aims to investigate the established link that exists between personality and team climate for a software development team of experts for a particular body. In this regard, the personal qualities were considered to be independent variables while qualities associated with the temperament and character inventory (TCI) were taken as the dependent variables. The study employed four variables that are dependent and individual perceived team climate (IPTC). The independent and dependent variables for the study includes the following (Vishnubhotla *et al* 2020):

    i. Neuroticism;
    ii. Extraversion;
    iii. Openness to experience;
    iv. Agreeableness;
    v. Conscientiousness.

Whereas the dependent variables are as follows:
  i. Participative safety;
  ii. Support for innovation;
  iii. Team vision;
  iv. Task orientation;
  v. IPTC.

Research context

This was motivated by the request of the industrial associates which happens to be a prominent telecom company providing multimedia and global telecom services situated in Sweden. The investigation was conducted in collaboration with a department in charge of developing software-intensive applications for charging and billing tasks for mobile networks. The department accommodates several agile groups that strictly follow scrum methods for the development of software. Two senior professionals from the organization having a different role of product owner and taking a decision that is strategic in recruiting individuals to groups is among the responsibilities that served as the sources of interaction (Vishnubhotla *et al* 2020).

Data collection instruments

Conducting a successful study on personality traits of distinct team members and understanding their personal views on team climate, requires mechanism for data collection to collect perceptions directly from numerous group members. For the purpose of this study, the survey mechanism was adopted to collect quantitative data by using questionnaires as the tool for data collection. The IPPIP-NEO personality test was used for the collection of personality traits. The questionnaire consists of 120 questions covering five different features of personality with each question answering across the five elements of the Likert scale over the range of 'very accurate' to 'very inaccurate'. The TCI questionnaire was used for a better understanding of the perception of team climate; it comprises four team climate factors with a total number of 38 items. The rating option for each item is given as: 'strongly disagree', 'to a very little extent', 'neutral', 'to a moderate extent', 'strongly agree', and 'to a very great extent'. An informed consent form has been incorporated in order to fulfil the required ethical norm. This proves that individual contribution in the research was voluntary as the signature of the participants on the consent form confirms their willingness to take part in the study. Information regarding the entire study such as the objective of the study, study benefits, data storage and processing, participants rights and the research team roles were captured. Demographic information for distinguishing a subject such as age, gender, email, team ID and so on were also included (Vishnubhotla *et al* 2020).

Data collection technique

A meeting was organized with the product owners following their request to investigate the issues affecting team climate. In the meeting, the purpose of the research and the information required were discussed. A formal approval was subsequently issued by the product owners for survey to be conducted in the organization. Subjects were selected depending on the subject accessibility and workload (note that there was no direct contact between the teams and the researchers). Eight agile teams working with the organization were contacted by the product owners and each of the team members was invited to take part in the survey. After an enquiry on the nature of the teams, the product owners specified that members from the entire eight teams worked as a group on many sprints. Hence, the acquired experience as a result of working in the team shows every individual acquired some significant level of awareness that facilitates their reflection on perceived level of team climate. A four-session series of interaction with the eight teams was organized. A presentation initiated every session to clearly explain the aim of the study and to reveal the benefits of the outcome. The study objectives and the information that would be collected were explained in detail during the presentation. Individuals participating were assured that all information collected using questionnaires would be anonymous and the data would be kept private such that none of their organization members would get access to it. Participants were also informed that participation was optional. After a clear presentation about the study, copies of informed consent forms were distributed to the participants after which pairs of questionnaires were distributed to the voluntary participants. The questionnaires were distributed in hard copies in order to tackle the non-response issue. The participants were given the chance to fill in the questionnaires at a personal pace and members of the research team were available at every session to respond to any question pertaining to the questionnaire or the study in general. This was necessary because the questionnaires were in English language and it was not the mother-tongue of most of the participants, hence, the need to explain meanings of some words to them. A distinct participant identifier is attached to each of the questionnaires (IPPIP-NEO and TCI) given to participants in the forms. The consent forms used the same identifiers that contained information about demographics. Responses and the consent forms were collected. To enable digital data storage, data entry forms were developed differently to store survey answers and demographic data. Responses to questions provided in the questionnaire were accepted as valid only when both fields in the IPPIP-NEO and the TCI questionnaires had been answered. In situations where unanswered questions were discovered, an email containing the question(s) was sent to the respondent requesting them to provide their response (Vishnubhotla *et al* 2020).

Subjects

The survey was conducted with a total of 43 software experts who volunteered to take part in the survey. These voluntary participants are the members from the eight agile teams that were invited to join the survey, 100% response rate was recorded. Out of the 43 participants, there were 37 male participants which is 86.0%, and the remaining six participants were female taking 13.95% of the participants. It was observed that the participating professionals belonged to different age groups within the range of 20–55 years. Among them, 30.23% of the participants were within the age range of 41–45 years, which is the majority, followed by young professionals within an age range of 21–25 years taking 18.60% of the participants. Considering the participants' roles, the responses provided have shown that up to 67.44% of the participants were software developers. Apart from the software developers, the remaining professionals played various roles in the organization. Looking at the aspect of countries, 31 of the participants indicated that they were from Sweden taking the majority with 68.88%. Others came from different countries including Ukraine and India, each with 4.65% of the participants, followed by Russia, Ethiopia, England, Iran, Lithuania, Turkey, Romania, and Scotland, each having 2.32% of the participants (Vishnubhotla *et al* 2020).

6.8.1.1 *Software engineering: Case study methodology*
Data was collected in two different phases: an interview was initially conducted to collect the topics significant to the research questions. An extensive survey on the topics identified was then conducted. An approval of the research design was obtained from Microsoft Ethics Advisory Board.

6.8.1.1.1 *Interviews*
There was no any systematic approach to identification of key stakeholders regarding the topics considered. This is due to the fact that the studies on development and integration of machine learning (ML) with software and services is still at an early stage and not standardized across product teams. In this case, snowball sampling approach was adopted in the following order: 1—leaders from teams experienced in ML application, Bing, for example; 2—leaders from teams where artificial intelligence is used as the main part of the user experience, Cortana, for instance; 3—individuals organizing in-house training on AI and ML across the company. As the informants were chosen, various teams were also selected in order to get diverse levels of skills in different aspects, including products having AI components, AI created for external companies, AI platforms and frameworks. The interview was conducted with 14 individuals who were software engineers and mostly senior leaders. A semi-structured interview approach was adopted based on the specialized role of the interviewee. For instance, participant number 13 was asked only issues relating to his role of supervising the teams developing the architectural components of the product.

6.8.1.1.2 *Survey*
The results obtained from the interview were used to design an open-ended questionnaire which targeted the traditions in this research, its challenges, and the best traditions. Questions on challenges were asked directly and indirectly by telling participants to picture 'dream tools' and upgrades or make changes that would enhance the work practice. The questionnaires on ML and AI were sent to 4195 individuals of the internal mailing list. Among them, responses were received from 551 software engineers, making a response rate of 13.6%. Responses provided in each of the open response items were analyzed using a card sort by 2–4 researchers. The card sort results were then analyzed by the general team for precision and

uniformity. The respondents were equally spread across all sectors of the organization and having a variety of tasks where 32% were from software engineering, 7% from research sector, 42% from data and applied science, 17% from program management, and the remaining 1% were from other sections. From the individual task aspect, 21% were managers, while the remaining 79% were volunteers assisting in balancing the perception of majority of the managers during the interviews (Amershi *et al* 2019).

6.8.2 Case study 2: cybersecurity

The methodology from the perspective of CyS is originally presented in Riera *et al* (2022). The stages involved in the procedure are presented below.

6.8.2.1 Dataset
SR-BH 2020 is a standard dataset developed for the experimentation and evaluation of various models and algorithms. This dataset contains 12 days' web requests gathered in July 2020 by the WordPress server. The server is embedded with Apache ModSecurity and core rule set installed in the mode of detection only. This was done to enable the recording of both malicious and legitimate requests in the records created by the ModSecurity without any blockage. The records generated by the ModeSecurity were stored on a daily basis while the state of the virtual machine was reset to clean. At the expiration of the web server time of exposure, manual and semiautomatic processing of the collected records was carried out to examine the web request labeling made by the ModSecurity, make necessary corrections, and ensure the proper CAPEC classification. The ultimate outcome was a multi-labeled dataset targeted at the detection of web attack containing a total of 907 814 requests. Among the total number of requests, 525 195 were normal while 382 619 were abnormal requests where every record has 24 features and 13 labels (Riera *et al* 2022).

6.8.2.2 Data pre-processing
Examining dataset and preprocessing is critical to detect and remove inconsistent/duplicated data, correct any error and modify the data for numerical coding to make the data compatible to ML algorithms. For each field of every web request, the average of the ASCII values is computed. By doing this, fields that have a high number of abnormal characters will be having average ASCII values different from the fields with a web request that is normal. The process of selecting the input variables with highly significant link to the target variable is known as feature selection. After computing the ASCII value average for each feature, a histogram is created for each of the fields such that features providing insignificant information can be easily identified and removed. The numerical values cookie_value feature is distributed in the range 80–90 and 100–110, hence, providing valuable information to allow web request differentiation. But all web requests for the do-not-attack value feature have the same value, thus, it does not provide valuable information. Features with insignificant information are discarded. A recursive feature elimination was

finally conducted by means of cross-validation to select the ultimate number of features. Having imbalanced classes (see chapter 5, section 5.1.3 on how to deal with imbalanced classes) is common when using a set of real data that can affect the various metrics of evaluation for the learning algorithms. Despite the existence of various methods that generate artificial data while maintaining an equal representation of the classifications in the dataset, only real data were chosen. Metrics that consider the different percentage of classes representation in the data were selected for the evaluation of the models (Riera *et al* 2022).

6.8.2.3 Models

The dataset (SR-BH 2020) was used, containing 13 different labels with normal and abnormal requests. It was assumed that a normal request value was 1 and the remaining labels were set to 0. Conversely, for a possible attack, the value at the first label was 0 and values at one or more of the other labels were set to 1. Single-phase classification where the model tries to make predictions on the whole labels without any dependence on the values found by the first label was established. This implies that the model attempts to predict the other labels even when the initial label indicates a normal request. Similarly, a two-phase model can be generated to predict only the remaining labels if the value of the initial label is 0, otherwise the remaining labels are automatically set to 0, if the value is 1 it indicates a normal request. Customized models can also be developed where the computation of the best hyper parameters can be done with CatBoost, LightGBM and GridSearch CV algorithms. Each label was predicted using a matching algorithm adjusted with the computed hyper parameters. LightGBM and CatBoost algorithms were evaluated (Riera *et al* 2022).

6.8.3 Case study 3: cybersecurity

6.8.3.1 Dataset

The labeled dataset containing samples from different domain generation algorithm (DGA) families is required for modeling the algorithm for different malicious attacks. The samples were gathered from NetLab360 and DGArchive. The benign domains containing the list of website domain name (DN) with high frequency of visits on the internet were collected. The two high ranking lists serve as dependable sources of standard domain names. The Majestic top million and the Alexa top million domain names were merged and duplicate names were removed. The aim wasn't targeted towards a particular DGA family. In view of this, the study mixed up all DGA families being malicious data samples before performing binary classification using the benign samples. To obtain a model with equivalent detection capability on samples with heterogeneous lengths, the dataset was constructed based on balance of the length. Benign and malicious sample number were equal per length of sample. The datasets were named in accordance with the samples' length range. The dataset was divided into two subsets taking 90% of the data for training of the algorithm and 10% was taken as test dataset for the evaluation of the models.

Figure 6.3. The HAGDetector flow processes.

6.8.3.2 Performance measure

The performance of DGA-based DN detection is influenced by the length of the DNs. Shorter DNs are difficult to detect. In an attempt to tackle the issue of the sensitivity of the models to length of DNs, a heterogeneous model named HAGDetector for detecting DGA-based DNs was developed for improving accuracy and reducing the rate of false alarms. The process of name detection involves three stages. In the first stage, the length of DN is calculated after which different feature extraction methods are selected depending on the length. Feature extraction is performed in the second stage. The final stage incorporates three methods of classification to differentiate between benign DNs and the DGA-based DNs. The HAGDetector is composed of three varying modules for processing DNs with distinct lengths as shown in figure 6.3.

6.8.3.3 Conflict of subdomain

DNs were divided into two sections; subdomain and public suffix, e.g. giving 'exam.ple.co.uk' as a DN, 'exam.ple' is the subdomain and 'co.uk' is the public suffix according to the public suffix list (PSL). The public suffixes can be concatenated with the subdomains that are developed by the DGA for building DNs that are malicious to launch action perceived to be harmful. The standard for measuring the subdomain length is the length of the DN, for example, let's say 6 is the length of the DN comprising 6 characters. Conflict occurred when malicious and benign DNs had the same subdomain with contradictory public suffixes. For example, given 'btgg' as a subdomain name, a normal DN is formed by adding the suffix 'org' but a DGA-based DN is formed when 'co.uk' is the suffix.

6.8.3.4 The extra short DGA

The extra short DNs are those domains that have subdomains with lengths within the range of 3–6 characters. An extra short DGA detection module was designed and implemented. The module is composed of the following different sections:

    i. Attention-based word embedding;
    ii. Side-by-side multi-way convolution;
    iii. Fully connected classifier.

The extra short DGA module for detection accepts a fixed length sequence usually set to 16 as its input. A start label is inserted at the beginning of the sequence while an end label is attached at the sequence end.

6.8.3.5 *Moderate-length DGA*

Moderate-length DNs are those DNs with subdomains with lengths within the range of 7–20 characters. In order to achieve a successful classification of moderate-length DNs, Right Shifted Tensor (RST) was designed for the representation of the DNs. In this regard, a CNN is proposed as the detection module that accepts the RST as input.

6.8.3.6 *Extra-long DGA*

The extra-long DNs are those DNs subdomains with more than 20 characters in length. The DNs of the extra-long normally present the DGA-DNs with characteristics that are abnormal. The more the number of characters, the more the difference between DGA domains and normal domains becomes apparent. For the detection of DGA-DNs, 14 features were manually generated.

6.8.4 Case study 4: data science

The method proposed in this study consists of different modules: first, the query statement specifying how to accomplish the task. Secondly, the rebuild index is a component used to build and subsequently rebuild the index whenever is necessary. Thirdly, the search index is the module used when searching the index by means of values specified in the query's predicate. The module searches for the data requested by the query and eventually returns its location. Lastly, the query processing module is also a component of the proposed approach that is in charge of doing the real processing of issuing queries (Abdullahi *et al* 2021).

In the proposed approach, the rebuild index module is first used to build an index based on the partitioning B+-Tree serving as the data structure. The input data provides the search keys and input-splits of the respective values. A temporary file is created on the HDFS to store the built index. For any query to be executed on a particular task, the search index module uses the predicates of the query to search the index to get the input-splits. The partitioned B+-Tree is also used by the search index module to re-build the index and utilize it to search for and return the search results. The query processing module is then employed to read and use the returned input-splits in processing of the specified query. The proposed method of indexing uses the input-split feature of the Hadoop Distributed File System (HDFS), which are the respective values of the input search keys. The input-split is an outstanding feature of the HDFS that distinctively recognizes the data chunks used by Hadoop. The input-split was adopted due to its ability to ensure balance between size of an index, the cost of searching and the size of the given data to be searched. This implies that the input-splits for the blocks of data have to be generated prior to extracting the IDs of the blocks from them even when the indexing is to be performed with the block-IDs. Index Rebuild in MapReduce: for the index to be used, it must first be built over the entire given data. The MapReduce package is used in the extraction of the HDFS features together with the values of the search key provided by the input data.

Input data kept on the HDFS is read by the rebuild index by means of Mapper class (Abdullahi *et al* 2021).

Nevertheless, when the file containing the input data is large, only the distinctive key values are obtained and treated as the search keys for indexing. The mapping function belonging to the Rebuild Index Mapper is invoked to utilize the specified key/value arguments of input files and read every record from the files. The values are passed to an external function as arguments. The major role of the external function is to extract and return values specified to be used searching keys for indexing. The map function combines the values returned and the filenames obtained by the setup function to create the distinctive search key values, otherwise the values returned by the extra function are taken to be the search keys. The extracted search keys for each record merged with the input-split are sent to the partitioned B+-Tree to build an index. The build function of the partitioned B+-Tree is responsible for the building of the index. The tree is built by the build function by having the Map function loops over the input data and forwards the key/value pairs to the build function (Abdullahi *et al* 2021).

Index search with MapReduce: The program in mapper class reads from the indexing file generated by the preceding component that is the rebuild indexing. The mapper class also has three functions such as the cleanup, setup and map. The range of the search keys is read by the setup function in the index. The map function is employed to read records from the index files. The function uses its distinct key/value arguments in rebuilding of the tree. The aim of this is to ensure that the Hadoop rebuilds and retains the tree for effective searching. The final stage of the tree is captured by the cleanup function. The function invokes the searchRange method belonging to the partitioned B+-Tree using the range of keys. The search range function of the partitioned B+-Tree was enhanced with the capability for searching and returning the suitable value that matches any specified search key. This becomes feasible because of the logic applied in the construction and the compression of the partitioned B+-Tree (Abdullahi *et al* 2021). The cleanup function loops and prints all the values returned in the output files of the HDFS as the result of the index. It does this using the context write function. Index in MapReduce: More MapReduce program is required for exploring index in main execution of MapReduce query. Apart from the adoption of a customized File Input Format, the program performs its operation as the common MapReduce function. Three different classes are used by the query processing; Mapper class, Reducer class, and the Index File Input Format class. The functions of the mapper are basically two: setup function that uses the configuration feature of its context class variable to obtain runtime arguments and the map function loops around the data for inputs associated to key/values in the records having upper bounds and lower limits for the predicates query. The map function returns only the records that satisfied the criteria setup by the query predicates. Subsequently, the getSplit method that invokes the Read Input Split From File is another feeder function responsible for reading the index results returned by the Search Index method (Abdullahi *et al* 2021).

6.8.5 Case study 5: computer science

The aim of the study is to improve firefly algorithm to solve unrelated parallel machines scheduling problem (UPMSP). Nevertheless, firefly algorithm was initially developed with the aim of solving continuous optimization problems. In this case, some alteration methods are needed to convert the basic firefly algorithm for continuous optimization to a firefly for solving discrete combinatorial optimization problems. The methodology proposed by this study employed two instances of conversion method, namely: Random permutation and the Adjusted Processing Times matrix . The Adjusted Processing Times matrix was developed and applied to enhance application of the continuous firefly in solving UPMSP. The random permutation is applied at the second stage of conversion and it uses a simple modulus function for the discretization procedure (Ezugwu and Akutsah 2018). Refer to section 7.5.2 for details on algorithm modification.

6.8.6 Case study 6: information systems

6.8.6.1 Data collection

The OUC of BMC was selected as the experimental setting. BMC is a highly recognized company with multiple years of experience in software development, provision services, and enterprises to different business organizations. The company's headquarters is located in Houston, Texas. An interview conducted with the community manager proved that most of the employees were urged to take part in the community to provide product support. Although employees from various roles may have varying goals, their contribution is still not compulsory. The employees from BMC participate by both answering product users' questions and contribution of content through writing documents. The documents contributed by the employees target the product's description and explanation, application and usage of the product's features and functions. Documents announcing the availability of a new product such as its date of release and category are not included because they are considered as not relevant to the functions and features of the product. The method of the data collection relates to employees (authors), employee-generated content (documents) and product users (readers). Identification of the employee-generated content was the first step in the data collection after which the data was collected from authors and readers. The employee-generated documents were collected over a period of two years (January 2014–January 2016). Links to the author's community profile alongside the document's interaction data such as bookmarks, comments, viewers, likes, and views were recorded for every document. Employees' community profiles may include demographic information, reputation record such as levels and points, social network information such as following and followers, and record of participation such as contributed documents or discussions. Additional information on participating in discussions, threads, and profiles of followers can be accessed by members via the 'connections', 'content', and 'reputation' menu option. At the completion of the process, contributions made by 231 employees generated 815 documents and the number of individual readers of the documents were 12 315 in total (Yan *et al* 2021).

6.8.6.2 *Variables and measures*

This study examined four major variables: circulation/readership of document among users of the product, reading of the document by users (of the product), knowledge contribution by the users of the product, and the employee's knowledge contribution. To obtain the aggregate document circulation/readership among users of the product, we considered some factors relating to the document's interaction information such as the number of likes, bookmarks, views, and comments. These data objectively reveal the amount of a document's circulation among targeted users. However, other behavioral factors were taken into consideration while measuring circulation/readership with the listed factors. Starting with the number of views, many readers may only skim through the document or just take a hasty glance without actually reading it, therefore, a document's circulation/readership may not be well represented by number of views only. Similarly, the same reader might bookmark, like, and comment while others may not make any attempt to like, bookmark or comment following reading a document. Again, a document with a high number of comments seems to be more popular than the document with same number of likes without any comments. Considering these factors, the circulation/readership variable was measured by computing the circulation/readership factor score by the number of bookmarks, comments, and likes received by each of the documents. The individual reading of the document by product users was collected from the profile information of the community and computed based on the count of documents liked, commented, or bookmarked by the product user throughout the period of two years. The assumption is that the product user must have read the document to some extent before deciding to like, comment, or bookmark. Content generation or knowledge contribution by employee was collected from the community profile of the employee and computed by considering the number of documents created and shared by the employee throughout the study period of two years. However, computing the content contribution of product users in providing support posed a challenge as the association between the reading behavior of the product users and their respective content contribution behavior could not be observed. A drawback of this measure is that it does not put into consideration the content contribution of product users constructed from employee content without citing it. Hence, discussion quantity was included as a control variable. The discussion variable was computed by summing the entire replies of a product user in the discussion. Aside from the discussion quantity, various control variables were included. The community tenure is a control variable for both the product users and the employees and was computed in months according to the profile data of each member. The writing experience is given by the complete number of documents contributed by an employee before sending their recent document. The place scope of product users was also controlled. Place scope sums the number of discrete places where contribution to product support was made by a product user. Some product users contribute only in one to two places while others contribute in various places. Particularly, it is expected that the likelihood of an employee's contribution to a new document is not only due to rise in readership but also as a result of new product release by the host organization. This simply implies that contributing employees get more inspired to write or discuss new products than the ones already in existence. In order to quantify this variable, the history database of BMC products was accessed, and the history of product release over two years (January 2014–January 2016) was downloaded. The aggregated number of releases per month was calculated for each category of product and knowledge is unclear: it could be from the contribution of an employee read by the user or from the users themselves. The links from each incoming document were used to solve the problem. The links include the citation history of the document. The link cited by a product user usually appears in a discussion thread. Information regarding the time, location, and the individuals that cited the document since it was first posted to the community were obtained through the link. The citation captures both behavior in reading and source for the contribution of the knowledge (Yan *et al* 2021).

6.8.6.3 Modeling strategy

Panel data was constructed to depict any probable endogeneity problems such as reversed connection and omitted variables. As participation is not compulsory, employees from various functions have varying motivation type and level to contribute knowledge. Contributions by employees also vary with some of the employees contributing more document content than others possibly due to deferent level of knowledge and expertise. The exceptional framework features and sources of data aids in the mitigation of bias. For instance, logically, the reading behavior of users is expected to come before the citation of the material that was read by the users. The employers may decide to contribute more content with the intention of gaining high readership and increased reputation within the community. In order to record probable reverse causality, readership was measured before measuring the writing behavior of employees. It is expected that the change of readership has substantial effect if the readership influences writing. The panel dataset was designed to have two levels; employee level and product users level. At the employee level, author–month pairs were created for two years (January 2014–January 2016). Readership among users was recorded for each of the authors by totaling all the factor scores of readership for all the documents from the author in the present month. Writing experience as a control variable was computed by getting the number of documents contributed by an employee up to the current month. Employee content generation as a dependent variable was recorded for each month by summing the number of new contents posted by the employee in the following month. The total count of releases made in the present month gives a record of the product release variable. A reader–month pair was created at the level of the reader to cover the period of two years. For every reader, the total count of documents bookmarked, commented, liked by the reader over the given month gives the reading variable. The knowledge contribution in support of the product as a dependent variable was calculated by summing the number of citations made by the product user in that same month. The place scope as a control variable was computed as the number of distinctive places a product user contributed in the same month. The total count of discussion replies (discussion quantity) in the month contributed by the product user was also considered as a control variable.

Community tenure was calculated for both user and employee in the panel to record the effect of time (Yan *et al* 2021).

6.8.7 Case study 7: computer engineering

The optimization methodology that cuts across hardware and software levels is proposed and the stages involved are below (Hanif and Shafique 2022).

6.8.7.1 Pruning at the software level

This is the most efficient technique used to optimize a deep neural network at the software level. In the first stage, iterative pruning was adopted to remove irrelevant weights in the deep neural network. The pruning is performed iteratively starting with the evaluation of the salient features of each weight or deep neural network collection of weights or the deep neural network layer. The small group of weights that are insignificant in the deep neural network are eliminated based on L1-norm/ L2-norm. The next step involves the fine tuning of the pruned network for a small number of iterations (note that this is optional). The process is iteratively continuing until a point is reached where additional pruning causes a decrease in the network accuracy beyond the accuracy bounds specified by the user. Iterative pruning has been chosen over one-shot pruning because it allows parameter pruning to be performed in chunks after which re-evaluation of significant weights can be conducted leading to decrease in the size and complexity of the network.

The proposed methodology for pruning of neurons/filters of a pre-trained deep neural network model is summarized. For the pre-trained model, the user-specified cost function defining the weight of neurons/filters and the accuracy limit is specified by the user as part of the settings. The summary of the steps is presented as follows (Hanif and Shafique 2022):

1. The significance of the filters in each layer of the deep neural network is computed based on salience method referred to as L1.
2. The deep neural network model copy is created for each of the layers.
3. Each of the pruned models is evaluated using validation dataset.
4. The user-defined function is used for the computation of cost for each layer after the accuracy of all the networks created are recorded.
5. The cost function is used to sort the models. Models with the optimal cost function are retained while those with poor cost function are discarded.
6. The network chosen in step 5, is fine tuned for maximum accuracy using the validation dataset.
7. The accuracy obtained in step 6 is compared with the accuracy specified by the user, if the network meets the specified accuracy, the pruned network replaces the pre-trained network and the process starts all over. In cases where the pruned model fails to meet the accuracy limit, the pretrained model is taken as the algorithm's output while the pruned model is abandoned.

6.8.7.2 Quantization

After the completion of the pruning, the second step involves searching for an efficient quantization procedure that reduces the weights bit width and the deep neural network activation in each layer. The quantization allows the deployment of simple logic units at the level of hardware in addition to decreasing the size of the deep neural network. Fine tuning could also be performed but is optional during the quantization to adjust quantization error that occurs as a result of the weight representation and activation with only a few bits. The combination of pruning and quantization can be used together in one framework to obtain optimum outcome. Sophisticated optimization algorithms are required by such types of frameworks for the exploration of the hybridized optimization space, hence, leading to increasing search complexity.

6.8.7.3 Hardware approximations

The third stage involves exploring designing of space for estimating the functional units of the hardware, for instance, approximate multipliers and adders to choose only those that present the optimal trade-off between quality and efficiency. Approximate modules considered the self-healing internally from the errors estimated in the whole design space. After reducing the design space based on the approximate units, the fourth step adopts behavioral simulations via implementation of functional units of the units estimated to precisely compute the effect of approximations on the functionality of the deep neural network. From the results, the designs offered optimal savings while maintaining the chosen accuracy limit. Fine tuning can be performed in this stage (but is optional) to balance the lost accuracy caused by the approximations.

6.8.8 Case study 8: information technology

This research was intended to investigate the technology acceptance model (TAM) in relation to work tasks with a website. TAM is developed based on well-grounded theories for predicting the acceptance and use of new IT. TAM has the following indicators:

  i. Perceived ease of use;
  ii. Perceived usefulness;
  iii. Attitude towards using;
  iv. Behavioral intent to use;
  v. Actual usage.

TAM is a theoretical model used for the purpose of conducting research (Lederer *et al* 2000, Habibie *et al* 2022).

6.8.8.1 Developing the data collection instrument

The email questionnaire containing questions for the respondent to identify website use mainly for the purpose of work was developed. The questionnaire is developed based on TAM capturing the factors enumerated in the preceding section. Questions about demography and website use for work were included (Lederer *et al* 2000).

6.8.8.2 Subjects and data collection
The focus of the subject in the research is a person who uses websites for job purposes. The subjects that participated in the study were drawn from a newsgroup related to work. The discussions of the newsgroup cut across finance, consulting, business, biology, law and science. The emails of the participants were extracted from the newsgroup website that archived submission. The emails were filtered to remove duplicates from the sorted email list. The program was used to send the online copy of the survey to the participant emails. The response rate was 5% (163 subjects completed and returned the survey), it is considered to be a low response compared to a paper and pen survey (Lederer *et al* 2000).

6.9 Summary
Research methodology is the core component of any valid research. However, there is no consensus on research methodology for computing, but this chapter provided a guide on research methodology from the perspective of computing instead of the commonly used general research methodology. Methodology differs from discipline to discipline in computing because of the peculiarity or nature of the research area. The chapter discussed the research methodology suitable for different computing disciplines to correct the perception of postgraduate students on the appropriate methodology for a particular discipline in the computing disciplines ecosystem. The chapter started by introducing different types of methodology in CS as it has relation to methodology in other computing disciplines in view of the fact that CS is well established compared to many disciplines in computing. Most of the disciplines in computing have their root in CS. The different types of the methodology in CS include formal, model, experiment, built and process. The core component of computing is the algorithm, thus, algorithms were discussed in the chapter, including the application of the algorithm in solving problems in the real world. Criteria for algorithm evaluation were discussed, as well as the effect of hardware on algorithm effectiveness and efficiency. To make the chapter easily understandable by readers, we presented different case studies for different computing disciplines, demonstrating the application of a suitable methodology to each of the computing disciplines: CS, SE, IS, DS, CyS, CE and IT. After reading the chapter, the reader can easily understand the suitable methodology for each discipline, thus, can avoid the use of inappropriate methodology in conducting research.

References
Abdullahi A U, Ahmad R and Zakaria N M 2021 Big data analytics: partitioned B+-Tree-based indexing in MapReduce *Machine Learning and Data Mining for Emerging Trend in Cyber Dynamics* (Cham: Springer) pp 217–39

Amaral J N, Buro M, Elio R, Hoover J, Nikolaidis I, Salavatipour M, Stewart L and Wong K 2011 About Computing Science Research Methodology. http://webdocs.cs.ualberta.ca/~amaral/courses/603/readings/research-methods.pdf (Accessed: 14 October 2021)

Amershi S, Begel A, Bird C, DeLine R, Gall H, Kamar E, Nagappan N, Nushi B and Zimmermann T 2019 Software engineering for machine learning: a case study *2019 IEEE/ACM 41st Int. Conf. on Software Engineering: Software Engineering in Practice (ICSE-SEIP) (2019, May)* (Piscataway, NJ: IEEE) 291–300

Cormen T H, Leiserson C E, Rivest R L and Stein C 2009 *Introduction to Algorithms.* 3rd edn (New York: MIT Press)

Demšar J 2006 Statistical comparisons of classifiers over multiple data sets *J. Mach. Learn. Res.* **7** 1–30

Ezugwu A E and Akutsah F 2018 An improved firefly algorithm for the unrelated parallel machines scheduling problem with sequence-dependent setup times *IEEE Access* **6** 54459–78

Glass R L, Ramesh V and Vessey I 2004 An analysis of research in computing disciplines *Commun. ACM* **47** 89–94

Habibie T J, Yasirandi R and Oktaria D 2022 The analysis of Pangandaran fisherman's actual usage level of GPS based on TAM model *Procedia Comput. Sci.* **197** 34–41

Hanif M A and Shafique M 2022 A cross-layer approach towards developing efficient embedded deep learning systems *Microprocess. Microsyst.* **88** 103609

Hira S, Bai A and Hira S 2021 An automatic approach based on CNN architecture to detect COVID-19 disease from chest X-ray images *Appl. Intell.* **51** 2864–89

Lederer A L, Maupin D J, Sena M P and Zhuang Y 2000 The technology acceptance model and the World Wide Web *Decis. Support Syst.* **29** 269–82

Levitin A 2007 *Introduction to the Design and Analysis of Algorithm* 3rd edn (London: Pearson)

Luo Y, Yin D, Wang A and Wu W 2018 Pedestrian tracking in surveillance video based on modified CNN *Multimedia Tools Appl.* **77** 24041–58

Oyelade O N, Ezugwu A E S and Chiroma H 2021 CovFrameNet: an enhanced deep learning framework for COVID-19 detection *IEEE Access* **9** 77905–19

Pedamkar P 2022 *What is methodology* https://educba.com/what-is-methodology/ (accessed 17 December 2022)

Pressman R S and Maxim B 2015 *Software Engineering: A Practitioner's Approach* (New York: McGraw-Hill Education)

Riera T S, Higuera J R B, Higuera J B, Herraiz J J M and Montalvo J A S 2022 A new multi-label dataset for Web attacks CAPEC classification using machine learning techniques *Comput. Secur.* **120** 102788

Vishnubhotla S D, Mendes E and Lundberg L 2020 Investigating the relationship between personalities and agile team climate of software professionals in a telecom company *Inf. Softw. Technol.* **126** 106335

Yan J K, Leidner D E, Benbya H and Zou W 2021 Examining interdependence between product users and employees in online user communities: the role of employee-generated content *J. Strateg. Inf. Syst.* **30** 101657

Zhao L, Wang J, Liu J and Kato N 2019 Routing for crowd management in smart cities: a deep reinforcement learning perspective *IEEE Commun. Mag.* **57** 88–93

Chapter 7

Scientific publishing in computing: beginners guide

New and novice researchers always confront challenges in avoiding desk rejection and lack understanding of the ingredients required in a research article to escape desk rejection. However, many postgraduate programmes require postgraduate students or postdoctoral fellows or research scholars to publish at least one paper in a high impact journal as a requirement for the award of PhD, MSc or contract renewal. From the perspective of the expert researchers, common mistakes committed by the researchers sometimes lead to desk rejection. Rejections can be frustrating for a researcher, thus, how to deal with rejections is sacrosanct. In this chapter, common mistakes that always lead to desk rejection of papers and what editors and reviewers are always looking for in a research paper are highlighted and discussed. Peer review process, responding to reviewer's comments, dealing with rejections, research highlights, cover letter, supplementary materials, and recommending reviewers for the researcher's own paper are all contained in the chapter. The chapter spells out the differences between thesis, journal paper and conference paper. A step-by-step guide on developing a journal paper is provided in a simplified approach. We believe that after reading this chapter, the confidence of the reader in drafting a manuscript will be boosted and they will be well equipped with the basic skills required to draft an excellent academic paper. On the part of expert researchers, common mistakes that always lead to desk rejection can be avoided.

7.1 Introduction

Research communication is done by means of publishing the research outputs in a journal, conference proceedings or any other reputable forum. The publication communicates the findings to the researcher's peers.

It is believed that every researcher must have confronted a blank page wondering what to write and confused on where to start the writing in the early days of the researcher's career. To write the description of researcher's own research in an acceptable format to be understood by other researchers for publication is a challenging task. The researcher becomes emotionally and intimately involved in the research if resources have been expended in the course of conducting the research. The researcher always has the biased mind that the research conducted by the researcher has a value and it is significant research. Subjectivity and deep involvement in the research by the researchers makes it difficult for the researcher to conceive the best approach to present the research in a clear and understandable way for peers and non-experts in the field to value the findings of the research. The 'publish or perish' syndrome is still valid in current times because of the pressure mounting on early stage researchers to publish for career progression or fulfill grant requirements or prove eligibility for funding requests or as a graduation requirement for PhD or MSc (Ecarnot *et al* 2015).

The current trend in academic publication is to publish in Institute for scientific information (ISI) Web of Science (WoS) indexed publications (journals, proceedings, book chapters, books, edited books, etc) owned by *Clarivate Analytics*. Clarivate Analytics have described WoS as *'the world's leading source of scholarly research data'*. The ISI publications are categorized into the sciences, social sciences, arts, humanities, etc. Journals indexed in ISI have impact factors and there are also those without impact factors. Presently, top scholars, including Nobel Prize winners across the world, publish in venues indexed by ISI. However, publishing in ISI, especially journals with impact factor is competitive and difficult, the rejection rate ranges up to 90%. The second category of publications regarded as reputable in the world academic circle is publications indexed in the Scopus database owned by Elsevier. ISI can be regarded as a subset of Scopus. ISI indexed publications are also indexed in Scopus but not all Scopus indexed publications are found in ISI. ISI and Scopus academic databases are venues for international reputable and rigorous peer review publications.

It is extremely difficult for a scholar without prior ISI WoS publication knowledge to get it right at the beginning of his/her submission without inputs from experienced hands. The ISI WoS indexed journals attract very high submissions from top universities across the globe and the publication space is limited for competing among researchers. Having a novel result is not enough to get published in ISI WoS indexed journals; how to present the results, convince the research community, justify the novelty, the structure of the manuscript, selection of the right target journal, etc all play a vital role for an author to get favourable reviewers' comments, and subsequently the editor's invitation to revise. However, on the other hand, there are thousands of blacklisted and fake journals that claim to be ISI/Scopus indexed journals just to defraud researchers. Also, the identity of some authentic ISI/Scopus indexed journals has been hijacked by fraudsters to extort money from their victims who are potential authors.

Bodies involved in world universities ranking use prestigious academic databases such as the ISI and Scopus for data collection. Top institutions across the world, funding organizations, research institutes, etc value research published in ISI/Scopus venues. Researchers at Stanford University and Elsevier publishing house use data from Scopus to rank the top 2% of active researchers in the world.

In view of the significance of publishing in ISI/Scopus venues, challenges facing early career researchers to publish in such competitive journals and the need for new researchers to be equipped with the techniques and skills required to get published in ISI journals, this chapter is intended to outlined and provide an easy guide for new and novice researchers for scientific publishing in ISI journals from the perspective of computing. A step-by-step guide on developing a journal paper is provided in a simplified approach. The chapter cover tips to avoid desk rejection from an editor's perspective, dealing with rejections, responding to reviewers' comments, cover letters, research highlights and the peer review cycle.

7.2 PhD/MSc thesis, journal and conference proceedings publications

As most of the target readers of this chapter are postgraduate students, the differences that exist among theses, journals and conference proceedings is high-lighted for students to understand them. In some cases, the student will be required to extract a journal or conference paper from a thesis, thus, this section can easily guide the student on such an exercise.

Typically, journal papers report research that has been concluded or significant scientific achievements or scientific discoveries, contrary to a conference paper that reports preliminary results of ongoing research at the early stage. Conferences accept early stage results of an ongoing research project. The conference proceeding papers undergo peer review similar to that of the journal but the conference proceedings peer review is always very fast within a short timeframe. The papers published in conference proceedings do not have the great reputation of journal papers, especially in natural science and social science, unlike in computing where there are prestigious conferences equivalent to journals. Most of the conferences are organized annually with some organized bi-annually. Conference proceeding papers after acceptance are presented in the venue of the conference. It is important for those intending to publish part of a thesis in a journal to note that the thesis was written to please the perception of the supervisors/ advisors, but when publishing in a journal, the paper should be written to please the editors and the target journal audience (Derntl 2014). A thesis is voluminous and more time is taken than for a journal article. Detailed procedure in developing a journal paper can be found in the next section. Students are recommended to always consults advisors or supervisor for a reputable conference venue because fake conferences without reputation and peer review process exist aiming to defraud any researcher submitting a paper. In such kind of conferences, any paper submitted is accepted without any form of peer review process as long as the authors can pay the conference fees.

Note: Postgraduate students are advised not to publish the thesis online before publishing the journal paper extracted from the thesis. Rarely would a reputable journal accept a paper extracted from a thesis that is already available online. A similarity report can always show that the thesis is already published online. Therefore, any student intending to publish a journal paper from a thesis should avoid publishing the thesis online until they have published the journal paper extracted from the thesis, after which they can make the thesis available online.

7.3 Tips for developing an excellent journal paper

Writing papers from research projects or theses is highly critical in validating the quality of the research. Good research work is expected to be publishable in a reputable/credible journal. Writing a journal paper is different from a PhD/MSc thesis because of different structure and length, as already explained in section 7.2. In this section, the content and the components that made up a journal paper, as shown in figure 7.1, are discussed to serve as a guide to novices and new career researchers. The structure is not exhaustive and static as other structures can be found in the literature. However, the structure presented can really provide a guide. The research results need to be written properly in a convincing manner to be published. All the components in the paper are critical, so should be taken with all the seriousness they deserve and scholars should invest precious time to understand the information required in each section of the paper. Publishing a journal paper before a viva really boosts the confidence of the examiners on the thesis/ dissertation and makes it easy to get positive feedback from the examiners.

7.3.1 Title of the paper

The title of a paper is crucial as it is the first line of encounter with the editors, reviewers and readers. The title should be short, not more than 20 words and informative conveying the novelty and summarizing the content of the paper. The title of a paper can make get paper rejected without scrutiny of the complete content. The words in the title need to be chosen with utmost caution for readers to easily find the work. If the words are not chosen properly, finding the work by readers will be difficult, thereby reducing the impact of the research Macdonald (2016). '*Sometimes it's not the content of a journal article that has it rejected, but the headline.*' (Gell-Mann (1969 Nobel Prize Winner in Physics.)

7.3.2 Abstract

The abstract is one of the core components of a journal paper that makes a reader decide whether to read the content of the paper or abandon it. Typically, the abstract summarizes the study, condensing the entire paper content into a concise form. The abstract is informative where it summarizes a brief introduction to the research, the problem description, objective, methodology, results, contributions, general conclusion and ending with the relevance of the study to society. It is in block form, and citations in the abstract are not required. Time should be invested in writing the abstract because editors always read the abstract before deciding to scan through the paper prior to taking an initial decision. On the other hand, there is another type of abstract called a graphical abstract. The graphical abstract is a representation of the paper content in graphical format, but it is not mandatory for many journals, is optional for some journals while

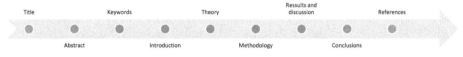

Figure 7.1. Flow of a journal paper content.

some journals do not have provision for graphical abstracts. Graphical abstract does not mean that an abstract in a text is to be converted to graphics. A figure in the paper that approximately represents the entire paper is selected as the graphical abstract.

7.3.3 Keywords

Keywords are significant especially for the indexing of the paper after publication, matching the paper with an appropriate editor and reviewers. Submission through the editorial system requires the author to supply keywords of the paper. It helps in the discovery of the work by readers after it has been published. Keywords does not mean to just pick words from the title of the paper. The keywords should be selected from the subsections of the paper and arranged in alphabetical order. The minimum and maximum number of keywords required in a paper are not agreed universally, they depend on the journal policy. It is advisable to read the journal guide to authors to see the maximum required keywords allowed by the journal.

7.3.4 Introduction

The introduction in writing a journal paper is different from the introduction in a PhD/MSc thesis. The literature review is embedded in the introductory section. However, if the literature is too much, a separate section should be created to conduct the literature review separately instead of embedding it in the introduction. The introduction in a journal paper includes the following items in paragraphs:
- Brief background information of the research and problem;
- Previous attempts by researchers to solve the problem (review of previous works, recently);
- Critique on previous methods to establish research gap;
- Suggested superior method with justification;
- Objective of the research;
- Brief structure of the paper;
- Summary of the contributions in the study.

7.3.5 Theoretical background

In computing research, especially writing a journal paper, theories about the algorithm, tools, technique or model adopted for the research are essential. The theory is required to show how the technique, tools, model or algorithm operate to achieve its objective. In writing the theory, it is highly recommended to include the mathematical background if applicable. For example, to present the theoretical description of an artificial neural network including the mathematical background. The theory can give the basic foundation before the contributions of the study.

7.3.6 Methodology

The methodology section should describe the detailed procedure used to arrive at the research results. All the equipment/tools used for data collection are described in the section before discussing the procedure of the data analysis. The methodology should be described in great detail in such a way that any scholar can reproduce it to get the same results. Sources of data, ethical considerations, subjects, tools, groups, case study, etc should be included in the section. The methodology depends on the computing discipline or research area. Refer to chapter 6 for details on methodologies from the perspective of computing.

7.3.7 Results and discussion

This section aims to present the observations derived from the experiment conducted based on the methodology and discusses the results. The results are expected to be explained using past tense. The results should be presented (tables and figures) in logical order according to the flow of the methodology. Tables and figures should be represented in such a manner that they will easily be understood by the reader. This will make the results easy to follow by readers. The results should be broken into subsections especially if the results are too much to be accommodated in one section. Each of the subsections should be explained according to the observations made on the results. For example, a modified algorithm outperformed the original algorithm with regard to convergence speed. If the result is negative (no improvement or new insight) it should be reported as it is and justified, one should not be afraid to present a negative result. Discussing the result entails interpretation, significance and comparing the result with the result already published. Subsequently, a possible reason why the reason appeared as it is should be given. Normally, one starts with the phrase 'likely', 'probably', 'possibly', etc in a given reason on why the result appears as it does. Lastly, the implication of the result to theory and practice should be discussed. Any limitations of the research should be pointed out. The summary of the major points in results and discussion are listed as follows:
- Present the results (tables and figures);
- Meaning of the results;
- Interpretation of the results;
- Compare your results with previous results if possible;
- Give reason why your results appear as they do;
- Implication/significance/relevance of the results to theory and practice;
- Limitations of the research.

In this section do not discuss any result not presented except during comparison of the current result with the result already published. Results in tables should not be represented in graph form as it will amount to redundancy, meaning that the same results should not be in tables and figures simultaneously.

7.3.8 Conclusions

The conclusion should be limited to the findings in the study, ensuring that it supports the data in the research. A summary of hints in writing conclusions are as follows:
- Objective of the research;
- Indicate how the objective of the research was achieved;

- Significance of the research;
- Give a general conclusion based on the findings;
- Future research direction.

7.3.9 References

All the references consulted in the course of conducting research should be listed in this section. The references indicate that the work is situated in the body of the mainstream literature. Those readers who may be interested in reading more details can easily locate the main literature. Once a statement is a claim, the researcher has to support it with a citation. For example, the number of female programmers is growing drastically. The references should be of high quality from reputable sources such as peer reviewed journals, conference proceedings, edited book, etc choosing the best references from the available references at the disposal of the researcher. Here is a summary of recommendations on citing references:

- Current references (last five years including current year);
- Old references can be included but very few and critical;
- Over 70% of the references should be top ISI indexed journals;
- Cite the most relevant papers only.

7.4 Common reasons for desk rejection and tips to avoiding it during initial screening

The editorial office of the top computing journals typically receives a high volume of manuscripts per year to process, running into the thousands. The authors of each of the manuscripts are expecting the journal to make a decision on the manuscript as quickly as possible. The editorial office of the journals typically conducts a preliminary screening to weed out papers that are poorly written and lack substance worthy of publication in a top journal. It is in this preliminary screening that many papers are screened out without going to the full peer review process as journals do not like sending out poorly written manuscripts without significant scientific contributions. At the initial screening stage many of the manuscripts received by the editorial office are rejected. Figure 7.2 depicts the reasons for desk rejection from top journals.

Dwivedi *et al* (2022) said that one of the difficult decisions confronting an editor is desk rejection. Both editors and researchers really appreciate the need for publication to enhance career progression. However, the editor has to make the decision on each paper assigned to either proceed to external review or desk rejection without sending out for external review. The desk rejection has the tendency of impacting negatively on researchers. It is believed that desk rejection is the most effective way to weed out poorly written papers to avoid diluting the literature. Before contacting external reviewers for peer review purpose, the editor always ensured that only quality papers are sent out for peer review. The common reasons for desk rejection are below (Dwivedi *et al* 2022).

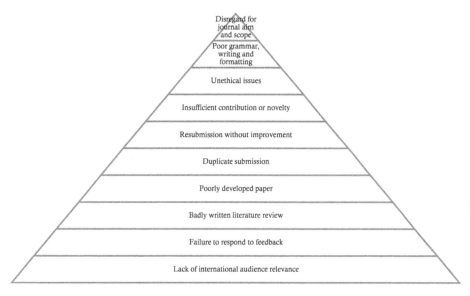

Figure 7.2. Reason for desk rejection in top computing journals.

7.4.1 Disregard for journal aims and scope

This is one of the top reasons why papers are being desk rejected by journals. Papers that do not fit into the journal aims and scope are desk rejected immediately for that reason. **Tips to avoid this:** the authors should always carefully read the aims and scope of the journal to ensure that the manuscript falls within them before making their submission. In addition, the authors can go through the recently published papers in the journal and make an effort to become a reviewer of the target journal.

7.4.2 Poor grammar, writing and formatting

First impression always matters for the manuscript submitted to the editorial office of a journal. Papers that contain obvious grammatical errors right from the abstract, poor writing and careless formatting trigger desk rejection as this shows a casual attitude and lack of seriousness from the authors in preparing the manuscript. **Tips to avoid this:** the authors should carefully proofread the manuscript thoroughly to correct any grammar, spelling and typographic error issues. The manuscript should be well formatted according to the journal author guide such as reference style, required length, format, etc.

7.4.3 Ethical issue: plagiarism/self-plagiarism

All top journals check for plagiarism when a manuscript is submitted; if it is found that the manuscript is plagiarized it is rejected immediately, in some cases leading to investigation and banning of the authors depending on the magnitude of the plagiarism. In some cases there is unintentional plagiarism. **Tips to avoid this:** all the necessary ethical issues regarding research should abide by it (refer to chapter 8 for research ethics). The authors can consider using a professional editing service. Authors should always do a self-screening by checking the manuscript through plagiarism detection tools such as Turnitin or iThenticate before submission to a journal.

7.4.4 Insufficient contribution or lack of novelty

The manuscript that lacks novelty or insufficient research contributions in the study conducted is likely not to pass the initial screening stage. **Tips to avoid this:** ensure that the study has novelty or sufficient contributions before preparing it for submission to a journal. For example, an internet journal considers manuscripts that have very strong theoretical foundation, address an important issue or advance theory to offer new insights. Such a paper is likely to escape desk rejection. Highlighting the novelty of the study in a cover letter to the editor ensures that it is well articulated. In addition, the abstract is another opportunity to communicate the novelty of the study for easy identification by the editor.

Submission length: submitting a paper that is too long with many too pages can be desk rejected because of excessive length. Journals have their required number of pages expected for a paper; when exceeded, the paper cannot be allowed to go for external peer review. Always submit the paper with the required number of pages. However, there are a few journals that don't have any page limit regarding number of pages. **Tips to avoid this:** to avoid desk rejecting manuscript because of the number of pages, always read the author guide of the target journal to see the page limit of the journal, then, ensure that the pages of the paper are within the allowed limit before submitting the paper.

7.4.5 Resubmitting a rejected paper to a new journal without modification

Typically, a rejected paper comes with reviewer's comments on the reason why the paper was declined publication in it is current form in a particular journal. If a paper is rejected from a journal, it is not expected that the paper should be resubmitted back to the same journal, to avoid another rejection. **Tips to avoid this:** the normal practice is to use the comments of the reviewers to improve the paper based on the reviewers' comments then submit to a new journal. This practice can improve the chances of the paper going through the initial screening without desk rejection.

From our personal experience as authors, that is not always true because in some cases a paper can be rejected from a journal but the author can disagree with the reviewer comments and resubmit to another new journal without any modification and the paper goes through in another new journal.

7.4.6 Duplicate submission

Duplicate submission to a journal is considered unethical. Submitting the same manuscript to two different journals is what is called a duplicate submission or the same paper might be submitted with few differences to another journal. Such kind of submission if detected is desk rejected immediately. **Tips to avoid this:** ensure that a paper is submitted to only one journal at a time and resist any temptation for duplicate submission because of pressure to publish. Complete the submission cycle in a journal before making submission to another new journal in case the paper is not accepted in the previous journal.

7.4.7 Poorly developed paper

Getting novel or groundbreaking results is not sufficient for publication in a top journal. When a manuscript is poorly developed, poorly organized with poor preparation it can be desk rejected. The manuscript can be rejected for premature submission. **Tips to avoid this:** the manuscript should be well developed and organized with all the necessary seriousness as first impression matters in the cycle of peer review. The researcher should try as much as possible to avoid premature submission and submitting a poorly organized as well as poorly developed paper.

7.4.8 Poor literature reviews

In-depth literature review is critical in the development of new knowledge. Poorly written literature review in a paper is one of the reasons for rejecting a manuscript because it gives a bad impression about the thoroughness of the study (Jackson and Bradbury-Jones 2020). Based on personal experience as an editor of *Computational and Mathematical Methods in Medicine*, I have turned down many papers from going for external peer review because of a poorly written literature review. **Tips to avoid this:** highly relevant papers should be reviewed in the introduction section of the paper. But if the literature review is long, a dedicated section in the paper should be created to present the literature review. The literature review should be critical, not just reporting the list of papers that have similar study. A critical literature review is required to situate the proposed research problem in mainstream literature.

7.4.9 Failure to respond to feedback

A manuscript submitted to a journal typically comes back with feedback. If the feedback is not rejection, authors are expected to respond to the feedback received from the journal. if the authors fail to respond to the feedback the paper will automatically be rejected by the journal (Jackson and Bradbury-Jones 2020). **Tips to avoid this:** to avoid rejection, the authors should adequately respond to the feedback received from the journal.

7.4.10 Lack of relevance to an international audience

The top journals are international in nature, so the editors expect research work that can attract an international audience to read it, not national or regional research that is only confined to a specific region or nation. **Tips to avoid this:** authors should always target international topic of discussions (Jackson and Bradbury-Jones 2020).

7.5 Cover letter

A cover letter or letter to the editor is a letter conveying the major contributions in your study with the intention of convincing the editor to send out your paper for external review. In the letter, the authors have to demonstrate that the paper is a good fit to the journal aim and scope, solely submitted to the journal and it has not

---

Haruna Chiroma
University of Hafr Al Batin
College of Computer Science and Engineering
Hafr Al Batin,
Saudi Arabia
charuna@uhb.edu.sa

Dr. Jamila Musa Umar
Editor-in-Chief
[Name of the journal]
January 15, 2023

Dear Dr. Jamila Musa Umar,

Malaria detection based on recurrent neural network with features extracted from blood smear.

Please find attached the above computational and experimental study investigating the use of a recurrent neural network for the classification of severity of malarial infection, for consideration for publication in *[Name of the journal]*.

Malaria remains a significant global health problem, particularly in sub-Saharan Africa. Although all clinical malarial infection requires prompt treatment, classification according to severity of parasitic infection remains important for tailoring treatment and predicting the clinical course of the disease. While severity can be established from the microscopic features observed on blood films, the optimal algorithm for accurately determining severity remains to be established. Furthermore, when machine learning algorithms have been applied to the classification and grading of severity of malaria, these have predominantly used feed-forward neural networks, which are known to perform less well than recurrent networks for classification tasks.

This prompted us to develop a novel recurrent neural network, based on the Jordan-Elman algorithm, for the classification of severity of malarial infection using blood film data from 450 patients with malaria in Maiduguri, Nigeria. We assessed the performance of our algorithm against standard classification from the clinical data using several criteria, including sensitivity, specificity, PPV, NPV, receiver operating characteristics, and multiple regression analysis. We show that the proposed neural has a sensitivity, specificity, PPV, and NPV of over 90%, and is superior in performance to other published algorithms.

We therefore believe that the global relevance, comprehensive clinical data, development of new analytical methodologies, and the significance of the findings makes this article an excellent fit for *[Name of the journal]*, and we hope that you will consider it for publication.

The manuscript has not been published or under consideration in any journal and there is no any conflict of interest to declare.

Yours faithfully,

Haruna Chiroma, *Ph.D.*
Department of Computer Science
University of Hafr Al-Batin

Figure 7.3. Sample of standard cover letter.

been previously published, and they should assure the editor that they don't have any conflict of interest when there is none. However, if any conflict of interest exists, it should be disclosed in the cover letter. The cover letter should be written with all the seriousness it deserves and not seen as just a mere formality. The cover letter is addressed to the editor-in-chief of the journal, dated, with the title of the manuscript, type of contribution—technical, review, report, etc, and the address and name of the corresponding author with signature should be contained in the cover letter. Figure 7.3 displays a typical sample of a cover letter.

The cover letter is a mandatory requirement when submitting manuscripts to journals as provision for uploading the cover letter is embedded in the editorial submission systems. However, in some journals a cover letter is optional, it is the prerogative of the authors to submit or not, whereas other journals don't have provision for submitting a cover letter as it is not part of the journal submission requirement. Therefore, submission of cover letter depends on the policy of the target journal.

7.6 Research highlights

Research highlight is the summary of the main contributions in the study presented in bullet points mostly not more than 80 characters per bullet point. However, the number of required characters can differ depending on the journal policy. It gives the editors and the reviewers a snapshot of the whole research paper even before reading the paper abstract. When the paper is finally published, it can give readers an overview of the work before reading the complete paper. An example of research highlights is from Almutairi *et al* (2023) in a study that hybridized two dynamic neural networks—deep recurrent neural network and long–short-term memory—to predict collisions in internet of vehicles. The proposed approach is able to predict collisions with an improved accuracy over state-of-the-art algorithms. The authors listed research highlights as below.

7.6.1 Highlights

- Fog-based internet of vehicles was designed and developed.
- Deep recurrent neural network and long–short-term memory were hybridized.
- The proposed hybrid algorithm is used to detect vehicles collision in internet of vehicles.
- The hybrid algorithm proposed in the study outperformed the classical algorithms.

The research highlights are typically listed in a separate file and uploaded in the editorial system during the submission process. However, the submission of research highlights is not mandatory in all journals. Other journals leave it open for researchers to decide whether to submit or not while some journals do not even have provision for submitting research highlights.

7.7 Supplementary materials

Supplementary materials are required to be uploaded by journals during the submission process. The supplementary materials are materials that supported the findings of the research but cannot be included in the report itself. Example of supplementary materials includes source code, datasets, simulated environment, questionnaire, artifacts, images, multimedia files, large tables, checklists, etc. However, the submission of supplementary materials is optional in most of the journals. Only a few of the journals in computing require the submission of supplementary materials as mandatory. For example, in *PeerJ* computer science journal, submission of source code and research data is mandatory except in circumstances where copyright or policy restriction limit the sharing of the data or source code. It is recommended to always upload the supplementary materials when submitting a paper to a journal because it adds more credibility and confidence to the research as the supplementary materials can be used to reproduce the research findings.

7.8 Suggesting reviewers for a researcher's own paper

In normal circumstances, if a researcher is given the opportunity to nominate reviewers for the researcher's own paper, what first comes to mind is who might give favorable comments to the manuscript. Some of the journals typically request authors to suggest reviewers for the author's paper during the submission process. In some cases, the journals contact the suggested reviewers but sometimes the journals do not contact the suggested reviewers, it is at the discretion of the editor. Some of the journals swap the suggested reviewers suggested by the authors during the submission process. Many papers were retracted because of compromising the review process by suggesting fictitious reviewers whose email address is created by the manuscript author themselves to review their own paper. In some cases, some of the authors unethically suggest reviewers from the pool of the author's friends/collaborators to get favorable comments.

We suggest that authors should resist the temptation of acting unethically in suggesting reviewers for the author's own paper. In our opinion, the best way to avoid conflict of interest or compromising the review process, is that the authors should find reviewers from the list of the paper's references. The author should just go to the reference list to suggest reviewers of the submitting paper because they have conducted similar research. Therefore, they possess the requisite expertise to review the paper.

7.9 Quality measurement in computing publications

In the research community, quality measurements are used to gauge the claims of researchers. Any discovery or significant scientific achievement recorded by a researcher must be passed through the quality measurement pipe for the discovery or achievement to be accepted within the research community. The oldest quality measurement pipe is referred to as peer review. The next subsections discuss the peer review cycle as a means of quality measurement.

7.9.1 Peer review in the research community

In the academic community, peer review is critical for validating the work of scholars. Peer review is defined as the cycle of validating the work of a scholar, proposal or idea for the purpose of scrutinizing it by the experts in the same research area. The main reason for peer review is to encourage researchers to maintain the standard of the research field, control the publication of research output, ensure acceptable interpretation, reject unwarranted claims and publication of personal opinion without the scrutiny of an expert. The peer review process is the pipeline that helps journal editors to select the best manuscripts with a high level of credibility, new contributions, novelty and papers interesting to readers to be published in scientific journals. In addition, it gives the opportunity for editors to correct any error or mistake in the paper before final publication. Scientific claims in the research community are not accepted until the claim or discovery is published in a credible scientific peer reviewed journal. For over 300 years, peer review has been established in the communication of scientific knowledge. The ISI only consider journals with well established peer review process as a candidate for inclusion to receive an impact factor (Kelly *et al* 2014).

7.9.2 Peer review cycle

The peer review cycle typically starts when researchers complete their research project. After that, researchers develop a manuscript describing the study by presenting the purpose of the study, experiment, output and conclusion. Subsequently, the researchers submit the paper to a target journal within the scope of the study for the peer review process to properly begin. The editor receives the manuscript for submission by the authors to the journal. The editors of the journal evaluate the paper to ensure that it meets the standard requirements of the journal. It is at this stage that papers failing the initial screening process are desk rejected, many papers do not survive this initial evaluation and only a few make it to the next round. For any paper that passes the initial screening by meeting all the journal set standards requirements and originates from a credible source, expert reviewers in the research field will be invited to provide a formal peer review. The reviewers are in different categories ranging from young, middle-aged to old reviewers with vast experience in the field. The most responsive with high quality reviews are young reviewers though this is not absolute. The reviewer is expected to conduct eight reviews per year on average. The main responsibility of the editor is to ensure the selection of the most suitable paper and handle the review process from the beginning to the end. The editor is expected to ensure a fair peer review process without conflict of interest, effectively handle papers and accomplish the peer review within a reasonable period of time (Kelly *et al* 2014).

The reviewer reads the paper to evaluate the science, scientific contributions, validity of the experiment, methods, originality and significance of the research. Scientific flaws and highly relevant missing references are expected to be identified by the reviewer before making a judgement as to whether the research work can contribute to the body of knowledge by evaluating the research findings.

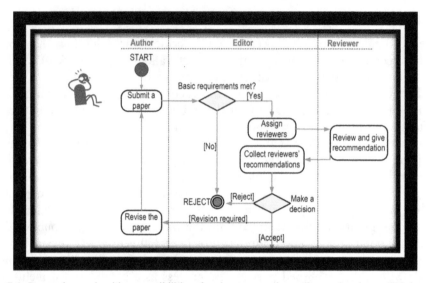

Figure 7.4. Peer review cycle with responsibilities of each actor—author, editor and reviewer. This image has been obtained by the authors from the Wikimedia website where it was made available by User:JanBoaNL79 under a CC BY-SA 4.0 licence. It is included within this article on that basis. It is attributed to User: JanBoaNL79.

The reviewer prepares a report based on the different components of the paper and makes recommendations to the journal editor on whether to accept, reject or improve the paper before publication. The editor carefully studies the report from the reviewer before clarifying the priority of the reviewer request, recommending components that should be strengthened and ruling over areas the editor feels is beyond the scope of the paper. The accepted papers are sent to the production department where the paper will be formatted according to the publisher's style before finally being published in the scientific journal (Kelly *et al* 2014). Figure 7.4 depicts the peer review cycle.

7.9.3 Types of peer review in the research community

Generally, there are three different approaches to peer review process adopted by different journals, conference organizers or edited books. The choice of the review process depends on the policy of the publication venue. Each of the review processes has its own advantages and disadvantages. Figure 7.5 shows a visual representation of the review process in the research community.

The three different approaches to peer review process are discussed below.

7.9.3.1 Double-blind review
The identification information of both reviewer and the author are concealed from each other. The paper does not have revealing information of the author as they are not allowed to append it during the submission process and the peer review cycle.

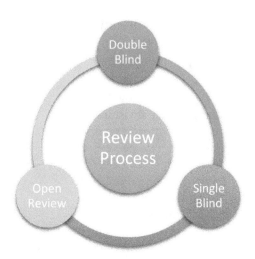

Figure 7.5. Different types of review process.

The paper quality is judged by the reviewer based on the content of the paper without being influence by the reputation of the author as the author information is not known to the reviewer. Reputation of the author has the tendency to influence the decision of a reviewer. The bias of a reviewer towards a particular country or published work is eliminated in double-blind review because the author's affiliation is not known to the reviewer. However, the reviewer can unmask the identity of the author through self-citation, subject of the research or style of the writing. Generally, it is believed that the double-blind review minimizes bias and sustains the quality of the review process (Kelly *et al* 2014).

7.9.3.2 Single-blind review
The identification information of the author—name and affiliation is revealed to the reviewer. On the other hand, the identity of the reviewer is concealed from the author. It is believed that the tendency of the reviewer to provide honest review comments is high if the identity of the reviewer is not known to the author. However, there is tendency of the reviewer to delay a paper that conducts similar research to that of the reviewer until the reviewer's own paper is published before releasing feedback on the manuscript (Kelly *et al* 2014).

7.9.3.3 Open review
The identity of the author and the reviewer are known to each other in the open review process. The open review has the tendency of preventing the reviewer from making nasty, careless or unethical feedback about the paper. It encourages honest review without disrespectful feedback. Plagiarism among authors is discouraged but it encourages dishonest favorable comment by withholding criticism to maintain a relationship with the author. Fewer reviewers are willing participate in an open review process (Kelly *et al* 2014).

7.10 Responding to reviewer comments

In most cases, a paper with potential to get accepted in a journal is returned with the decision from the editor inviting the authors to revise and return the manuscript within a certain period of time. The author should always ensure that the revision is completed within the timeframe specified by the journal. In case the authors feel that the time is not enough to complete the revision, the authors can write to the journal to request additional time. The editor reserves making a final decision on the manuscript until the authors have revised the manuscript and returned it to the journal where the revised manuscript will be sent back to the reviewers to evaluate the revision made to the manuscript based on the reviewer's initial feedback. This is normally the case in the situation where the revision is a major one. On the other hand, in the case where the decision is a minor revision, if the feedback is properly responded to convincingly, the editor can decide to make a final decision without sending it back to the reviewer, or the editor may wish to send it back to the previous reviewers to ascertain the revision.

Response to a reviewer's comments is one of the challenging stages in the peer review process because, if not appropriately handled, the paper can be rejected at this stage. A separate file named *letter of response to reviewer comments*, an example of which is shown below, has to be prepared for responding to the reviewer's comments. The response to the reviewer's comments must be done point by point in a systematic manner that can easily be understood by the editor and the reviewer. The response must be done in a polite manner explaining exactly what has been revised in the manuscript, the page where the revision can be found in the revised manuscript should be referenced in the response. In responding to the comment, saying 'it has been resolved' is a bad response, see table 7.1 for the proper way of responding. All the portions revised in the manuscript should be painted with a unique color e.g. yellow or red so they can easily be located. In responding to the reviewer's comment, the author may not agree with the reviewer on certain points but the rebuttal should be in a highly polite and respective manner explaining your reason for disagreeing with the reviewer. Many scholars get their manuscript rejected at this stage, in many cases due to insufficient work requested by the reviewer, lack of politeness in responding to reviewers' comments and rebuttal of a point.

Table 7.1. Point-by-point response to reviewer comments.

Reviewer comment	Agreement	Response
Perform more experiment to compare similar algorithms on some datasets.	Disagreed	Thank you very much for this observation. How we wish we could have performed the experiment. However, the focus of our study is a systematic literature review and the methodology is provided in section s1 on page p1. The advantages and disadvantages of the deep learning architectures are provided in table t1 on page p2.

(Continued)

Table 7.1. (*Continued*)

Reviewer comment	Agreement	Response
The paper has grammatical errors and incorrect citation	Agreed	Thank you very much for this observation. The article has been proofread and discovered grammatical errors have been corrected and the citations are now corrected. You may wish to refer to the manuscript to see the corrections scattered throughout the paper indicated with yellow background color for easy identification.
The structure of the paper is weak and simple.	Disagreed	Thank you very much for this observation. We tried as much as we could to make the article easy to understand by any reader with interest in the research area while maintaining the major components of a survey paper: concise summary, synthesis and analysis, taxonomy, challenges and future research directions. This is because the area is new, therefore, a survey paper in this domain is required to easily attract interests of new researchers to serve as initial reading material for them, while expert researchers can easily identify areas that need further development of the area to propose novel approaches.
The discussion of article is very weak.	Agreed	We have strengthened the discussion of the article by adding more discussion in the discussion section on the implication of the results on theory and practice. You may wish to refer to pages p19–23.
The best solution is denoted as g∗, this is not correct, amend it.	Agreed	The correct symbol is g∗ and it has been modified and clarified in the manuscript. You may wish to refer to page p4.
I suggest to run the experiment more than 15 times for each algorithm.	Agreed	This is an excellent observations made by the reviewer. As such, we have increased the independent runs to 25. An additional 10 experiments were conducted to make it 25 runs. Now, the runs are 25 as suggested. You may wish to refer to page p6 running to p9 to see the additional experiments and discussion.

Letter of Response to Reviewer Comments

Dear Editor,

We would like to show our profound appreciation to the anonymous reviewers for taking their valuable and precious time to rigorously scrutinize the manuscript. The comments of the reviewers have been addressed, which significantly improved the quality, presentation and English standard of the manuscript. The responses to the reviewers' comments are outlined point by point in table 7.1 and the modified version of the manuscript incorporating the changes has been uploaded.

Thank you very much on behalf of the authors.

Note to reviewers: All the modifications/changes made in the manuscript were highlighted in yellow for easy identification.

7.11 Handling of rejections

A new career researcher coming into the research world must prepare their mind to face rejections and tackle rejection head-on without been demoralized. Receiving a rejection letter from a journal editor can be devastating for authors, it is demoralizing and makes the authors feel discouraged about the research, especially new career researchers. In reality, rejection is part of the peer review process that one cannot shy away from. It is extremely rare for any researcher to never experience rejection throughout their academic career, especially at the early stage of their career. Even the top researchers who have established a reputation over the years can experience rejections. Authors under pressure to publish for career progression, awards of degree or fulfilled grant requirements feel rejection badly, especially if the manuscript remained with the publisher for a long period before being returned with a rejection letter. Despite all these challenges about rejections, in a real sense, there is nothing to worry about with rejection as this is not the end of the manuscript.

There were researches rejected for publication but later moved on to be published in another journal and won the Nobel Prize. Table 7.2 presents the summary of the

Table 7.2. Papers rejected but moved on to win the Nobel Prize.

Title	Rejected journal	Published Journal	Award
An attempt of a theory of beta radiation	*Nature*	German journal *Zeitschrift für Physik*	Fermi won the 1938 Nobel Prize in Physics
The role of citric acid in intermediate metabolism in animal tissues	*Nature*	*Enzymologia*	Hans Krebs won the 1953 Nobel Prize in Medicine
Isotopic spin and curious particles	*Physical Review Letters*	*Physical Review Letters*	Gell-Mann awarded the 1969 Nobel Prize in Physics

(*Continued*)

Table 7.2. (*Continued*)

Title	Rejected journal	Published Journal	Award
Spontaneous symmetry breakdown without massless bosons	*Physics Letters*	*Physical Review Letters*	Peter Higgs awarded the 2013 Nobel Prize in Physics
Application of Fourier transform spectroscopy to magnetic resonance	*Journal of Chemical Physics*	*Review of Scientific Instruments*	Richard Ernst received the 1991 Nobel Prize in Chemistry
The discovery of quasicrystals	*Physical Review Letters*	*Metallurgic Transactions A*	Dan Shectman won the 2011 Nobel Prize

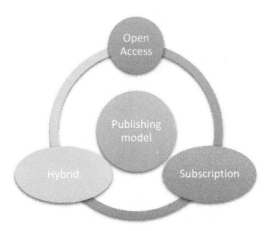

Figure 7.6. Visual representation of the three major publishing models.

papers that were once rejected but later won the Nobel Prize (Macdonald 2016). Rejection can be handled in such a way that the authors can turn it to advantage instead of disadvantage. When a manuscript is rejected from a journal, the authors should carefully read the reviewers comments and use them to enhance the manuscript, even if it means conducting additional experiments. Then, they should submit it to another new journal instead of to the journal that initially rejected the manuscript, except if the journal invites the manuscript for resubmission.

7.12 Understand different publishing models—open access, subscription, and hybrid

Different publishing models exist in the publishing world. The three main publishing models are shown in figure 7.6. When submitting a paper to a journal, the researcher has to consider the publishing model of the journal before making submission.

This is because some of the journals require heavy payment before the paper is published after acceptance, as such, the researcher has to consider financial status of the research group or individual researchers before making submission. The different publishing models are discussed as follows.

7.12.1 Open access journals

With open access publishing, authors that submitted paper for publication are expected to pay for publication fees after the paper has been accepted. When the paper is published, anyone can access the full published paper without making any payment. In the mid-1990s when the open access journals were building dominance in the publishing world, academics did not consider such journals as a serious alternative to the subscription journals. The open access publishing models were in doubt because the sustainability and peer review quality of the journals were perceived to be low. At that time, the open access journals were not indexed in the WoS and the journals lacked the prestige required by researchers. The second generation of the open access journals was the established subscription journals that decided to make the content of the published papers free online to readers. This category of journals is very important in some regions of the world, especially Latin America and Japan, and they are mostly owned by societies. The third generation of the open access journals pioneered by BioMedCentral and Public Library of Science introduced article processing charge for financing the sustainability of the open access model of publication. Since then, the article processing charge grew rapidly (Björk and Solomon 2012).

7.12.2 Subscription journals

In subscription journals, authors submit the paper free of charge; if the paper is accepted for publication after the peer review cycle, the paper is published free without requiring the authors to pay publication fees. However, readers cannot have full access to the published paper until they pay to obtain access to the full published paper, but the title, keywords, and abstract are mostly free to readers to access.

7.12.3 Hybrid journals

Hybrid is where subscription publishers have an open access option where authors of the accepted manuscript can decide to pay for publication fees typically up to US $3000 to have the published paper electronic versions of the accepted articles as open access despite the fact that the journal is a subscription based journal (Björk and Solomon 2012).

7.13 Summary

Early career and novice researchers always confront challenges in writing an excellent academic paper with the potential to avoid desk rejection. Having a breakthrough research result is not a guarantee for publishing the results in a reputable journal. Despite this challenge, some postgraduate programmes require the candidate to publish the results in a reputable journal as a prerequisite for graduation. On the other hand, postdoctoral fellows or research scholars in some institutions are required to publish at least one paper in an academic journal as a requirement for contract renewal. From the perspective of expert researchers, common mistakes committed by researchers sometimes lead to desk rejections. Rejections can be frustrating for a researcher, thus, how to deal with rejections is sacrosanct. We discussed guides for new researchers on how to deviate from the hammer of the editor and move to the external review process. One of the top challenges in the publishing process is dealing with reviewer comments. The chapter clearly spelled out how to respond to reviewer comments in an acceptable language as well as the best approach to disagree with the reviewer. Rejection can be devastating for researchers and can discourage their zeal, especially young researchers and expert researchers under pressure to publish for grant requirements or career progression. Therefore, the chapter dedicated a section to discussing how to deal with rejections without feeling any pressure. Research highlights, cover letter and recommending reviewers for the researcher's own paper are all outlined and discussed. Common mistakes that always lead to desk rejection of papers and what editors are always looking for in a research paper were explained. Tips to avoid desk rejection are contained in the chapter. The chapter contained the sample of cover letter and response to reviewer comments to guide new researchers. Desk rejection can be avoided if the tips provided in the chapter are properly followed. We believe that after reading this chapter, the confidence of the reader in drafting a manuscript will be boosted and they will be well equipped with tips to deal with reviewer comments and rejection.

References

Almutairi M S, Almutairi K and Chiroma H 2023 Hybrid of deep recurrent network and long short term memory for rear-end collision detection in fog based internet of vehicles *Expert Syst. Appl.* **213** 119033

Björk B C and Solomon D 2012 Open access versus subscription journals: a comparison of scientific impact *BMC Med.* **10** 1–10

Derntl M 2014 Basics of research paper writing and publishing *Int. J. Technol. Enhanc. Learn.* **6** 105–23

Dwivedi Y K, Hughes L, Cheung C M, Conboy K, Duan Y, Dubey R, Janssen M, Jones P, Sigala M and Viglia G 2022 How to develop a quality research article and avoid a journal desk rejection *Int. J. Inf. Manage.* **62** 102426

Ecarnot F, Seronde M F, Chopard R, Schiele F and Meneveau N 2015 Writing a scientific article: a step-by-step guide for beginners *Eur. Geriatr. Med.* **6** 573–9

Jackson D and Bradbury-Jones C 2020 Top ten reasons papers are rejected during initial screening and some tips to avoid early rejection *J. Clin. Nurs.* **29** 3899–900

Kelly J, Sadeghieh T and Adeli K 2014 Peer review in scientific publications: benefits, critiques, & a survival guide *EJIFCC* **25** 227

MacDonald F 2016 8 Scientific papers that were rejected before going on to win a Nobel Prize *ScienceAlert* https://www.sciencealert.com/these-8-papers-were-rejected-before-going-on-to-win-the-nobel-prize

Chapter 8

Research ethics in computing

Integrity in the academic community is determined by the ethical conduct of the research activities. Research activities are guided by research ethics to protect the researcher from involvement in misconduct, in some cases unknowingly. This chapter focuses on research ethics from the perspective of computing instead of the general research ethics mostly found in the literature. Research ethics in computing is dynamic as a result of rapid technological development. The chapter explores issues surrounding research ethics in the computing ecosystem. Research ethics is discussed in the context of different disciplines in computing—information systems (IS), information technology (IT), data science (DS), cyber security (CyS), computer science (CS), software engineering (SE), and computer engineering (CE). Negative research findings and tips to get them published are presented. Research misconduct, its implications and preventive measures are outlined and discussed. We believe the chapter will serve as a guide to the computing research community, especially novices or new career researchers and promote conducting research in any computing discipline ethically to avoid unethical behaviours, thereby maintaining and improving the integrity of research in computing.

8.1 Introduction

Research ethics is of great significance in the research community. Novices or new researchers may not be aware of research ethics and its implications for the researcher's career, reputation and institution. As such, there can be engagement in unethical issues without knowing they are unethical in the research community or intentionally engaging in research misconducted without knowing the consequences of unethical behaviour in research. Research ethics differs depending on the type of research and the discipline with which the research is associated. The internet has revolutionized research in computing.

The internet has developed to the extent that it is seen as basic infrastructure for communication both locally and globally. Access to it is advocated to be considered as a basic fundamental ethical part of human rights similar to freedom of expression and a free press (Capurro 2009).

Personal data publication via online user universal resource locators (URLs) through private and secure means is a growing issue and is attracting special attention; for instance, social networks are gaining increasing attention daily (Günther *et al* (2011)). Researchers' behaviour is greatly affected because of the freedom in using online resources to perform different activities, such as: observing social interaction at scale; invisible data gathering on the web; computational data processing via machine learning models, automated sentiment analysis, natural language processing; and sharing of datasets. These activities are used in social computing to analyse and comprehend the technologically mediated behaviour of societies, groups, individuals and new understanding of human behaviour. These practices give room for more questions pertaining what constitutes ethical research (Boyd and Crawford 2012). The simultaneous rise of big data intelligence which involves the use of AI technologies to collect, analyze, and draw conclusions from huge varieties of user data has enhanced and expanded data intelligence, social computing research, investigating digital traces to comprehend mediated behaviours of societies, groups, and individuals. On the other hand, the different techniques deployed to access these data have raised worries on the ethics of research practice (Vitak *et al* 2017). The evolution of new technologies and right to access data is posing great difficulty and making research ethics even more complex in the fields of social computing and human–computer interaction (Bjorn *et al* 2018).

Research activities are guided by research ethics to protect the researcher from being involved in misconduct, in some cases unknowingly. Research ethics available in the literature is mainly general research ethics and medical. Computing research ethics is mostly found in different literature for different disciplines within the computing ecosystem. This makes it difficult for researchers to have the opportunity to compare the different research ethics in different disciplines in the computing ecosystem.

This chapter focuses on research ethics from the perspective of computing instead of general research ethics mostly found in the literature. It intends to present research ethics in the context of different disciplines in computing—IS, IT, DS, CyS, CS, SE and CE. Lastly, it is an attempt to centralize research ethics for different disciplines in computing. The chapter can provide a guide for early career researchers, novice researchers, postgraduate and undergraduate students on research ethics in computing.

8.2 Research ethics from the perspective of computing

The integration of artifacts and computing technologies into most parts of our private, social, and professional lives comes with ethical concerns that require the attention of professionals (Stahl *et al* 2016). Ethics means regarding something being good or right or acceptable. As such, an ethical use of computing may refer to it being acceptable, proper, socially appropriate, or right. Such intuitive reasoning of the ethical value of an action is often largely or to some extent seen as customs and principles that are recognized across a culture or social group. And in situations where such customs and principles become conflicting or simply applicable, well-defined consideration on the bases and assumptions connected to ethical judgement is considered. This is a major role of ethics as an aspect of moral philosophy. The term 'computer ethics' dates back to the 1970s, but ethical matters surfacing from digital computing are as old as the development of the technology. The founder of cybernetics, Norbert Wiener who is also a notable figure in the advancement of digital computers, predicted the potential of technology to change several facets of life that were critical to ethical implications. He predicted possible significant ethical changes. Additional notable development in identifying computing ethics started with the use of AI to make computers communicate with people and it was interesting that people considered using computers in psychological consultations. Weizenbaum considered this as fundamental to an investigation of the connection between humans and computers. Although early instances of top consideration to the relationship between computers and ethics were in existence, a more comprehensive address only commenced around the 1980s to 1990s. Through this period, computer ethics advanced into an area of applied ethics. Core courses on computing ethics were added in syllabuses and textbooks, and academic conferences were initiated. Professional computing organizations such as the British Computer Society or ACM, generated ethical codes to serve as a guide to associates. Research ethics is intensely linked to involvements of consent (Stahl *et al* 2016). The major ethical consideration in computing is shown in figure 8.1.

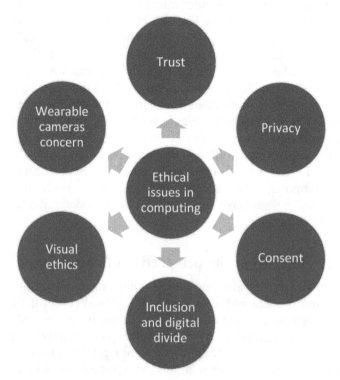

Figure 8.1. The ethical consideration in computing research.

8.2.1 Trust

This is a broad concept usually linked to security and privacy, relating to a great extent to data processing. Trust and privacy are often jointly discussed together. Trust is considered to be a constituent of privacy, trust is the characteristic of the bonds among data owners, authors, data analysts and controllers in which there is confidence that the information system is properly utilized for data processing in an appropriate way. Trust is an assessment of the distinguished reliability, enthusiasm, transparency, and accountability of a system, the system's designers, and its operators. In this case, reliability affects reputation; the system operators and the system itself have to be adequately responsible to appropriately handle data. Motivation concerns how the operators plan and intend to use the data, some degree of transparency is needed for such communication. When a trustful relationship is established, data processing can progress unobstructed within an approved outline of norms (Stahl *et al* 2016).

8.2.2 Privacy

Privacy has become a widely used ethical concern and concept. Based on diverse theoretical history and applications to technologies through the years, privacy predates 'computer ethics' as a discipline. Privacy is seen as what is considered ethically treasured, or sources its value from interrelated rights, often autonomy or freedom. Privacy in computing technologies can broadly and basically be categorized into two: personal privacy and data privacy. Data privacy is related to data of an individual, in which appropriate rules of ownership, alteration and movement can easily be tracked. On the other hand, personal privacy is more about rights for oneself whereby it does not clearly address data about oneself, such as a 'right to be left alone,' differentiates between 'public' and 'private' contexts and spaces. As technologically mediated interactions dominate over private and public digital spaces and communication modes, the distinction inevitably is not too clear. The distinction is still useful in ontological words, differentiating between privacy as a regulator to informational depictions of the personal and associated phenomena and as limitations on access to physical bodies and spaces (Stahl *et al* 2016). There are privacy concerns about the data generated because of the development and diffusion of computing technologies in society such as smart phones, GPS, cameras, health wearable devices and internet of things (Ess 2013).

8.2.3 Consent

Informed consent is two-dimensional: the participant is first presented with the possible participation risks and benefits; next, the participant is then given a chance to take the decision on whether to partake or not (Johnson *et al* 2011). The issues of informed consent have attracted a great deal of attention both in the commercial and research contexts. Informed consent dominates discussions relating to the medical technologies in cyberspace such as e-health and bio-ICT. Informed consent is a standard research and development control mechanism designed to prevent misuse in research where participation is voluntary. Informed consent was purposely designed to control medical research. Hence, it requires users to be given sufficient information and support to comprehend the extent, rationale, and probable results of the study. These include the probability of identified dangers and benefits occurring (including degrees of uncertainty), the identity of persons participating in planning and conducting the study, conflicting interests if any, and the rights of participants, such as the right to withdraw from the study at any time. Consent processes also give the chance to incorporate protections to users, such as the ways to avoid identity revelation, such as anonymity. The recent increase in development and deployment of information systems by commercial entities beyond research settings is subjected to ethical governance. Consent can also be referred to as the agreements reached by operators and users of a system describing satisfactory uses and roles. Equivalent ethical supervision may be essential in commercial settings owing to likely risks being comparable throughout commercial and academic usage. Numerous informed consent challenges have emanated from the emerging computing technologies. Outlining technology-specific thresholds for informed consent remains contentious with regard to consent practices of the emerging computing technologies (Stahl *et al* 2016).

8.2.3.1 Waiving consent

In order to promote a common good, there are usually justifiable reasons to restrict autonomy. Arguably, at times involving human subjects in research without any consent is ethically acceptable by the following conditions:

  i. The study deliberates significant issues of public interest.
  ii. The study cannot be carried out if consent must be provided by the subjects.
  iii. Including subjects in the study without their approval does not substantially give up their autonomy.

For instance, institutional research boards may support ignoring the requirement for consent to conduct experiment about phishing as they may produce vital information regarding matters that are of serious concern to the public and may likely satisfy all the criteria for waiving consent. Conducting an experiment on phishing is not possible without consent being waived or modification of the consent criteria. The reason for waiving consent in this type of research is that the result of the research will be invalidated if the participants are aware of it. Secondly, after the completion of the experiment, the subjects would be provided with the detailed information regarding their participation. Thirdly, risk involving phishing experiments is probably minimal without any serious concern (Stahl *et al* 2016).

8.2.4 Inclusion and digital divides

The increasing value of computing as a major component of economic activity and social communication, entails that the inability to take part in these activities can be a substantial ethical concern. The issues of inclusion and divides is found within and among societies or countries. There are numerous causes of digital divides whose different causes often signal wider social divisions, such as those triggered as a result of the financial and economic system, or other types of inequality, such as those caused by socioeconomic status, age, or education (Stahl *et al* 2016).

8.2.5 Visual ethics

This involves individuals explaining the ethical concerns to persons they photograph, even though not being trained researchers. Wang and Burris suggested that photo voice participants training should include talks focusing around ethics, power, and cameras, as well as deal with questions involving whether one can take a photograph of people without their knowledge (Mok *et al* 2015).

8.2.6 Research ethics using wearable cameras

Technological advancement includes the design of automated tools such as wearable cameras for monitoring and investigation of health behaviours in the public health setting. The use of such automated, wearable cameras to conduct experiments is intrusive and generates a plethora of image data, of which some are unwanted. The participants and third parties involved might think they are being spied on or might feel their privacy is being jeopardised (Kelly *et al* 2013). There are four suggestions to mitigate the problem of using wearable cameras, listed as follows (Mok *et al* 2015):

  i. Reducing the scope and detail, integrating and retaining the data collected, and restricting its access.
  ii. Devising an ethical method that considers the common rule methods favouring anonymity and privacy along with the ethics of contextual judgement and consent as an ongoing process.
  iii. Development of more powerful ethical guidelines of study outside the academic world.
  iv. Employing research participants and the public to take part in developing ethical regulations.

8.3 The six domains of research ethics

The six domains presented in table 8.1 are not hermetically sealed. There are items that cut across a single domain or category. A typical example can be seen in a lot of the items under animal welfare and human protection also applying to regulatory compliance. However, ethical matters related to protection of animal welfare and human subjects are not exactly similar to matters related to regulatory compliance. At some point, the two often interrelate, and are usually meant to interrelate, but at times obeying rules fulfils no ethical value other than that of abiding by the rules. Certainly, at times, rules do not meet the requirement of morality and sometimes morality requires actions that go against the rules. Abiding by the rules does not exactly imply being ethical (Pimple 2002).

The six domains of research ethics as presented in table 8.1 include scientific integrity, which establishes the relationship between the truth and the research. Collegiality ensures relationships among researchers. Protection of human subjects ensures avoidance of violation to human subjects in the research, typically, showing

Table 8.1. The six fundamental research ethics domains.

Scientific integrity	Collegiality	Human protection	Animal welfare	Social responsibility	Institutional integrity
Basic technical competence	Authorship	Protection from harm	Replacement, reduction, refinement	Research priorities	Conflict of interest
Unintentional bias	Mentorship	Access to treatments	Animal 'rights'	Forbidden knowledge	Institutional demands and support
Fabrication	Candor	Research risks and benefits	Enrichment	Environmental impact	Institutional oversight
Falsification	Confidentiality	Debriefing	Pain and suffering	Advocacy by researchers	Data retention
Statistical methods	Peer review	Deceit		Public education	Regulatory compliance
Data manipulation	Plagiarism	Confidentiality and anonymity		Public service	Conflict of commitment
	Data sharing and timely publishing	Assent		Fiscal responsibility	
		Informed consent			

connections between human subjects and researchers. Animal welfare refers to the connections between animal subjects and researchers. Institutional integrity refers to connections between researchers, the government, supporting institution, and their funding agencies. Social responsibility defines the relationship between the common good and research (Vitak *et al* 2017).

8.4 Research misconduct

In 1989, the federal government of India in an unenthusiastic manner laid out policies to address unethical research practices among researchers. Misconduct in research involves the following scenarios: fabrication of result or data; false claims or outcome; and plagiarising someone else idea in a proposal, conducting, or reviewing of research, or plagiarizing results of research. All these acts constitute research misconduct and are not tolerated. In more detail, fabrication is the act of creating dubious or fake data or research results disguised as original data or results. On the other hand, falsification constitutes the manipulation of materials used for the research, equipment or the research processes, or research data alteration or misrepresentation of the research outcome. Plagiarism is the stealing of someone else's literature, research processes, outcome of research, or text without properly citing the source of the text (Debnath 2016). A summary of research misconduct is shown in figure 8.2.

8.4.1 Plagiarism

Plagiarism is serious scientific misconduct among scientific researchers today and is one of the factors why a good number of manuscripts get rejections and why there is retraction of published papers. It is necessary for the research community to adopt a strict policy against any form of research misconduct, such as fabrication, falsification, or plagiarism, in order to ensure integrity and accuracy in research. Both the authors and editors are responsibility and accountable for making sure a manuscript

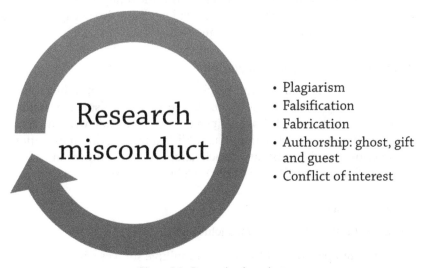

• Plagiarism
• Falsification
• Fabrication
• Authorship: ghost, gift and guest
• Conflict of interest

Figure 8.2. Research misconduct.

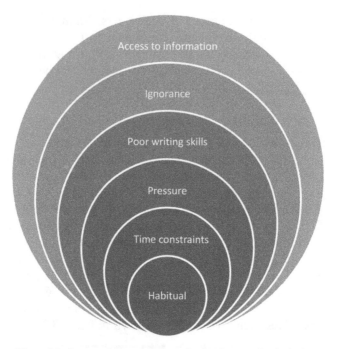

Figure 8.3. Some well-known reasons for involvement in plagiarism.

is plagiarism-free. Plagiarism is one of the most prevalent examples of scientific misconduct and a serious challenge to the scientific publication process across all fields of study.

The increase in instances of plagiarism in recent times can be attributed to a variety of reasons, such as the ease of access to information, pressure to publish for academic advancement, lack of writing skills, time constraints, lack of understanding about what constitutes plagiarism, and a mentality that using one's own work without citation is acceptable. Some individuals may also engage in plagiarism habitually (Debnath 2016) as shown in figure 8.3.

8.4.2 Disciplinary action against plagiarism

The severity of the punishment for plagiarism can vary depending on various factors, such as the journal's policy, the degree of plagiarism, the status of the author, and the author's intent. Possible penalties may include written reprimands, rejection of the manuscript, retraction of a published manuscript, notification to the author's superiors, and temporary blacklisting of the author in the journal (Committee on Publication Ethics (COPE); Debnath 2016).

8.4.3 Plagiarism types

There are several types of plagiarism, including:

    i. Copying and pasting text from one or multiple sources without giving credit.
   ii. Using a significant amount of text from another work without proper citation.

iii. Reproducing text word-for-word.
iv. Changing the wording of text but keeping the same meaning without giving credit.
v. Reusing text from an author's previous work without proper referencing.

8.4.4 Authorship

Writing authors' names on a scientific paper is a way to give appropriate credit to each individual and means they are answerable, for the study. Excluding an author's name from their work is also considered misconduct in proper reporting of scientific research. Although, there has not been a universal acceptable definition of authorship, an 'author' is someone who has intellectually contributed to the research.

The recommended guidelines for authorship by the International Committee of Medical Journal Editors (ICMJE) also referred to as the Vancouver protocol, which is widely adopted across disciplines, state that all individuals listed as authors must:

i. Have made a significant contribution to the study's concept, design, data acquisition, analysis, and interpretation.
ii. Have been involved in the manuscript drafting or revision of the article that improved the content of the article intellectually.
iii. Approved the final manuscript version.
iv. Be willing to take responsibility for accuracy and integrity of all the aspects of the work.

Here is a general guide to authors that can vary across research areas:

i. Authors' arrangement should be determined through a collective agreement made by all the co-authors.
ii. Those whose contributions are not sufficient for authorship should be acknowledged as contributors or acknowledged individuals. This includes those who provided advice, research space, oversight, and funding.
iii. For trials in large multiple centres, the names of the clinicians and centres involved are often included in the published study, along with details about the specific contributions made by each individual. Some groups choose alphabetical arrangement of author names while indicating the contributions of the authors are equal in both the research work and the publication.

8.4.4.1 Unethical authorship

The three different categories of authorship that are unethical and unacceptable are as follows (Elsevier 2019):

- *Ghost authorship*: This is a situation where professional writers are just paid for the services rendered but not acknowledged for the contributions. Unattributed contributions to data analysis can fall in this authorship category.
- *Guest authorship*: This is where individuals are listed as authors despite not making any significant contributions to the study. Usually the name of the

author is added to increase the chance of the manuscript acceptance because of the prominence of the author in the research field.

- *Gift authorship*: This is where individuals are listed as authors due to a weak association with the study, rather than the actual contributions.

If not properly handled, authorship problems could cause serious misunderstanding. Most of the misunderstandings arise as a result of ethical misconduct such as lying about an author's role, interpretation of the degree of contribution and if authorship is rationalised. Additional possible problems might include: excluding a contributor name; someone taking an idea from another and claiming full authorship; and unauthorized inclusion in a publication. If a disagreement is brought to the attention of the journal, an inquiry may be conducted with the journal editor and the author's organization to resolve the matter. In order to avoid possible collisions and confused expectation, it is appropriate authors involved in a scientific research meet to discuss authorship and clearly state the order of name arrangement on the paper before starting a research. If you're unsure how to handle a difficult situation involving authorship, it's best to seek guidance from a mentor or supervisor who can provide you with more information about journal guidelines and industry requirements. Additionally, if a complaint is raised, an investigation may be conducted by the journal editor and the author's institution to resolve the issue. It is important to remember that these situations can be sensitive and complex, and early career researchers may be hesitant to speak up for fear of damaging their reputation or career (Elsevier 2019).

8.4.5 Conflict of interest

In academic research, a conflict of interest (COI) is when financial or personal considerations may influence an author's professional judgment in conducting or reporting the research. This can occur when an author has competing interests that could potentially compromise objectivity. A COI is based on the circumstances and not the actions or character of an individual researcher. It is pertinent that investigators in human research related investigations avoid any form of COI to any of the studies that they participate in (University of California San Francisco 2022).

8.4.5.1 Researcher conflict of interest
Researcher COI is the conflict other than the usual financial conflicts. For instance, researchers could be offered either a grant or a huge financial reward for conducting a study if the study finding is positive. However, researcher conflict of interest covers conflicts such as career development or responsibilities to friends or family.

8.4.5.2 Editorial conflict of interest:
To ensure credibility, scholarly publications should strive for transparency in regards to potential biases in research, reporting, and publication. The COI can contribute to bias, and it is important to identify and disclosed. Based on the ICMJE, a COI is defined as a situation where an individual has competing interests that may influence the work they are presenting. The COIs are seen as an

inevitable aspect of the publication process, as they can potentially impact all the stakeholders such as the editors, authors, manuscript editors, journal guest editors, journal staff, reviewers and service providers (COPE).

8.5 Tips to avoid conflict of interest

The individuals responsible for making decisions about the content of the publication, policies of the publication venue and managing the affairs of the publishing venue must ensure that decisions taken are not influenced by COI. Declaring conflicts of interest is considered the main way to mitigate this bias. Although many journals require authors to disclose COI. However, the editors and members of the editorial board are not always mandated to declare the potential COI. Few journals disclose the editors COI openly on the journal website. This is despite the recommendations of reputable organizations like the council of science editors, COPE, ICMJE, etc to declare editorial COI. The COPE even suggests that potential editors should declare conflicts of interest including current editorial positions when applying to join the editorial board (COPE).

8.5.1 Participation in editorial board

The COPE Guidelines provide general information about the appointment and engagement of editorial board members, outlining roles and responsibilities, and highlighting important factors to consider during recruitment, such as involvement on multiple editorial boards. These Guidelines are official COPE policy and intended to guide editors and publishers on ethical publication practices. The key point raised by the COPE are as follows:

- The responsibilities and expectations of editorial roles should be clearly outlined, including the number of reviews required, the standards for review quality, the level of editorial decision-making involved and the process for making decisions.
- The terms of appointment should be clearly established and include information such as the qualifications and requirements for appointment, the duration of the term, the conditions for renewal and the reasons for which an appointment may be terminated before the end of the term.
- Journals should establish guidelines for COI that are not acceptable from the editors, and if an editor has such a conflict, the editor should not be allowed to join the board or the editor should be removed if they are already on the board and the conflict is not resolved.
- Journals should request that potential editorial board members disclose any potential COI if any.
- When recruiting editors for any level, journals should consider whether it is appropriate for an individual to serve on multiple editorial boards simultaneously within the same field, with similar decision-making or commissioning responsibilities.

8.6 Avoiding research misconduct

According to a study on researcher responsibility found that most of the participant (53.4%) agreed that the ethical standard held by researchers is high compared to others who use data generated online, and majority (51.7%) indicate that researchers should maintain the high ethical standards than others. The study also found that a clear majority (69%) of the participants agreed that currently researchers consider ethical issues regarding data than many years ago. The following statement 'I think researchers collecting online data are more interested in data than the people behind the data,' response remain unclear, where 40.4% agreed, 19.3% disagreed, while the other 40.4% were neutral (Vitak *et al* 2017). Researchers are expected to maintain very high ethical standards in conducting research, as such, any form of research misconduct must be avoided.

The different ways to prevent the occurrences of research misconduct as outlined in University of Saint Diego (2016) are as follows:

Good scientific practices can reduce the likelihood of misconduct and these include:

- Adhering strictly to the scientific method.
- Keeping clear and detailed records.
- Clearly defining collaborations.
- Understanding authorship roles and responsibilities.
- Providing guidance and mentorship to new researchers.
- Fostering an environment that encourages asking questions and open discussion.

Steps in managing researchers' COI:

- *Complying with the regulations:* The researcher is expected to always comply with institutional and government regulations to identify, disclose, and manage COI.
- *Avoiding and minimizing conflict:* Researchers should strive to ensure avoiding and minimizing conflicts, recognize the conflict before taking action to neutralize or reduce it when it occurrs.
- *Disclosing interests:* In the case of unavoidable conflict, the conflict needs be declared to the institution and any party involved and information provided about the exact conflict nature and magnitude.
- *Management of conflicts:* Managing COI involves more than just disclosure, action should be taken by isolating the individual involved in the conflict from the processes of decision-making during all the stages of the research.
- *Keep learning:* It is important to stay informed and continuously learn about potential COI and strategies for addressing COI, as they are constantly evolving. It is essential to actively seek out information and comply with both the intent and requirements of current regulations to avoid misperceptions of a researcher's motives.

8.7 Ethics committees and institutional research boards

Ethics committees and IRBs remain vested with the responsibility to protect the well-being of human subjects, such as assessing if the subjects are fully aware of the potential benefits and dangers of the research, whether the probable dangers have been significantly reduced, and whether the probable potential risks do not prevail over the expected benefits. These constitute the significant aspect of the concerns including other factors that can be considered. Knowing that it is a field of special-ization for the members of IRBs and not essentially for the researchers, for what reason would our community be recommended to get fully involved in deliberating on how the terms relate to our research? It is obvious that IRBs have skills in aspects where security researchers do not, it is still not safe to depend on the structure in existence to be the principal basis of moral guidance (Johnson *et al* 2011). The authors take the responsibility of recording data from researches involving animals or human participants by providing an official evaluation and approval, or in some cases review and waiver officially granted by a standard IRB or ethics committee is needed. This formal review and approval is explained in the methods/methodology section of the research manuscript. Authors who may not have access to formal ethics evaluation committees, should follow the outlined principles in the Helsinki Declaration. Those involved in investigating human subjects are required to mention the methods (i.e., oral or written) used to seek consent from the subjects involved in the study in the methods/methodology section of the work. Editors may demand the investigators present the documents of the official evaluation and approval from the ethics committee or IRB responsible for the supervision of the study (Aycock *et al* 2011).

8.8 Research ethics in the context of disciplines in computing

This section presents different research ethics in the context of each discipline in computing to guide readers on the appropriate research ethics to adopt for different research in different disciplines within the computing ecosystem. Of course the research ethics in each discipline is not static for a single discipline, the same research ethics can be adopted in different disciplines depending on the nature of the research. For example, research in IS and CS can require human subjects for experiments. In view of the fact that human subjects are involved in the two researches from different disciplines, evaluation and approval of the ethics committee is required. Figure 8.4

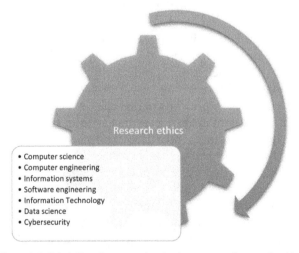

Figure 8.4. Disciplines in computing in the context of research ethics.

shows a pictorial representation of the disciplines in computing in the context of research ethics.

8.8.1 Ethics in software engineering

The issue of study ethics in empirical studies for SE has grave effects that the potential subjects, researchers, and corporate sponsors ought to be concerned about. Researchers stand the risk of losing cooperation or morality if they disappoint the subjects. Also, researchers who stand against the managers of the subjects risk losing access to the funding, the subjects or other resources. Researches from academia in Canada, Australia, and America funded by government jeopardize the funding if the researcher violates any specified ethical regulations. It is pertinent also for the sponsors of empirical studies of SE research to recognize how research ethics directs the actions of the researchers, and how immoral actions, from both the researchers and the sponsors can thwart the success of the project. For instance, convincing employees to be involved in a project as research subjects could render the data void. Potential subjects should also be highly concerned with ethical issues to be sure they are protected from the risks of losing their job. There may be varying reasons for researchers, potential subjects, and sponsors to be concerned about ethics, however, it is important they do nonetheless (Singer and Vinson 2002).

Informed consent: To buttress informed consent concept, consider an example of student subjects; Dr Joyce, a faculty member from a research university, was studying the impact of various perceptions on understanding a program based on source code. She created a platform that provides flow view on data, control and architecture of the system. She was interested in finding out which view is most effective for software engineers when designing and maintaining source code. However, she had no access to software engineers in the industry to test the tool she created. Thus, she resorted to using the students in her class of SE as the research subjects for testing the tool. The students in the class were categorised into four different groups. Three groups among the four were given different views of the tools created by Dr Joyce. On the other hand, the last group of the students were given the tool typically used by the University programming community. The students in all the four sections were given the same mid-term project. The result of the research indicates that only a slight increase in productivity was achieved by some of the views (Singer and Vinson 2002).

Based on the example in the previous paragraph, it is obvious that Dr Joyce did not seek for informed consent from the students, thus violating the standard of informed consent. In this research situation, even if the participation was made optional by Dr Joyce to the students, Dr Joyce could still influence the informed consent in view of the fact that there is potential impact on the student's grade. Therefore, it is challenging to get valid informed consent in the research conducted in a classroom setting because of the power dynamics between the professor and students (Singer and Vinson 2002). In this situation, SE from a different university could be used as the subjects of the research following research ethics guidelines or develop a proper ethical guideline for the research stating clearly in the guidelines that opting out of the research will not have any negative impact on student grades and participation will not in any way have positive impact on student grades. Participation should be purely for research purpose and independent from the semester activities.

8.8.2 Ethics in computer science

In computer science research, the discussions of ethics in human–computer interaction most likely come first when it has to do with human participants. The next likely discussed area may be the assessment of educational procedures or analytic/modeling methods in developing software. However, there are more research areas that involved human participation. Considering a case of a study concerning open-source software (OSS), it was noted that researchers and software developers find it more appealing to analyse large software systems source code because of their public accessibility and they do not need to be purchased. It was pointed out that the primary purpose of OSS was not to be analysed or for any research purposes, and hence, informed consent must be sought before using the source code. Nevertheless, obtaining consent from every developer of a given OSS project is tedious work. The numbers of contributors are so many and a researcher may not be aware of the specific individual's contributions that would be analysed next. El-Emam highlighted concerns regarding minimizing harm and maintaining confidentiality. This is because the version of the control systems typically used in the project for OSS has a way of marking and recording the contributor responsible for any segment of the code added. If the outcome of the research in the published code segments is negative, it could potentially lead to professional or personal harm because the author of the segment of the source code could be traced (Wright 2007).

Reacting to the challenge, Vinson and Singer highlight that while removing individual ID from data can assist in maintaining the confidentiality of the individual involved, it does not necessarily eliminate the need for informed consent. It was also noted that the process of removing identifiers can be difficult, as in the case of a popular open-source email client like Mozilla Thunderbird, even without mentioning the name of the program, it can still be easily identified through searching the repository of the source code and the identity of the individual who contribute to the development. Vinson and Singer argue that removing the identity in research on open-source software can make it difficult for other researchers to replicate the study because it cannot be confirmed if it is the evaluation of the same software. In this case, the compatibility of the first outcome and the later outcome can be reduced. It is concluded that research on open-source software raises many ethical concerns and researchers are advised to exercise caution when developing ethical guidelines for this type of research (Wright 2007).

In today's digital age, algorithms are being utilized more frequently to perform tasks that were once done by humans. These algorithms are used to make decisions, analyze data, and guide actions. These algorithms are becoming more prevalent in various areas including social interactions, business operations, and government decision-making. However, as these algorithms play a larger role in our lives, there is a growing concern about the ethical implications of their use. The gap between how algorithms are designed and how they are used can lead to negative consequences for individuals, groups, and the entire society. Automating decision-making can raise ethical concerns about consistency between the actions of algorithms and those of human decision-makers. To address this, it is important to ensure that algorithms are guided by the same ethical principles as the human counterparts. However, it can be challenging to define and implement these principles in a computable form. One approach to addressing this issue is to use virtue ethics, which offers a set of rules that can be easily applied to algorithmic decision-making structures (Mittelstadt *et al* 2016).

8.8.2.1 *Ethics for artificial intelligence in the medical domain*
Artificial intelligence (AI)-based systems have been penetrating every part of society with successful outcomes (refer to chapter 9 for details on recent developments in AI). The advancement in AI research has attracted media and public interest recently. As AI systems are transforming into autonomous agents and team mates, the impact of the AI need to be understood ethically through research and development (Dignum 2018). Focus on AI research is shifting to its ethical reliability (Carman and Rosman 2021). Ethical concerns about AI-based systems, especially in the medical domain are gaining momentum. The following are ethical issues to look out for in developing an AI system for medical applications (Jackson *et al* 2021):

1. AI-based systems developers are required to be transparent in their data collection, analysis and evaluation/validation of the AI-based system. The general public and patients should be informed about the processes.
2. In the development of an AI-based pathology system, the patient and individuals should be the determinant factors on the way the personal data can be used for developing the systems. The developers and clinical organizations should take the responsibility of ensuring that the control of the personal data is on the patient and individuals.
3. The pathology AI systems developers, validators, and implementers have the responsibility of ensuring measurable benefits to the public and patients while risk and harm are greatly minimized.
4. There should be fairness for the population that supplied the data used for the development process of the AI systems. Benefits, risk and harm should be shared among all the stakeholders: the population that supplied the data and those who the system has impact on.
5. Pathology AI systems should have sufficient transparent and auditable processes to ensure that the principles guiding pathology AI system development are abided by. For example, publication of the pathology AI systems can be used to establish a formal auditing process for transparency to the public. The developers and implementers are to ensure the transparency and the auditing.
6. Research integrity and scientific standards must be strictly adhered to by the developers, validators, and implementers of pathology AI systems. They should be ready to share information openly.

7. Pathology AI systems stakeholders should create a formal IRB to serve as a guiding board for the development of pathology AI systems.
8. The organizations engaged in the development, validation, implementation, sale, or purchase of pathology AI systems should hold each other accountable to those who violate ethical principles via mechanisms that are formal, such as through contracts. The required guidelines should include transparency, auditability and auditing requirement, prohibition against re-identification and misuse in other forms.

8.8.3 Ethics in information system

The field of IS that combines aspects of management, organizational studies, and computer science has a history of considering ethical issues. It is categorized under the broader category of business ethics, specific ethics code and professional conduct within the field, such as the one created by the ACM (Herwix *et al* 2021). Designing systems with a strong focus on ethical considerations is an effective way to promote human and social well-being. The Aristotelian ethics approach that stresses human values importance and virtues, can serve as a useful guide for ethical system design. This perspective emphasizes the importance of striving for 'eudaimonia', or self-actualization to achieve a state of well-being (Spiekermann *et al* 2022).

Increasingly, there are concerns about the potential risks associated with decision-making that is controlled by algorithms, as it may lead to unintended and negative outcomes for society. The core issues in this area include bias, fairness, and transparency, which are also key areas of research in the field of IS. Biases can arise from various sources, such as biased training data, flawed algorithms, unfair data presentation, and user error. To address these issues, policymakers suggest implementing measures to increase transparency and explainability in the models. There have been instances where autonomous systems such as recruitment systems have been found to have a gender bias, or decision support systems used in law enforcement with a racial bias. These discriminatory decisions that arise from flawed algorithm or data are a prime instance of the importance of research that takes a technical approach to these issues. This line of research recognizes that technology has a significant impact on social findings and human decision-making process. Researchers in the field of IS should acknowledge that biased data is often a reflection of discrimination in the physical world, and that it highlights the way humans design organizational systems. It is important to note that algorithm bias can be unintentionally infused by the developers based on the developers' background and experiences. Central to IS research is the ability to understand fairness and bias because of the interplay between socio-technical factors. To promote fairness and prevent bias of decision-making performed by algorithms, policymakers and researchers identify transparency as the key factor. By addressing the issue of transparency, researchers in the field of IS can play a role in creating a more equitable society by mitigating biases and discrimination (Spiekermann *et al* 2022). Therefore, conducting research in IS requires strong ethical issues to be considered carefully to avoid negative impact of the result findings in society.

8.8.4 Ethics in cyber security

In computer security research, the actual computer systems and the users are the main components that are being studied. Studying deployed systems in the real world and testing potential solutions with would-be users is crucial for understanding and addressing real-world problems. This often involves collecting data from users, which may involve direct interactions or analyzing data from the user's devices. For instance, the collection of data can involve the installation of software for monitoring a user's personal device, website instrumentation, or conducting an experiment in the laboratory for a study. Computer security researchers often engage in research involving human subjects through direct interaction or through the collection of data generated by humans. In any case, high ethical standards should be upheld by the researchers because the research involves human subjects as a relationship is established between the researchers and users (Johnson *et al* 2011).

The main goal of cyber security practices is the protection of data, software and hardware from harm or accessing the system without authorization. It is not only about securing data and systems that have economic or other value, but also protecting the integrity, functionality, and reliability of the human institutions and practices that rely on them. In protecting institutions and practices, the cyber security expert plays a critical role in protecting the lives and well-being of patients in hospitals and healthcare workers. It implies that as a security professional, the hospital critical data and networks depend on the formidable security services put in place to ensure patients' data are not compromised. This is because the privacy, health, and even survival of patients depends on the effectiveness of the cyber security practices. The patients' families, patient and caregivers are often protected by these cyber security practices. While this example is particularly stark, cyber security professionals are essential for protecting the broader population who are directly or indirectly related to health. Because cyber security practices are essential for protecting people, ethics are at the core of these cyber security practices. As the methods for securing online data and systems become more advanced, in a landscape that includes cloud services, Wi-Fi enabled devices, and 'smart' objects, the ethical concerns of protecting others is becoming a heavier burden and complex for cyber security professionals (Vallor *et al* 2017).

Consent: A concern arises when testing the security of a system. In some cases, researchers must assume the role of a hacker to test the system's vulnerabilities. For example, using phishing tests, where the researcher impersonates a fake agent, can be an effective method of identifying vulnerabilities. However, using phishing involves deception and obtaining prior consent from subjects can be difficult. In small-scale study involving limited participants participating in an experiment, not obtaining prior consent and/or using deception is within acceptable practice as long as the potential harm is highly minimized. However, when the experiment involves many research subjects, it is challenging to predict the harms and the lack of consent becomes a significant ethical concern. The use of phishing and vulnerabilities for systems testing can cause significant harm to the stakeholders, especially when informed consent has not been secured. It is generally recommended to avoid all potential harm as much as possible, and if it is not possible, seeking guidance from ethics committees can help to find a balance between the harm caused and the value of the research (Macnish and van der Ham 2020) (refer to section 8.1 for details about waiving informed consent).

Risk in computer security research: The security of human subjects research is of paramount importance, considering the wide range of risks that can be found in computer security research. The assessment of risks involved is a vital component of IRB review, and relevant to the two primary ethical theories: consequentialism and deontology (Johnson *et al* 2011). Traditional research ethics built its foundation on human respect, beneficence, and justice. The IRB is responsible for safeguarding human subjects involved in a research processes and functions as intermediary between the human subjects and providing evaluation as well as process of review. One of the areas of concern in computer security research is risk. For any research involving human subjects it must be proven that the benefits to the subjects or society outweigh the potential risk as argued by the office of human research protections. The IRB is responsible for reviewing a research proposal to ensure compliance to the human research protections principle. This principle is contained in all research ethics code and it is one of the fundamental aspects of federal regulations. The regulations mandate that researchers should attempt to reduce the potential risks to the human subjects to the lowest tolerance level instead of completely eradicating them (Aycock *et al* 2011).

8.8.5 Ethics in data science

The global and distributed manner of DS introduce challenges in the evaluation of the credibility, significance, and potentiality of the impact of the data and knowledge generated. This has major implications for managing and monitoring responsibilities and accountability in the field of DS (Leonelli 2016). Critical ethical questions are raised as a result of new techniques of ML used in DS, and the possibility of using algorithms to perform tasks carried out in the past by humans, as well as to generate new knowledge. These questions not only relate to the potential harm caused by the misuse of data, but also issues such as preserving privacy for sensitive data, avoiding bias in data selection, preventing disruptions and unauthorized access to data, and ensuring transparency in data collection, research, and dissemination. The central issues of these questions are ownership of data, who is authorized to access it, and the circumstances under which access is granted (Stanford University 2023).

While using data science tools to learn something useful, valuable, and reliable, data scientists are involved in lots of implicit ethical deliberations. For instance, using dirty and incomplete data has both moral and practical concerns. During ML training of data, a series of decisions need to be made, such as how was the data collected? How complete is the data? Some decisions in DS can be difficult, requiring careful thought at every step. This is true for validating a model and determining an acceptable error rate. For example, what criteria are needed to demonstrate that a model will be effective? How do data scientists determine if a reported error is acceptable and justifiable? When making fundamental decisions about the selection of a learning algorithm, ethical considerations come into play, and practitioners often find it challenging to find a balance between maximizing the performance of the resulting model and ensuring interpretability. In what situations is the capability to thoroughly test a model important enough to justify a decrease in performance? What kinds of real-world decisions prompt data scientists to prioritize developing models that are interpretable even if it means a lower level of accuracy in the results? These are complex decisions that must be carefully managed to meet ethical standards. It is unfortunate that most data scientists are not fully aware of these ethical concerns. The following ethical issues in data science should adhered to by researchers in DS (Barocas and Boyd 2017):

Accuracy of the data and validity: Ensuring accuracy of the data and validity are main responsibilities of the data scientist. It involves assessing the accuracy of the data, relevance and suitability in the context in which it will be used. In another words, the data scientists must guarantee that the data is suitable for its intended purpose to avoid it being misused or taken out of context.

Data misuse: Just simply because a data scientist has access to a dataset does not automatically guarantee the use of the data ethically (Boyd *et al* 2014). There are many websites that deny access to data on the website using a crawler and where using the crawler to access the data on the website violates the condition for using the website. Additionally, gathering big data is shrouded with ethical issues such as concern on the issue of privacy. It is recommended that the ownership of the date sources should be taken into control by the organizations. There should be no agreement on confidentiality that prevents disclosure of data partners and one should ensure that misuse of the data is prevented by guaranteed visibility of the data supply chain.

Privacy and anonymity: Data scientists must be aware of the person ability to select which of the data is shared with a third party, including what the person wishes to make public. The person should have the ability of controlling access to the data. The issue of privacy concerns mainly focuses on data control and ownership, not only the issue of the collected data ownership, right of transferring the data and what is the covenant involved in the collecting or receiving of the data.

8.8.6 Ethics in information technology

Ethics in IT research is similar to other disciplines in computing. For the purpose of illustrating research ethics in IT, a surveillance system is considered.

When it comes to ethical issues surrounding the automation of surveillance, there are three options to consider: manual surveillance (MS), automated surveillance (AS), and partially automated surveillance (PAS). Privacy and distance are relevant factors in PAS. The more automation is used, the more privacy concerns arise. However, as automation increases, the divide increases between the individual being surveilled and the device operator. This can limit the opportunities for flexible behavior or interacting with humans. Blinkered surveillance (BS) is considered more privacy-friendly than unblinkered surveillance (UBS). Distance is a more complex moral anxiety compared to privacy, the distance increases with BS having positive and negative effects. PAS systems are considered to be more ethical than fully MS or fully AS. They have greater processing capacity. Issues such as bias and false positives/negatives may still exist but the false positives/negatives concerns are considered insignificant compared to the issues surrounding MS. It is believed that in an ideal scenario, a BS system would be preferred generally compared to UBS systems in the case of a PAS system. BS systems reduce the scope for discretion and interaction, and limit opportunities for prejudice. Given the current limitations in computer processing technology, it may not be practical to implement a BS system as it would likely result in too many false negatives. As a result, it appears that a UBS PAS system would be the most ethical option in most cases under the current conditions (Macnish 2012).

8.8.7 Ethics in computer engineering

Researchers and engineers in the field have an ethical responsibility to consider the potential impacts of the research work and make decisions accordingly. Ethics plays a crucial role in engineering research as it often impacts human lives. What may be considered ethical in one situation or by one group of people, may not be viewed the same way by others. The availability of vast amounts of data and the various methods for analyzing it also brings ethical considerations in engineering research. Engineering research is closely tied to technological developments and must take privacy and data connected to surveillance systems into account for ethical consideration. Researchers have the responsibility for the effect of their research and must make ethical decisions that influence the impact of technology. This can be done through setting ethical requirements at the beginning of the research, designing technology with ethical considerations in mind, and making informed choices among several alternatives that serve similar functions. Ethically, it is the responsibility of the researchers to ensure minimal potential hazards and risks connected to the research outcomes, adopt alternative and safer methods if necessary. This includes designing the research in a way that it manages and controls any potential side effects and implementing factors that are safe, multi-facial independent barriers for safety, or a mechanism as a supervisor to take control in the situation where the main process breaks down (Deb *et al* 2019).

8.9 Negative research results and tips to get published

Compared to the negative results, the percentage of positive results published in journals or conferences is higher (Murudka 2021). In the research community, researchers often expect positive findings/results at the end of the research work. Positive results referred to as hypothesis are always expected at the beginning of a research work. Researchers celebrate positive findings and the bias of the scientific research community is towards positive results. Positive results are celebrated by publishing them or use without publishing, especially in industry. Figure 8.5 depicts a typical cycle of research findings. A result is referred to as negative finding if it goes contrary to the positive expectation of the researcher or the hypothesis. In other words, if the finding rejected the hypothesis and supported the null hypothesis.

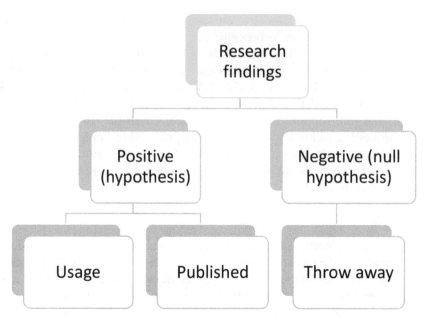

Figure 8.5. Typical scenario of research findings.

Mostly researchers feel bad or frustrated if the research findings supported the null hypothesis and rejected the research hypothesis. As a result of that, many researchers become demoralized and do not proceed with the project because it is believed that the scientific community has a bias towards positive findings and the benefits of negative results are lower compared to those of positive results.

If the research results are negative, a researcher should resist the temptation of tampering with or manipulating the negative results to be positive. There is no cause to worry if the research finding becomes negative because it can be published as long as the researcher can defend the results and proves that its actually negative. It is highly unethical to manipulate or alter negative results to be positive results. Manipulating negative results to positive and publishing them contribute to the accumulation of falsified/fake data in the scientific literature. This is unacceptable, unethical and gross misconduct in the scientific research community.

8.9.1 Publishing negative results

The good news is that negative results are publishable and the number of journals or conferences publishing negative results are increasing rapidly to encourage honest scientific research discussion; this prevents other researchers from conducting similar study, thus saving time, resources and effort. It encourages sharing information with the scientific community to give the opportunity to other researchers to tackle the same problem from a different perspective. Many journals now published negative results but the examples of journals given in this section were selected because they published computing research findings. For example, *Journal of Universal Computer*

Sciences for Negative Results, PLoS One, Nature, etc. An example of negative research findings emanated from computer science is published in Onah *et al* (2021).

If a research finding is negative and the researcher decides to publish the negative findings, it must be done with precautions. The data involved in the research must prove beyond any doubt that the results are indeed negative statistically after rigorous data analytics. To ensure the negativity of the findings, an experiment free of technical flaws should be conducted repeatedly. In addition, the experiment can be further conducted with peers, colleagues and experts in the research area to be sure of the negative findings. If after all the efforts confirm the negativity of the results, it would give confidence to the researchers that the findings are negative and the results can have a chance of getting published in high impact journals (Murudka 2021).

8.10 Summary

Integrity in the academic community is determined by the ethical conduct of the researchers. Research ethics guides the conduct of research ethically. Research ethics in computing is dynamic as a result of advancement in computing technology. This chapter explores issues surrounding research ethics in computing ecosystems. The origin of research ethics in computing was elaborated and major ethical issues from the perspective of computing in relation to privacy, informed consent, security, inclusion and digital divide, trust and visual ethics were pointed out. The six domains of research ethics discussed are as follows: scientific integrity, collegiality, human protection, animal welfare, social responsibility and institutional integrity. Research misconducts were discussed in the chapter such as plagiarism, falsification, fabrication, unethical authorship and COI. Its implications and preventive measures were explained. Research ethics was discussed in the context of different disciplines in computing—CS, CE, IS, DS, CyS, IT and SE. Negative research findings (null hypothesis) and tips to get them published were discussed. The chapter discusses ethics in computing research to inform readers, especially new or novice researchers, about the ethics involving research. The chapter can equip researchers with the required ethical information to conduct research in any computing discipline and avoid unethical behaviours, thereby preserving and improving the integrity of research in computing.

References

Aycock J, Buchanan E, Dexter S and Dittrich D 2011 Human subjects, agents, or bots: current issues in ethics and computer security research *Int. Conf. on Financial Cryptography and Data Security* (Berlin: Springer), 138–45

Barocas S and Boyd D 2017 Engaging the ethics of data science in practice *Commun. ACM* **60** 23–5

Boyd D and Crawford K 2012 Critical questions for big data: provocations for a cultural, technological, and scholarly phenomenon *Inf. Commun. Soc.* **15** 662–79

Boyd D, Levy K and Marwick A 2014 The networked nature of algorithmic discrimination. Data and Discrimination: Collected Essays *Open Technology Institute*, 53–7 http://www.danah. org/papers/2014/DataDiscrimination.pdf (Accessed 16 October 2021)

Bjorn P, Fiesler C, Muller M, Pater J and Wisniewski P 2018 Research ethics town hall meeting *Proc. 2018 ACM Conf. on Supporting Group Work* 393–6

Capurro R 2009 Digital ethics *Global Forum on Civilization and Peace* 1 (Karlsruhe: Steinbeis-Transfer-Institut Information Ethics (STI-IE)) pp 207–16

Carman M and Rosman B 2021 Applying a principle of explicability to AI research in Africa: should we do it? *Ethics Inf. Technol.* **23** 107–17

Deb D, Dey R and Balas V E 2019 Ethics in engineering research *Engineering Research Methodology. Intelligent Systems Reference Library* vol 153 (Singapore: Springer)

Debnath J 2016 Plagiarism: a silent epidemic in scientific writing—reasons, recognition and remedies *Med. J. Armed Forces India* **72** 164–7

Dignum V 2018 Ethics in artificial intelligence: introduction to the special issue Ethics *Inf. Technol.* **20** 1–3

Elsevier 2019 *Factsheet: Authorship* https://elsevier.com/__data/assets/pdf_file/0006/653883/Authorship-factsheet-March-2019.pdf (accessed 27 April 2022)

Ess C 2013 *Digital Media Ethics* (Cambridge: Polity)

Gelinas L, Wertheimer A and Miller F G 2016 When and why is research without consent permissible? *Hastings Cent. Rep.* **46** 35–43

Günther F, Manulis M and Strufe T 2011 Cryptographic treatment of private user profiles *Int. Conf. on Financial Cryptography and Data Security* (Berlin: Springer) pp 40–54

Herwix A, Haj-Bolouri A, Rossi M, Tremblay M C, Purao S and Gregor S 2021 Ethics in information systems and design science research: five perspectives *CAIS* **50** https://doi.org/10.17705/1CAIS.05028

Jackson B R, Ye Y, Crawford J M, Becich M J, Roy S, Botkin J R, De Baca M E and Pantanowitz L 2021 The ethics of artificial intelligence in pathology and laboratory medicine: principles and practice *Acad. Pathol.* **8** 2374289521990784

Johnson M L, Bellovin S M and Keromytis A D 2011 Computer security research with human subjects: risks, benefits and informed consent *Int. Conf. on Financial Cryptography and Data Security* (Berlin: Springer) 131–7

Kelly P, Marshall S J, Badland H, Kerr J, Oliver M, Doherty A R and Foster C 2013 An ethical framework for automated, wearable cameras in health behavior research *Am. J. Prev. Med.* **44** 314–9

Leonelli S 2016 Locating ethics in data science: responsibility and accountability in global and distributed knowledge production systems *Phil. Trans. R. Soc.* A **374** 20160122

Macnish K 2012 Unblinking eyes: the ethics of automating surveillance *Ethics Inf. Technol.* **14** 151–67

Macnish K and van der Ham J 2020 Ethics in cybersecurity research and practice *Technol. Soc.* **63** 101382

Mittelstadt B D, Allo P, Taddeo M, Wachter S and Floridi L 2016 The ethics of algorithms: mapping the debate *Big Data Soc.* **3** 2053951716679679

Mok T M, Cornish F and Tarr J 2015 Too much information: visual research ethics in the age of wearable cameras *Integr. Psychol. Behav. Sci.* **49** 309–22

Murudka S 2021 *Enago Academy* https://enago.com/academy/top-10-journals-publish-negative-results/#:~:text=Why%20do%20Researchers%20Get%20Negative%20or%20Null%20Results

%3F,confirm%20the%20findings%20obtained%20from%20earlier%20published%20reports (accessed 27 January2023)

Onah J O, Abdullahi M, Hassan I H and Al-Ghusham A 2021 Genetic algorithm based feature selection and Naïve Bayes for anomaly detection in fog computing environment *Mach. Learn. Appl.* **6** 100156

Pimple K D 2002 Six domains of research ethics *Sci. Eng. Ethics* **8** 191–205

Resnik D B and Finn P R 2018 Ethics and phishing experiments *Sci. Eng. Ethics* **24** 1241–52

Singer J and Vinson N G 2002 Ethical issues in empirical studies of software engineering *IEEE Trans. Software Eng.* **28** 1171–80

Spiekermann S, Krasnova H and Hinz O *et al* 2022 Values and ethics in information systems *Bus. Inf. Syst. Eng.* **64** 247–64

Stahl B C, Timmermans J and Mittelstadt B D 2016 The ethics of computing: a survey of the computing-oriented literature *ACM Comput. Surv. (CSUR)* **48** 1–38

Stanford University 2023 Ethics and Data Science https://datascience.stanford.edu/research/research-areas/ethics-and-data-science

University of California San Francisco 2022 *Huma Research Protection—Conflict of Interest in Research* https://irb.ucsf.edu/conflicts-of-interest-research

University of Saint Diego 2016 *Resource for Research Ethics Education* http://research-ethics.org/topics/conflicts-of-interest/ (accessed 27 April 2022)

Vallor S S, William J and Rewak S J 2017 *An Introduction to Cybersecurity Ethics* https://scu.edu/media/ethics-center/technology-ethics/IntroToCybersecurityEthics.pdf

Vitak J, Proferes N, Shilton K and Ashktorab Z 2017 Ethics regulation in social computing research: examining the role of institutional review boards *J. Empir. Res. Hum. Res. Ethics* **12** 372–82

Wright D R 2007 Motivation, design, and ubiquity: a discussion of research ethics and computer science *arXiv preprint* arXiv:0706.0484

Computing Research Survival Manual
A practical handbook for beginners
Haruna Chiroma and Jemal H Abawjy

Chapter 9

Emerging research trends in computing

It is a challenge for many researchers, especially novice researchers, to identify emerging and trending topics appealing to the research community and industry. Research conducted in emerging and trending topics maximizes the impact of the research. On the other hand, research in obsolete, declining or exhausted research areas minimizes the impact of the research as the research community and grant awarding organizations are no long interested in the research area. In this chapter, we present hot selected research problems and emerging research directions in different aspects of computing for researchers, postgraduate students, early career faculties and industry practitioners' to easily identify the trending emerging topics in computing. The emerging research problems were selected from recent surveys/ systematic literature review (SLR), metadata analysis, and narrative review published in top computing journals cutting across computing disciplines: computer science (CS), computer engineering (CE), information systems (IS), data science (DS), cyber security (CyS), information technology (IT) and software engineering (SE). After reading this chapter, the reader will be able to easily identify research problems and directions in hot emerging research fields.

9.1 Introduction

Right from the early stage, computing has been dynamic in nature, which was why conference publications took the center stage at first, because of the need to showcase the dynamics in the computing world. CS and IS are the oldest disciplines within the computing ecosystem. Currently, seven disciplines exist in the computing ecosystem focusing on different aspects of computing because of the technological advancement witnessed in recent years. The era of computing is experiencing dramatic changes as a result of technological advancement in different aspects of the computing ecosystem.

Technological development of hardware and software has reached an impressive level, improving education, daily life activities, the healthcare system, production,

doi:10.1088/978-0-7503-5017-4ch9

industries, etc (Mishra *et al* 2014). The drastic dynamics and challenges associated with innovations in the computing industry make it extremely difficult to correctly predict the future of the computer industry. The state-of-the-art is disruptive with just a few fractions of the innovations in the computer industry. Some of the innovations in the computer industry are ahead of their time or not cost effective or lack a market for them. There are innovations that were never adopted for use because other innovations arrived on the market at a better time to put the early innovation on the disadvantage side (IEEE Computer Society 2022).

It is computing advancements that give birth to projects, such as leading to the development of self-driving vehicles, quantum computing, developing robots that can build themselves, smart offices, with the biggest breakthrough in Singapore, flying cars, etc.

With computing advancements sustainable cities projects have sprung up across the world, such as Neom project in Saudi Arabia expected to cost over $500 billion, and housing the longest skyscraper of 170 km. There will be no cars and it will be zero carbon emissions. Malaysia is building biodiverCity without a car in the city where transportation is strictly autonomous water, air and land public transportation. Akon smart city in Senegal, to be powered by renewable energy, will house a technology hub. Blockchain and cryptocurrency will be used to stimulate the local economy. Telosa in USA is expected to house 5 million people and commuting in the city will take a maximum of 15 min, expected to be powered by renewable energy. Woven smart city in Japan is currently under construction by Toyota, where everything will be fully autonomously driven by artificial intelligence (AI) technology. A floating smart city is planned in the Maldives, which will be floating and resistant to climate change (Jalal 2022).

Computing research in obsolete, declining or exhausted research areas minimizes the impact of the research as the research community and grant awarding organizations are no long interested in the research area. Researchers, especially students and early career researchers, are often challenged in deciding the research area to start a research. Delving into research in an area that is already outdated or rapidly declining can put the researcher at a disadvantage, especially in seeking grants, a PhD/MSc proposal, journals or conference publications.

In this chapter, we intend to outline the emerging research areas in different computing disciplines: CS, SE, IS, DS, CyS, CE and IT. The emerging research areas are believed to have the potential that can shape the future of the computing world, which in turn changes the way people in society operate and interact with the environment. It can help students, new career researchers and expert researchers looking for hot research areas to easily identify research problems and future directions. The emerging research areas outlined and discussed in the chapter are not in any way exhaustive but can serve as a starting point.

9.2 Emerging research topics in computing

The emerging topics in different computing discipline ecosystems are presented in this section for readers to easily identify the trends in computing. For each of the disciplines, a taxonomy is created to show a visual representation of the emerging research topics. Those emerging research areas presented for each of the disciplines in the taxonomy are not in any way exhaustive, as earlier stated in the introduction section, but provide an overview of some major areas. Current global research trends cause research to be interwoven between disciplines. As a result of that, a particular research area from any of the computing disciplines can be tackled from different perspectives. In our taxonomy, massively open online courses (MOOCs) is under IS as the domicile domain. However, a research problem in MOOCs can be tackled from the perspective of CS, IS, CyS, etc depending on the nature of the problem, or a team can be formed with members from different disciplines to tackle a particular research problem. For example, it was argued by Uddin *et al* (2021) that deep learning and natural language process in combination with analytics and ontology design can be an excellent technology in solving research challenges in MOOCs. Another example, assisted transportation solutions can be developed from the perspective of CS, SE or CE. Similarly, additive manufacturing challenges can be tackled from the perspective of SE, CE, CS, etc. However, the additive manufacturing is domiciled in CE. The next subsections discuss emerging research trends in different disciplines.

9.2.1 Computer science

This section presents the emerging research areas in computer science. The research areas discussed in this section are trending in the literature with a lot of research opportunities. Figure 9.1 represents the visualization of emerging research areas.

9.2.1.1 Artificial intelligence
AI is the machine that operates based on natural intelligence to solve problems intelligently. It has witnessed tremendous attention from the industry and academia. AI has penetrated different domains for solving challenging problems that

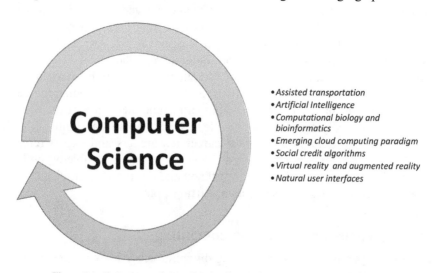

• Assisted transportation
• Artificial Intelligence
• Computational biology and bioinformatics
• Emerging cloud computing paradigm
• Social credit algorithms
• Virtual reality and augmented reality
• Natural user interfaces

Figure 9.1. Taxonomy of the emerging research areas in computer science.

conventional methods fail to solve, and incredible results have been recorded. Under AI, we group any topic related to AI that is found in the different IEEE Computer Society reports on the prediction of technology trends: computer vision and pattern recognition; adversarial machine learning (ML); the challenges of safety and reliability in dealing with intelligent systems; cognitive skills for robots; medical robots and AI for critical systems. All these are emerging topics worth exploring by researchers to further develop the AI research area.

9.2.1.2 Social credit algorithms

These are a set of algorithms that try to identify an individual based on biometric traits with the purpose of collecting data about the individuals from digital platforms and social media with the aim to grant or reject access to online (IEEE Computer Society 2019). The Chinese government has been at the forefront of implementing these algorithms since the early 2000s. The so-called 'Social Credit System' is believed to fundamentally transform the life of Chinese citizens (Mac Síthigh and Siems 2019). The Social Credit System is expected to function encompassing mechanisms in the public and private platforms. It rewards individuals who engage the system with good behavior while punishing those with bad behavior, including businesses and professional sectors. China's Social Credit System is attracting much interest from the research community and developers (Kshetri 2020).

9.2.1.3 Assisted transportation

The vision of fully self-driving vehicles is at an advanced stage, and it could fully be operated in public spaces in a few years. Full automation of vehicles is taking place in both public and personal vehicles. Assisted transportation acceptability and usefulness will usher in the development of self-driving vehicles (IEEE Computer Society 2019). Already there are great efforts from different perspectives in improving the effectiveness and efficiency of the autonomous vehicles with remarkable achievements. Despite the achievements recorded, a lot of unresolved challenges still exist, creating gaps for further research opportunities (Gidado *et al* 2020).

9.2.1.4 Virtual reality and augmented reality

Recent decades have witnessed different technologies related to virtual reality and augmented reality. A popular example is the game called Pokemon Go. The game has the ability to create a fictional object in the real-world environment using the camera of a smartphone (IEEE Computer Society 2019). Several areas for future research in virtual reality and augmented reality exist, such as the issues of accessibility, physical and virtual settings interplay, etc (Scavarelli *et al* 2021). Haptic technologies in mobile augmented reality require improvement. Some of the challenges include design, network requirements for future mobile augmented reality application, design for the elderly and visually impaired people, etc (Bermejo and Hui 2021).

9.2.1.5 Next generation cloud computing

Cloud computing represents the infrastructure as a '*cloud*' which is provisioned as-a-service to businesses and users where they access applications across the globe on demand over the internet (Buyya *et al* 2009). The next generation of cloud computing was proposed to deviate from the conventional cloud computing limitations. It is intended to bring computing nearer to the users compared to conventional cloud computing to improve quality of services and experiences from the side of users. Emerging cloud computing architecture includes serverless, volunteer, edge, software-defined networks and fog (Buyya *et al* 2018). The emerging cloud computing requires a lot of research efforts to develop the research area (Jauro *et al* 2020).

9.2.1.6 *Natural user interfaces*

The application of natural user interfaces for devices is increasingly becoming mainstream because the interaction of humans with devices has become more natural as people interact with devices using natural gestures. As a result of that, embedding sensors, a powerful processor, device connectivity with the environment become much easier (Norman 2010). The natural user interface becomes reality because of the researches conducted in the area of big data, computer vision, natural language processing, machine learning, speech recognition and user interfaces for years, which makes it possible for the development of the software that runs these technologies. The computer applications that have adopted the natural user interface need to address the following challenges: predictive, anticipatory, adaptive, contextual awareness, multisensory input, language and inference, and augmented reality (IEEE Computer Society 2022). These challenges can form bases for future research directions in new perspectives.

9.2.1.7 *Computational biology and bioinformatics*

The application of computation in biological systems ranging from analysis, collection of data and modeling has been increasing for decades because of its significance. Computational biology and bioinformatics are two distinct research fields sharply divided based on data collection and analysis. Genomic bioinformatics currently occupies a very wide area in the research field, whereas bioinformatics and computational biology remain broad areas (IEEE Computer Society 2022). Template-free protein structure prediction is still an open research problem in computational biology (Outeiral *et al* 2021). Despite the progress made in the area of bioinformatics, many problems remain unresolved (Chiroma *et al* 2020). Research directions from the perspective of quantum computing for solving challenges in computational biology are provided in Outeiral *et al* (2021). Managing and analysis of the explosive growth in genomic data constitute a challenge (IEEE Computer Society 2022). It will be interesting for researchers to explore the untapped areas of computational biology and bioinformatics to develop the research field.

9.2.2 Computer engineering

CE is another discipline domiciled in the computing ecosystems with different emerging research areas. The research areas extracted from the literature for CE are shown in figure 9.2.

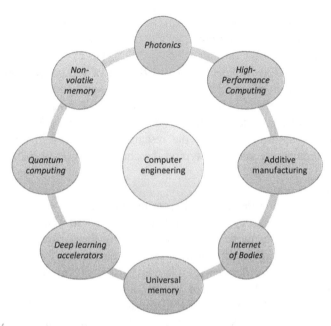

Figure 9.2. Emerging research areas in computer engineering.

9.2.2.1 Deep learning accelerators

These are architectures purposely designed and optimized to enhance efficiency and speed of computers running deep learning models. These include graphics processing units (GPUs), field-programmable gate arrays (FPGAs), and more recently tensor processing units (TPUs). There are different companies that have set out to design the accelerators for use in data centres. Edge devices can also use the accelerators. This development will facilitate the operation of smart devices incorporating ML to be used in internet of things (IoT) devices and appliances (IEEE Computer Society 2019). It was found that running deep learning on TPUs outperforms the GPU and CPU (You *et al* 2019). Embedded intelligence (EI) is a trending research field that aims at combining ML and intelligent decision-making into mobile devices and embedded systems. Hardware accelerators for energy efficient neural networks are considering the use of FPGA-based EI solutions instead of solely relying on software solutions. However, to ensure efficient practical use of FPGA-based EI solutions, there is the need to address the issue of high computing cost and energy efficiency. In addition, the scalability for different network size and topologies requires further work to address the issues (Seng *et al* 2021). The acceleration of large artificial neural networks processing can best be performed by the FPGAs. Automated partitioning tools and resource-rich FPGAs should be made available (Mittal 2020). Researches in this direction, especially EI, is recommended for researchers to explore.

9.2.2.2 High-performance computing

High performance computing (HPC) comprises hardware, software, tools and services. From the perspective of the hardware, the HPC is designed to have farms of processors for intensive processing, large-scale memories and interconnection that match up low latency and high bandwidth requirements. The new level of scale has the challenge of programming models (IEEE Computer Society 2022). The extreme heterogeneity of the architectural specialization is expected to end the era of the conventional technology scaling (Shalf 2020). It is believe that the metal–oxide–semiconductor (CMOS) circuits are approaching physical limits, however, the non-volatile memory (NVM) inspired neuro computing chips are making inroads and are promising. This development has prompted tremendous attention from the research community in making efforts to develop device engineering and prototyping the chip (Zhang *et al* 2020).

9.2.2.3 Internet of bodies

The IoT-based monitoring devices are becoming more commonplace and promising, and convenience and efficiency for businesses are improved. The people using these technologies are becoming more comfortable in using them either on or inside their bodies. Consumers now find it convenient to use external devices for self-tracking as well as using augmented reality devices for playing games. However, there are areas of concern for users such as the issues of security and privacy, possibility of physically harming the user, and lastly, abuses (IEEE Computer Society 2019). Therefore, research in IoT security, privacy and safety remain the focus (Ogonji *et al* 2020, Alferidah and Jhanjhi 2020). Future researches are expected to explore the area of security and privacy, physical harm, safety and abuses related to the use of external devices for self-tracking.

9.2.2.4 Non-volatile memory

It expected that in the future, NVM Express (NVMe) solid state drives (SSDs) can be substituted with SATA and SAS SSDs and the dominant protocol for network storage will be NVMe-oF (IEEE Computer Society 2020). The emerging NVM block is used as a buffer pool for database extension. Experimental results have revealed that the NVM block device produces 75% higher performance (Yang *et al* 2021). The challenge associated with dynamic random-access memory (DRAM) in consumer devices is efficiently handled by the emerging NVMs. This finding will open up opportunities for the optimization of hardware and software in a device developed based on future NVM (Oliveira *et al* 2021).

9.2.2.5 Additive manufacturing

The production of special purpose components and prototype has dominated 3D printing since the advent of the 3D printer in the 1980s. 3D printing is currently coming into mainstream manufacturing, especially mass production of customized components because of the advancement in hardware, processes, software, materials and workflow. In the case where the production of a large volume of unique components is required, additive manufacturing is cost effective compared to conventional manufacturing. For example, thousands of customized molds are being produced daily by SmileDirect company using 3D printing for making orthodontic aligners for different individuals (IEEE Computer Society 2020). By 2030, Dubai will have used this technology to construct about 25% of its buildings, and 3D printing is expected to be adopted in other countries. The cost of infrastructure is the major barrier in the adoption of large-scale 3D printing (Hossain *et al* 2020). Research and development on additive manufacturing leading to cost effective 3D printing in the future is required. Researchers can focus on the 3D design, modeling, material, quality control and construction to produce cost effective 3D printing machines.

9.2.2.6 Quantum computing

The principle of quantum theory has motivated the concept of quantum computing and is expected to offer higher computational capabilities significantly better than the existing supercomputers. Both industry and the academic research community have delved into developing the pioneer quantum machine in the world. Research and development on the development of the largest quantum machine is already an active race among the technology giants (e.g. IBM, Microsoft, Google and Intel) and start-ups that are ambitious (e.g. IonQ and Rigetti) (Gill *et al* 2022). There is tremendous potential using quantum computing technologies for future computations and communications (Gyongyosi and Imre 2019). The challenges facing quantum computing are as follows: design, fault-tolerant and reliability; large number of physical qubits; energy consumption; and high cost (Gill *et al* 2022). These areas from quantum computing can form the bases for future research from different perspectives of computing.

9.2.2.7 Universal memory

It is predicted that there will be a tremendous change in the IT infrastructure, especially in the architectures of memory and processors within the next five years. By 2022, it is expected that a new form of NVM will replace DRAM. This new 'universal memory' will possess the non-volatility properties of Flash and the fast random-access characteristics of DRAM. While it cannot be said when and how this transition will take place, it is definite and the signs are already being manifested (IEEE Computer Society 2020). Research in this direction may likely spring up in the future.

9.2.2.8 Photonics

The technology in silicon photonics has introduced an improved CMOS-compatibility with the capability to deviate from the bottlenecks associated with the conventional CPU and GPU like the CMOS scaling slowdown. Silicon photonics performs better than the metallic interconnection for data transmission because it doesn't scale properly and causes inefficient bandwidth, latency and energy in the conventional processor (Sunny *et al* 2021). Silicon photonic technology is promising for interconnection fabrics that has different performance characteristics compared to the solutions by the CMOS. With silicon photonics, lower power and higher bandwidth density can be achieved as well as eliminating the link-length restrictions associated with the electronic interconnects (IEEE Computer Society 2022). Researchers at the Technical University of Denmark have demonstrated the transfer of data for 1.84 petabits/second over 7.9 km (4.9 miles) using a photonic chip connected via fiber-optic cable. This is compared to the approximately 1 petabit/second internet bandwidth used by the global population (Tyson 2022). Energy efficiency in many core computing areas with silicon photonics has been receiving attention over the years. There are lots of open research opportunities in energy efficiency in many core computing areas that can be explored (Pasricha and Nikdast 2020). A novel package for photonic devices is needed to allow the large number of single-mode connections for the waveguide to be placed between the photonic device and the subassemblies. Therefore, research and development into technologies like the packaging and connector and waveguide need further exploration (IEEE Computer Society 2022). The area of silicon photonic device reliability is a promising research direction to improve the reliability of the device. Thus, urgent research is required to develop energy efficient and high speed controllers for the photonic neural networks. To achieve improved resolution for photonic deep learning accelerator, further research in crosstalk mitigation, noise correction and resilience is highly required. Scalable photonic accelerator design is an additional area that requires extensive research to explore it (Sunny *et al* 2021).

9.2.3 Cyber security

There are different emerging research areas in CyS that deserve the attention of researchers to explore. The CyS solutions can be developed from different perspectives to protect enterprise systems from hackers and saboteurs. Figure 9.3 is the taxonomy of the emerging research areas in CyS as extracted from the literature.

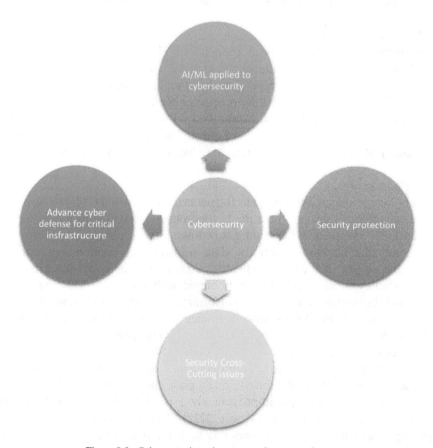

Figure 9.3. Cyber security science emerging research areas.

9.2.3.1 Advanced cyber defense for critical infrastructure

The need to protect critical infrastructure from different forms of cyber attacks has continued to be critical and requires urgent responses and solutions. The development of innovative cyber defense mechanisms can mitigate emerging cyber weapons with capacity to cause physical harm on a massive scale, intrusion and the critical infrastructural systems failure (PR Newswire 2020). The most targeted cyber attacks in recent years have been focusing on critical infrastructures from all sides of industry (Chowdhury and Gkioulos 2021). The proliferation of IoT devices and the control of critical infrastructure, medical devices, experimental equipment, and data collection introduces vulnerabilities due to hacking or bugs. Digital vulnerabilities on the other hand, escalate destruction or disabling of infrastructure such as power sources, water sources, ground transportation, dams, air traffic, hospitals, military bases/equipment, shipping and environmental monitoring. Therefore, improved IoT cyber security is required to protect the critical infrastructure (IEEE Computer Society 2021). In recent years, the need for protecting critical infrastructure from cyber intrusion attacks has become a hot research area that requires more urgency (Panagiotis *et al* 2021).

9.2.3.2 Applications of artificial intelligence in cyber security

CyS science is paramount to any business today because of its vulnerability to risks. This is due to the growing concern about different cyber attacks like threats from amateurs, distributed denial of service (DDoS), that is, sophisticated and nation-state actors with skills. To counter these attacks from different threats, there is the need for cyber security analysts. The number of cyber security experts is not adequate for the growing demand. In addition, there is lack of sufficient cyber security training and the turnover rate is high. The innovative applications of AI/ML are a promising solution in the detection of security threats and are helping security analysts to take decisions by offering informed recommendations (IEEE Computer Society 2020). Therefore, research should be conducted on improving current CyS training (Chowdhury and Gkioulos 2021). Also, novel security protection solutions for AI should be explored in the future (Li 2018). The development of an autonomous CyS defense mechanism based on AI/ML with capacity to stop cyber attacks in progress should be the focus of the next generation research on CyS defense systems. The use of AI/MLS in CyS threat response is an underexplored research area (Kamoun *et al* 2020).

9.2.3.3 Security cross-cutting issues

Individuals, private and public entities are concerned with the emergence of powerful forces. These forces can make groups, businesses and people rethink before making certain information available to merchants, the government and citizens in view of the fact that there may be consequences. The first force is considered to be the large-scale data that is growing at an exponential rate containing both corporate and personal information. The second force is the subjecting of the data to analytics with enhanced capability to detect different patterns. The third force refers to the technological advancement in the collection of a variety of data about citizens, government and non-governmental organizations from various sources. These data can be generated from personal activities, commercial transactions, people and assets mobility, and the relationships that exist with businesses. Institutional and crowd sourcing of information is the fourth force expected to be the pioneer exploration of such data and it can have an impact on society. Finally, it is the growing capacity of intruders/hackers to hack into information about businesses, critical infrastructure and people. These intruders/hackers can be insiders working in government agencies, criminals, enemies of individuals and businesses, and malcontents. Combining all these forces needs the issue of privacy and security to be a tradeoff in making decision. Thus, striking a balance between security and privacy cutting across the forces enumerated above is a challenge because different forces require a different level of privacy and security, therefore, it is an interesting research area to explore for researchers (IEEE Computer Society 2022).

9.2.3.4 Security protection

The conventional techniques for protecting computer systems are mostly passive and involve the utilization of a mechanism for protection like anti-virus software. However, the anti-virus protection software is relegated to the background as the hackers/intruders advance their skills as a result of technological advancement and effectiveness of the protection mechanism decreasing. To mitigate such challenges, new security features such as hook are embedded to detect new forms of attacks. In addition, ML-based detection systems can adapt to detect advanced attacks automatically. Although attacking the security attacker is technologically possible, it is discouraged because it is almost always illegal (IEEE Computer Society 2019). Therefore, researchers are recommended to propose new protection mechanisms with the ability to detect sophisticated attacks while maintaining ethical issues.

9.2.4 Software engineering

As already explained, SE can be applied in different aspects of computing research areas. Figure 9.4 presents the taxonomy of the areas classified under SE for the purpose of this chapter. Only the digital twins and SE in ML systems are discussed

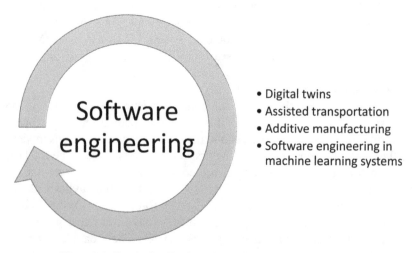

Figure 9.4. Simple classification of emerging research areas in SE.

because assisted transportation and additive manufacturing were already discussed in the previous sections. SE plays a critical role in assisted transportation and additive manufacturing.

9.2.4.1 Digital twins

A digital twin is a model of a physical entity, product or process including humans. It is a software representation with the purpose to study, understand, predict, and optimize performance for improved business outcomes. The characteristics that are selected to be represented digitally depend on the purpose for which the twin is proposed to achieve. The adoption of digital twins by many companies is on the rise with 48% of companies in the IoTs community already implementing it. This includes digital twins for very large complex entities such as an entire smart city (for example, Digital Singapore). Digital twins are expected to transform the healthcare sector within the next three years (IEEE Computer Society 2019). Digital twins, being an incipient technology, comes with certain technical and domain-dependent challenges that require exploration and further study. Although digital twin technology depends on IoTs, ML and data at the same time, a seamless integration of all these leads to the powerful and efficient product that makes up digital twins (Sharma *et al* 2022). There are research opportunities that can be explored for future developments in digital twins technology (Mihai *et al* 2022).

9.2.4.2 Software engineering in machine learning based systems

ML-based systems are already penetrating society, changing the way people interact with the environment. However, there have been reported cases of ML-based system malfunctions and catastrophic failure leading to loss of investment and life in some instances. The constant failure of ML-based systems across different projects is a call for concern among the stakeholders. For example, an investment of $60 million was lost because of poor outcome from a project for IBM's oncology expert advisor. To mitigate these failures, it is proposed to introduce SE techniques such as explicit requirements elicitation, testing, and continuous integration that has been established for the last 50 years to build reliable, robust, fair and safe ML-based systems (Isbell *et al* 2023). It was reported that a software team in Microsoft developed an AI-based application (Amershi *et al* 2019). The balance between ML and SE best practice that can lead to a successful ML-based project is a promising research direction for researchers to explore.

9.2.5 Information systems, information technology and data science

This section present taxonomy for different disciplines: IS, IT and DS because the classifications are few and can be accommodated in a single taxonomy. Here, only big data analytics and MOOCs are discussed as others were discussed in the preceding sections. Figure 9.5 depicts the emerging research areas in the different disciplines.

9.2.5.1 Big data analytics

There is an increasing volume of data being uploaded on the internet every day and there is demand for intelligent inferences and gaining insight from the data. This has

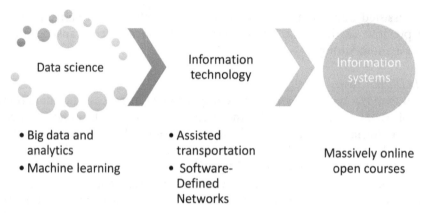

Figure 9.5. Emerging research areas in IS, IT and DS.

made big data analytics a promising research area to enhance business decision making. However, while benefiting from the advantages of big data analytics, there is a need for special consideration on the significant challenges it poses on both societal and technological aspects. Drastic transformation in data collection, storage and processing is posing new challenges as the result of unprecedented generation of data, thus, these challenges such as complex privacy issues should be addressed to harness the surge of data to beneficial use (IEEE Computer Society 2022). Research on personal data regarding ethics, legal and privacy concerns is recommended to researchers (Hassani *et al* 2020).

9.2.5.2 Massively open online courses

MOOCs is an online learning platform for disseminating knowledge to thousands of students. The university high quality course content delivery is free without payment; only access to the internet and a device is required to enroll in the online classroom. MOOCs is also an avenue for courses on continuing education with credit-bearing undergraduate courses. Enrolment in MOOCs leads to degree programs and graduation (IEEE Computer Society 2022). There are basically three areas of research identified by the discussion forum of MOOCs: participant's behavior and course learning outcome; content analysis, monitoring and organization; and interaction among learners. This brings to light some of the research opportunities that are promising and innovative that if properly harnessed can develop the research area and further make MOOCs a better platform for teaching and learning (Almatrafi and Johri 2018). Therefore, researchers are recommended to conduct research from different perspectives in MOOCs with the aim of improving the entire platform.

9.3 Selected research problems

Research problems are selected for researchers to easily identify them for developing a research area. Continued development of research can help in solving real-world problems that can lead to practical applications. The next subsections present the discussion of different research problems from different emerging research areas.

9.3.1 New generation artificial neural networks

There are limitations on using the conventional ML techniques for the processing of natural data without automatic pre-processing. For years it has been the practice in building an ML system to conduct thorough feature engineering requiring an expert in the field under study to extract the relevant and required features for transforming the raw data suitable for processing by the ML algorithm. ML has transformed different aspects of society such as the recommender system embedded in e-commerce websites, web search, and social media content filtering. In addition, ML has empowered products such as cameras and smartphones. The systems developed based on ML can be used for speech transcribing into text, matching the interests of users to news items or products, identifying objects in images, and selecting relevant results of search. The most successful ML technique called deep learning is the new generation artificial neural network that has gained tremendous popularity compared to the conventional ML because of its ability to automatically classify raw data without going through the stress of manual data engineering. Deep learning is expected to develop in the future because it has automated data engineering capability and offers an improvement in performance with an increase in volume of data. Therefore, it can process the increasing volume of data as a result of computation. The new architectures and learning algorithms in the process of development currently can enhanced the progress of deep learning for processing a voluminous amount of data (LeCun *et al* 2015). The new elements introduced into artificial neural networks in the early 2000s ignited the interest of the research community on deep learning architecture of the artificial neural network. The new elements added make it simple to train deep learning architecture. The availability of a voluminous amount of data and the technological advancements that lead to the development of GPUs are enhancing the interest in deep learning. Open source platforms such as TensorFlow, PyTorch, Caffe, Theano and Torch for the running of the deep learning architecture are opening up a lot of opportunities for deep learning to be explored. A perception task such as speech and object detection typically records success with the deep learning architecture in view of the fact that the many layers in deep learning architecture allow complex nonlinearities (Bengio *et al* 2021). The effective and efficient hardware platform for the training of convolutional neural networks is the GPU (Stoica *et al* 2014). The GPU was initially developed for the processing of graphics before being re-designed as general purpose massive parallel processor. Frameworks like CUDA allow execution of various algorithms on the hardware platforms (Strigl *et al* 2010).

9.3.1.1 Fundamental deficiencies of deep learning

Despite the successes achieved by the deep learning systems, they still suffer from some deficiencies, as summarized in figure 9.6, that scaling alone cannot address. Compared to human intelligence, AI requires tremendous improvement. The following are the directions that need attention from the research

Figure 9.6. Summary of the challenges facing deep learning.

community for enhancement of the performance of deep learning models (Bengio *et al* 2021):

    i. There is need for large-scale data and many trials for training supervised learning and for model-free reinforcement learning to achieve success. However, humans can generalize very well without too much experience.

    ii. The deep learning model lacks robust distributed adaptation compared to humans that rapidly respond to adaptation with little exposure to experience.

    iii. Deep learning in its present state achieves success at perception tasks referred to as system 1 tasks. However, deep learning application in solving problems for system 2 tasks requires a sequence of steps that is deliberate; it is in an early stage and it is an interesting research area.

    iv. The ML community has the assumption that test cases are in distributed form as with training cases. But, in real-world applications, it is not feasible for the assumption to stand because of dynamics of the agents in the real-world environment that always expand the horizon as a result of new knowledge. For instance, the AI-based systems that perform excellently in the laboratory may perform poorly in the real-world environment.

9.3.2 Emerging Internet of Things research areas

Modern society has been penetrated by IoT with the objective of improving quality of life. The emerging IoT connects devices to become smart. The smart devices, applications and technologies are connected for improving the ways humans interact in society for quality of life (Al-Fuqaha *et al* 2015). The science community has embraced the fact that forensics is critical in our world today. As such, studies have acknowledged the relevance of forensics tools to be connected to the IoT domain. At the same time, it is important to maintain the legality and principles of forensics for extracting and preserving electronic evidence that is admissible. Acceptable security regulations and agreed standards require IoT systems explicitly. Therefore, an inter-disciplinary approach cutting across research, business and law needs to collaborate to expand the development of IoT as challenges are expected to expand continuously (Stoyanova *et al* 2020). Federated learning (FL) is a distributed ML approach developed for preserving privacy and scalability services and applications for IoT. The combination of FL and IoT has ignited new directions for research and is still ongoing, expected to drastically improve privacy protection in the FL–IoT-based systems with new innovative privacy protection solutions. The FL–IoT systems aim to provide privacy to clients like the IoT device and communications such as the wireless server–client links (Nguyen *et al* 2021). In IoT applications, top priority is given to privacy and security before considering the issue of performance, management and reliability. The IoT protocols and standards in different layers require optimization. Advanced analytic algorithms and tools suitable for the processing of big data generated and collected from IoT are required to advance the applications of IoT (Al-Fuqaha *et al* 2015).

9.3.3 The role of emerging 6G in unmanned aerial vehicle cellular communications

Compared to 5G, 6G is expected to offer ultra-reliable C2 and aerial passengers with high-speed connectivity at the same time to swarms of unmanned aerial vehicles possessing 3D localization. Attention of industry and academia is now focusing on the five major disruptive innovations that are anticipated to be part of mobile systems in the future such as: architectures without cell; pervasive application of AI; non-terrestrial networks; deployment of reconfigurable intelligent surfaces; and communication at the frequencies of THz. Commuting will be redefined by self-driving cars as a service as well as flying taxis. Thus, the new commuting system can redefined where people live and work with great opportunities for the entrepreneur as the societal implication of the emerging commuting system. In the near future of the 2020s decade, the public road will witness the launch of autonomous driving vehicles. Thus, transit will be from from semi-autonomous vehicles to fully autonomous vehicles moving to every part of society without human driver intervention. In the 2030s, it is projected that we will witness flying cars overcoming traffic congestion all autonomously powered by 6G mobile communication systems connectivity. However, challenges such as the issue of regulation for safety, concern over noise pollution and the required infrastructure are militating against the smooth takeoff of the new mobility projects. Already more than 100 cities across the globe are targeting flying mobility with many companies executing projects to make flying mobility a reality in the urban community, targeting a $1.5 trillion market by the year 2040 (Geraci *et al* 2022).

The unmanned aerial vehicles communication system is to be modeled and enhanced by AI: future communication systems are targeting higher bands having more antennas and AI-based modeling, design and operations to usher in a new paradigm. Future research about unmanned aerial vehicles communication systems for development is required in the following areas (Geraci *et al* 2022):

- Presently there is a lack of statistical aerial models operating at high frequency. Therefore, generative networks modeling for air-to-ground channel spatial consistency is needed.
- The unmanned aerial vehicles travelling at high speed require ML-based systems that can predict the time series to minimize the need for acquiring high frequency channel state information.
- It is necessary to sufficiently tackle high unmanned aerial vehicles mobility. Thus, an ML-based system for mobility management and allocation of radio resources dynamically is required.
- Lack of voluminous unmanned aerial vehicles data: the design and operation of unmanned aerial vehicles networks based on AI requires a voluminous dataset.

9.3.4 Nature inspired algorithms for global optimization problem

Conducting research in Nature inspired algorithms for problem solving has been filling the literature with a variety of new Nature inspired algorithms since the pioneering algorithms appeared in the 1970s and 1990s. The pioneer algorithms include genetic algorithm, particle swarm optimization, simulated annealing, ant colony and tabu search. Over 300 such algorithms exist including smarm-intelligence-based algorithms and evolutionary (Ezugwu *et al* 2021). Particle swarm optimization has the popular smart algorithms for solving numerical association rule mining problem. Other algorithms that solve similar problems include ant colony and Cat Swarm Optimization, Bat Algorithm. Making software frameworks and source code for the algorithms freely available can help advance the execution of the algorithms in solving issues in the real world and implementation in society (Fister and Fister 2021). The performance of those meta-heuristic algorithms heavily depends on parameter settings and no systematic framework for realizing the optimum parameters. We recommend researchers to propose parameter-free Nature inspired algorithms (meaning an algorithm whose performance does not depend on parameters).

9.3.5 Software requirement engineering for blockchain applications

Stakeholders' (ranging from blockchain engineers to real IT experts) orientation viewpoint in the blockchain application is required during the software requirement engineering practice. As such, a communication gap is created in the conventional techniques. Therefore, the software requirement engineering modeling for the blockchain application from the perspective of the blockchain stakeholders is highly needed for the improvement of the blockchain lifecycle. The lack of empirical studies in the domain makes it a challenge for the software requirement engineering practitioners to really understand the requirement tools, and criteria for the selection of the requirements of the blockchain application are needed to advance it for stakeholders. The publications of software requirement engineering for blockchain are limited as the area is still in the early stages of development. Therefore, massive studies in this area are needed for effective comprehension of the domain core rudiments and modules. The development of blockchain requires the involvement of both technical stakeholders and non-technical stakeholders more than many of the traditional forms of software development. Stakeholders have diverse goals, cooperation, stewardship, incentives and engagement at different levels. Future research is required at the level of the blockchain technical analysis for the framework on software requirement engineering (Farooq *et al* 2022).

9.3.6 Network security

9.3.6.1 *DoS/DDoS attacks in software-defined networks*
There are areas that require further research to mitigate denial of service (DoS) and DDoS attacks (DoS/DDoS) in software-defined networks that are discussed below (Eliyan and Di Pietro 2021).

First, only a limited number of cyber attacks solution mainly focuses on working under attacks situation or preventing the attacks. Cyber solutions mainly concentrated on detection or attack mitigation. Detection or mitigation of attacks is inferior compares to prevention of attacks while the network operates under the attacks. In such a prevention approach, it stopes the attack from propagation in the network and subsequent consumption of the network resources before detection and mitigation triggering is needed. In summary the preventive approach is more robust with capacity to operate under cyber attacks and subsequently survive the attacks. Therefore, focus should be on the preventive solutions rather than detection and mitigation. Secondly, the use of lightweight approach should be the focus in the future. The lightweight approach uses statistical driven approach to the solution in which the status of the network can be identified in view of the fact that the resource consumed can be measured as well as the request received. Thirdly, the approach that identified client identity should be a new direction for research because only limited works focus on it for DoS/DDoS attack solution. The approach has the advantage of simultaneously reducing efforts required for the detection and mitigation of attacks while maintaining the network services availability (Eliyan and Di Pietro 2021).

9.3.6.2 *Exploring anomaly-supervisory signals*
Deep anomaly detection key component is informative signal for learning the scores or representation of the anomaly accurately. Learning the representation has been explored by using unsupervised or self-supervise signals in which the major issue in the formulation is the objective function that is generic not tailored specifically for the detection of anomaly. The issue of measure dependent learning of the features for anomaly can be addressed by the imposition of conventional anomaly measure constraints. Unfortunately, there are challenges facing these constraints such as the anomaly measures implicit assumptions. As such, it is sacrosanct to explore alternative sources of the anomaly-supervisory signals to deviate from the limitations of the widely use data reconstruction and generative adversarial network that have weak assumption on the distribution of the anomaly. Large-scale normality

learning is another area in anomaly detection that requires attention despite the successes recorded especially for large-scale learning in the domain with a challenge of getting sufficient labeled dataset (Pang *et al* 2021).

9.4 Artificial intelligence future prediction

Figure 9.7 depicts technology success against the impact on humanity for different research areas predicted as the future research direction by the IEEE computer society technology prediction for 2023. It clearly indicates that AI is at the forefront of the technology development success expected to dominate the world of technology in the future. This is because AI has the highest number of related research areas, as shown in figure 9.7.

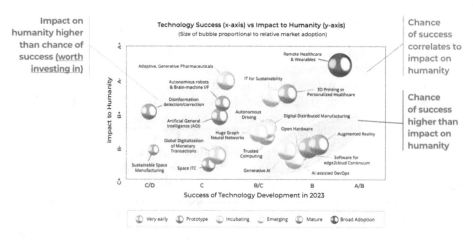

Figure 9.7. Technology success versus impact to humanity. Copyright IEEE. Reprinted with permission from Computer Society (2023).

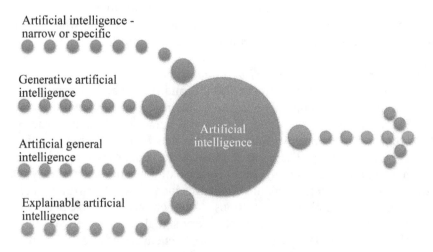

Figure 9.8. Types of artificial intelligence.

Therefore, heavy investment in AI by different organizations, research institutes, academia and companies is expected. However, the AI research areas in figure 9.7 listed as follows: autonomous robots and brain–machine interface; AI assisted DevOps; generative AI; adaptive, generative pharmaceuticals; autonomous driving; artificial general intelligence; and huge graph neural network, can be categorized into one or more of the different types of AI depicted in figure 9.8.

9.5 Summary

Computing is an evolving discipline with frequent new innovations from different perspectives of technological advancement to improve computing. Research conducted in emerging and trending topics maximizes the impact of the research. On the other hand, research in obsolete or declining or exhausted research areas minimizes the impact of the research as the research community and grant awarding organizations are no long interested in the research area. This chapter presents the emerging research areas from different computing ecosystem disciplines such as CS, SE, IS, DS, CyS, CE and IT. We created taxonomy of the emerging research areas from different disciplines for postgraduate students, new career researchers, post-doctoral fellows, industry practitioners and many others to easily identify hot areas that require research and development leading to practical applications. In addition, we selected some research problems in survey/review/systematic literature review (SLR) papers published in top computing journals cutting across the computing disciplines. The reader can decide to choose from the available hot research topics to develop SLR and develop problem formulation or select research problems from the available areas outlined in the chapter. Lastly, the future of AI is predicted.

References

Al-Fuqaha A, Guizani M, Mohammadi M, Aledhari M and Ayyash M 2015 Internet of Things: a survey on enabling technologies, protocols, and applications *IEEE Commun. Surv. Tutor.* **17** 2347–76

Alferidah D K and Jhanjhi N Z 2020 A review on security and privacy issues and challenges in Internet of Things *Int. J. Comput. Sci. Netw. Secur.* **20** 263–86

Almatrafi O and Johri A 2018 Systematic review of discussion forums in massive open online courses (MOOCs) *IEEE Trans. Learn. Technol.* **12** 413–28

Amershi S, Begel A, Bird C, DeLine R, Gall H, Kamar E, Nagappan N, Nushi B and Zimmermann T 2019 Software engineering for machine learning: a case study *2019 IEEE/ACM 41st Int. Conf. on Software Engineering: Software Engineering in Practice (ICSE-SEIP)* (Piscataway, NJ: IEEE) 291–300

Bengio Y, Lecun Y and Hinton G 2021 Deep learning for AI *Commun. ACM* **64** 58–65

Bermejo C and Hui P 2021 A survey on haptic technologies for mobile augmented reality *ACM Comput. Surv.* **54** 1–35

Buyya R, Yeo C S, Venugopal S, Broberg J and Brandic I 2009 Cloud computing and emerging IT platforms: vision, hype, and reality for delivering computing as the 5th utility *Future Gener. Comput. Syst.* **25** 599–616

Buyya R *et al* 2018 A manifesto for future generation cloud computing: research directions for the next decade *ACM Comput. Surv.* **51** 1–38

Chiroma H, Usman A M, Jauro F, Gabralla L A, Adewole K S, Dada E G, Shittu F, Umar A Y, Okesola J O and Oludele A 2020 Deep learning solutions for protein: recent development and future directions *Int. Conf. on Emerging Applications and Technologies for Industry 4.0 (2020, July)* (Berlin: Springer) 254–71

Chowdhury N and Gkioulos V 2021 Cyber security training for critical infrastructure protection: a literature review *Comput. Sci. Rev.* **40** 100361

Eliyan L F and Di Pietro R 2021 DoS and DDoS attacks in software defined networks: a survey of existing solutions and research challenges *Future Gener. Comput. Syst.* **122** 149–71

Ezugwu A E, Shukla A K, Nath R, Akinyelu A A, Agushaka J O, Chiroma H and Muhuri P K 2021 Metaheuristics: a comprehensive overview and classification along with bibliometric analysis *Artif. Intell. Rev.* **54** 4237–316

Farooq M S, Ahmed M and Emran M 2022 A survey on blockchain acquainted software requirements engineering: model, opportunities, challenges, and future directions *IEEE Access* **10** 48193–8228

Fister I Jr and Fister I 2021 A brief overview of swarm intelligence-based algorithms for numerical association rule mining *Applied Optimization and Swarm IntelligenceSpringer Tracts in Nature-Inspired Computing* ed E Osaba and X S Yang (Singapore: Springer) pp 47–59

Geraci G, Garcia-Rodriguez A, Azari M M, Lozano A, Mezzavilla M, Chatzinotas S, Chen Y, Rangan S and Di Renzo M 2022 What will the future of UAV cellular communications be? A flight from 5G to 6G *IEEE Commun. Surv. Tutor.* **24** 1304–35

Gidado U M, Chiroma H, Aljojo N, Abubakar S, Popoola S I and Al-Garadi M A 2020 A survey on deep learning for steering angle prediction in autonomous vehicles *IEEE Access* **8** 163797–817

Gill S S, Kumar A, Singh H, Singh M, Kaur K, Usman M and Buyya R 2022 Quantum computing: a taxonomy, systematic review and future directions *Softw. Pract. Exper.* **52** 66–114

Gyongyosi L and Imre S 2019 A survey on quantum computing technology *Comput. Sci. Rev.* **31** 51–71

Hossain M A, Zhumabekova A, Paul S C and Kim J R 2020 A review of 3D printing in construction and its impact on the labor market *Sustainability* **12** 8492

Hassani H, Beneki C, Unger S, Mazinani M T and Yeganegi M R 2020 Text mining in big data analytics *Big Data Cogn. Comput.* **4** 1

IEEE Computer Society 2019 *IEEE Computer Society Technology prediction 2020* https:// computer.org/publications/tech-news/trends/IEEE-Computer-Society-Predicts-the-Future-of-Tech-Top-10-Technology-Trends-for-2019 (accessed 20 October 2022)

IEEE Computer Society 2020 https://www.computer.org/2021-top-technology-predictions?source=pressrelease Available online (accessed 20 October 2022)

IEEE Computer Society 2021 *IEEE Computer Society Technology prediction 2022* https://ieeecs-media.computer.org/media/tech-news/tech-predictions-report-2022.pdf available online (accessed 20 October 2022)

IEEE Computer Society 2022 *IEEE Computer Society Technology prediction 2023* https:// computer.org/2022-top-technology-predictions/ (accessed 20 October 2022)

IEEE Computer Society 2023 *IEEE Computer Society Technology prediction 2023* https:// computer.org/2022-top-technology-predictions/ (accessed 20 January 2023)

Isbell C, Littman M L and Norvig P 2023 Software engineering of machine learning systems *Commun. ACM* **66** 35–7

Jalal M 2022 *12 Futuristic cities being built around the world, from Saudi Arabia to China* https://thenationalnews.com/arts-culture/2022/08/02/12-futuristic-cities-being-built-around-the-world-from-saudi-arabia-to-china/ (accessed 23 November 2022)

Jauro F, Chiroma H, Gital A Y, Almutairi M, Shafi'i M A and Abawajy J H 2020 Deep learning architectures in emerging cloud computing architectures: recent development, challenges and next research trend *Appl. Soft Comput.* **96** 106582

Kamoun F, Iqbal F, Esseghir M A and Baker T 2020 AI and machine learning: a mixed blessing for cybersecurity *2020 Int. Symp. on Networks, Computers and Communications (ISNCC) (2020, October)* (Piscataway, NJ: IEEE) 1–7

Kshetri N 2020 China's social credit system: data, algorithms and implications *IT Prof.* **22** 14–8

LeCun Y, Bengio Y and Hinton G 2015 Deep learning *Nature* **521** 436–44

Li J H 2018 Cyber security meets artificial intelligence: a survey *Front. Inf. Technol. Electron. Eng.* **19** 1462–74

Mac Síthigh D and Siems M 2019 The Chinese social credit system: a model for other countries? *Mod. Law Rev.* **82** 1034–71

Mihai S *et al* 2022 Digital twins: a survey on enabling technologies, challenges, trends and future prospects *IEEE Commun. Surv. Tutor.* **4** 2255–91

Mishra K K, Misra A K, Mueller P, Martinez Perez G, Bhatia S K and Wang Y 2014 Recent advancements in computer and software technology *Sci. World J.* **2014** 609512

Mittal S 2020 A survey of FPGA-based accelerators for convolutional neural networks *Neural Comput. Appl.* **32** 1109–39

Nguyen D C, Ding M, Pathirana P N, Seneviratne A, Li J and Poor H V 2021 Federated learning for internet of things: a comprehensive survey *IEEE Commun. Surv. Tutor.* **23** 1622–58

Norman D A 2010 Natural user interfaces are not natural *Interactions* **17** 6–10

Ogonji M M, Okeyo G and Wafula J M 2020 A survey on privacy and security of Internet of Things *Comput. Sci. Rev.* **38** 100312

Oliveira G F, Ghose S, Gómez-Luna J, Boroumand A, Savery A, Rao S, Qazi S, Grignou G, Thakur R, Shiu E and Mutlu O *et al* 2021 Extending memory capacity in consumer devices with emerging non-volatile memory: an experimental study *arXiv preprint* arXiv:2111.02325

Outeiral C, Strahm M, Shi J, Morris G M, Benjamin S C and Deane C M 2021 The prospects of quantum computing in computational molecular biology *Wiley Interdiscip. Rev.-Comput. Mol. Sci.* **11** e1481

Panagiotis F, Taxiarxchis K, Georgios K, Maglaras L and Ferrag M A 2021 Intrusion detection in critical infrastructures: a literature review *Smart Cities* **4** 1146–57

Pang G, Shen C, Cao L and Hengel A V D 2021 Deep learning for anomaly detection: a review *ACM Comput. Surv.* **54** 1–38

Pasricha S and Nikdast M 2020 A survey of silicon photonics for energy-efficient manycore computing *IEEE Des. Test* **37** 60–81

PR Newswire 2020 *IEEE Computer Society reveals its 2021 technology predictions* https://prnewswire.com/news-releases/ieee-computer-society-reveals-its-2021-technology-predictions-301194163.html available online (accessed 20 October 2022)

Rindell K, Ruohonen J, Holvitie J, Hyrynsalmi S and Leppänen V 2021 Security in agile software development: a practitioner survey *Inf. Softw. Technol.* **131** 106488

Scavarelli A, Arya A and Teather R J 2021 Virtual reality and augmented reality in social learning spaces: a literature review *Virtual Real.* **25** 257–77

Seng K P, Lee P J and Ang L M 2021 Embedded intelligence on FPGA: survey, applications and challenges *Electronics* **10** 895

Shalf J 2020 The future of computing beyond Moore's law *Philos. Trans. R. Soc.* A **378** 20190061

Sharma A, Kosasih E, Zhang J, Brintrup A and Calinescu A 2022 Digital twins: state of the art theory and practice, challenges, and open research questions *J. Ind. Inf. Integr.* **30** 100383

Stoica G V, Dogaru R and Stoica E C 2014 Speeding-up image processing in reaction-diffusion cellular neural networks using CUDA-enabled GPU platforms *Proc. 2014 6th Int. Conf. on Electronics, Computers and Artificial Intelligence (ECAI) (2014, October)* (Piscataway, NJ: IEEE) 39–42

Stoyanova M, Nikoloudakis Y, Panagiotakis S, Pallis E and Markakis E K 2020 A survey on the internet of things (IoT) forensics: challenges, approaches, and open issues *IEEE Commun. Surv. Tutor.* **22** 1191–221

Strigl D, Kofler K and Podlipnig S 2010 Performance and scalability of GPU-based convolutional neural networks *2010 18th Euromicro Conf. on Parallel, Distributed and Network-based Processing (2010, February)* (Piscataway, NJ: IEEE) 317–24

Sunny F P, Taheri E, Nikdast M and Pasricha S 2021 A survey on silicon photonics for deep learning *ACM J. Emerg. Technol. Comput. Syst.* **17** 1–57

Tyson M 2022 Record 1.84 petabit/s data transfer with photonic chip, fiber-optic cableTom's Hardware https://www.tomshardware.com/news/record-184-petabit-per-second-data-transfers-achieved-using-photonic-chip-and-fiber-optic-cable

Uddin I, Imran A S, Muhammad K, Fayyaz N and Sajjad M 2021 A systematic mapping review on MOOC recommender systems *IEEE Access* **9** 118379–405

Yang J, Li B and Lilja D J 2021 HeuristicDB: a hybrid storage database system using a non-volatile memory block device *Proc. 14th ACM Int. Conf. on Systems and Storage (2021, June)* 1–12

You Y, Zhang Z, Hsieh C J, Demmel J and Keutzer K 2019 Fast deep neural network training on distributed systems and cloud TPUs *IEEE Trans. Parallel Distrib. Syst.* **30** 2449–62

Zhang W, Gao B, Tang J, Yao P, Yu S, Chang M F, Yoo H-J, Wu H and Wu H 2020 Neuro-inspired computing chips *Nat. Electron.* **3** 371–82

Printed in the USA
CPSIA information can be obtained
at www.ICGtesting.com
JSHW060712031123
51216JS00004B/92

9 780750 350150